GREAT PSYCHOLOGISTS AS PARENTS

Does it make you a better parent if you have pioneered scientific theories of child development? In a unique study, David Cohen compares what great psychologists have said about raising children and the way they did it themselves. Did the experts practise what they preached?

Using an eclectic variety of sources, from letters, diaries, autobiographies, biographies, as well as material from interviews, each chapter focuses on a key figure in historical context. There are many surprises. Was Piaget, the greatest child psychologist of the twentieth century, the only man to try to psychoanalyse his mother? How many sons of great gurus have had to rescue their father from a police station as R.D. Laing's son did? And why did Melanie Klein's daughter wear red shoes the day her mother died?

The book covers Charles Darwin, the first scientist to study child psychology methodically, psychoanalysists such as Freud and Jung and founders of developmental psychology including Piaget and Bowlby as well as Dr Spock. It gives a vivid, dramatic and often entertaining insight into the family lives of these great psychologists. It highlights their ideas and theories alongside their behaviour as parents, and reveals the impact of their parenting on their children. Close bonds, fraught relationships and family drama are described against a backdrop of scientific development as the discipline of psychology evolves.

Great Psychologists as Parents will be absorbing reading for students in childhood studies, education and psychology and practitioners in psychology and psychoanalysis. It will also interest general readers looking for a parenting book with a difference.

David Cohen is a prolific writer, film-maker and trained psychologist, as well as the founder of *Psychology News*.

GREAT PSYCHOLOGISTS AS PARENTS

Does knowing the theory make you an expert?

David Cohen

Routledge
Taylor & Francis Group
LONDON AND NEW YORK

First published 2017
by Routledge
2 Park Square, Milton Park, Abingdon, Oxon OX14 4RN

and by Routledge
711 Third Avenue, New York, NY 10017

Routledge is an imprint of the Taylor & Francis Group, an informa business

© 2017 D. Cohen

The right of David Cohen to be identified as author of this work has been asserted by him in accordance with sections 77 and 78 of the Copyright, Designs and Patents Act 1988.

All rights reserved. No part of this book may be reprinted or reproduced or utilized in any form or by any electronic, mechanical, or other means, now known or hereafter invented, including photocopying and recording, or in any information storage or retrieval system, without permission in writing from the publishers.

Trademark notice: Product or corporate names may be trademarks or registered trademarks, and are used only for identification and explanation without intent to infringe.

British Library Cataloguing in Publication Data
A catalogue record for this book is available from the British Library

Library of Congress Cataloging in Publication Data
A catalog record for this book has been requested

ISBN: 978-1-138-89990-2 (hbk)
ISBN: 978-1-138-89991-9 (pbk)
ISBN: 978-1-315-70759-4 (ebk)

Typeset in Bembo
by Wearset Ltd, Boldon, Tyne and Wear
Printed and bound by CPI Group (UK) Ltd, Croydon, CR0 4YY

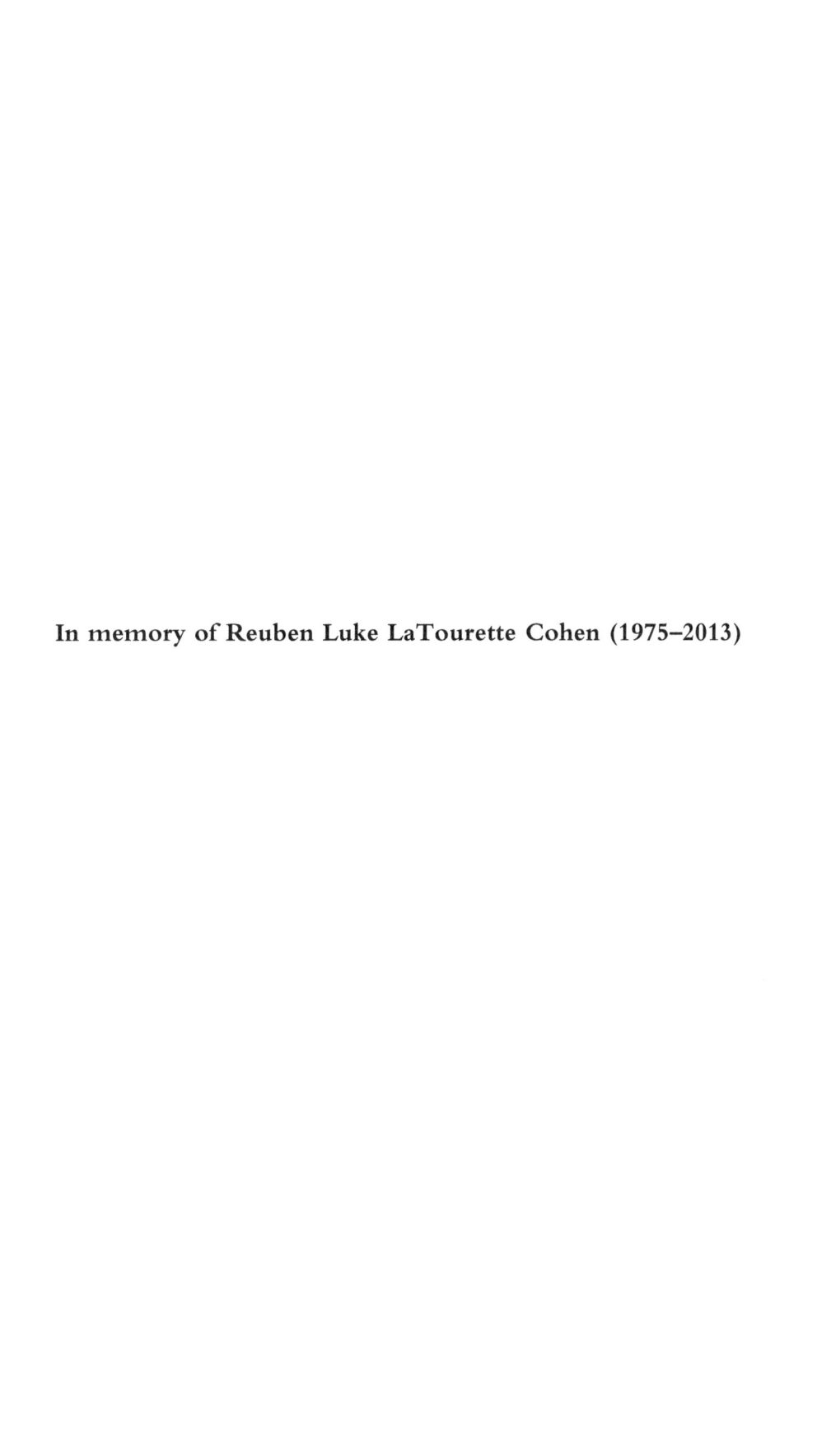

In memory of Reuben Luke LaTourette Cohen (1975–2013)

CONTENTS

1 Introduction   1

2 Charles Darwin: the first child psychologist   14

3 John B. Watson: a behaviourist's tragedies   31

4 Sigmund Freud: the man who analysed his daughter in secret   45

5 Carl Jung: the archetypal prick, a provocative title   63

6 Melanie Klein and her daughter   75

7 Jean Piaget: his mother and psychoanalysis   86

8 Benjamin Spock: the conservative radical   96

9 John Bowlby: the man with the bowler hat   105

10 Burrhus Skinner: the man who caged his daughters?   113

11 R.D. Laing: violence in the family   119

12 Carl Rogers and unconditional personal regard   133

13 The good enough psychologist?   143

Index   146

1
INTRODUCTION

In August 1916, Sigmund Freud wrote to his daughter, Anna, to tell her he had arrived at Bad Gastein, one of the most fashionable spas in Europe. His wife Martha and her sister Minna were with him. Visitors who bathed in the healing waters included the Habsburg Emperor, Eleanor Roosevelt, the writer Thomas Mann and Bismarck, the German Chancellor, who said of Disraeli at the Congress of Vienna 'der alte Jude, dass is der Mann' ('the old Jew, he is the man').

From 1916 to 1923, that other old Jew, Sigmund Freud, stayed a few weeks every summer at the villa of Dr Anton Wassing, a Jewish doctor who took in paying guests, presumably because not enough patients needed his medical services. The very hospitable owner today, Christian Ehrlater, showed me the record for 31 July 1920 when, as well as Freud, a Jewish pharmacist from Vienna was staying there. That July was six months after Freud had suffered the blow of losing his daughter tragically young: Sophie was just 27 years old when she died.

Freud worked on two of his books at Wassing's villa. Christian showed me the small single room 17, where the founder of psychoanalysis slept. 'The bed is the same, though the mattress is new', Christian pointed out. He added that, in 1920, Freud's wife did not accompany him, but her sister Minna did. She stayed next door in room 16; Christian smiled as he said that back then there was a door connecting the two rooms. One of the unresolved issues about Freud's life is whether he had an affair with his sister-in-law. That summer of 1920, six months after Sophie died, he was certainly in need of some comfort.

Many letters between Freud and Anna are likely to reflect the close, perhaps too close, relationship between father and daughter. We cannot judge for sure because so much of the correspondence between them in the Library of Congress is embargoed, either until 2056 or in perpetuity. When her father died, Anna was at his bedside trying to persuade him to wait a little longer before his doctor gave him the morphine Freud wanted. It was a loving leave-taking.

By contrast, Melanie Klein's daughter did not just refuse to go to her mother's funeral but wore special red shoes as her mother's death seemed a cause for celebration. Adrian Laing, the son of R.D. Laing, called his childhood a 'crock of shit'. Fortunately not all the relationships between a famous psychologist and his or her children were dramatic failures. The book looks at ten psychologists, psychiatrists and psychoanalysts. Charles Darwin was neither because these professions as we know them did not exist in his day, but he was a pioneer of development psychology.

In many ways, this is a book about more than a century of failure. Thousands of psychologists have studied how children develop, what makes them secure, insecure, confident, inadequate, eager to achieve or not; we should have learned something from all this effort. Psychologists should have more knowledge and insight than 'ordinary' parents and should be able to use that to be at least 'good enough' parents, a term devised by the English analyst, D.W. Winnicott. He believed that the way to be a good mother is to be 'a good enough mother'. As men in the Western world are more involved parents now, I have changed the phrase to 'the good enough parent'; this all-too-human person worries about being a parent and does not neglect his or her child, giving them physical and emotional security. That does not mean he or she does not sometimes get fed up, feel under pressure or even, Winnicott claimed, shout because the little one is leaping up and down in the supermarket wanting the latest fizzy drink. The good enough parent is a three-dimensional human being, both selfless and self-interested. At times the good enough parent may even hate the baby. It was foolish, even destructive, for parents to try to be perfect. Children learned from seeing that their parents were flawed – and plenty of these eleven subjects were.

Most historians date the start of scientific psychology to 1879 when laboratories were set up at Harvard by William James, and at Leipzig by Wilhelm Wundt. In the 135 years since, probably not one day has passed when children have not been studied by some psychologist. Yet no one has examined how psychologists put their ideas into practice with their own daughters and sons. I am a little nervous making such a claim, but there really seem to be no empirical studies of psychologists as parents. Some memoirs touch on the subject but they are very personal; two examples, Martin Freud's reverential book on his father, *Glory Reflected*, and Adrian Laing's absolutely not reverential biography of his father R.D. Laing. Natalie Rogers in a number of interviews has discussed her memories of her father. Deborah Skinner Buzan has written on her father Burrhus Skinner, as has her sister Julie Vargas; both think he was a fun father and defend him against accusations that he brought them up in some kind of 'Skinner box' as if they were the rats or pigeons so beloved of behaviourists. Keynes' *Annie Box's* on the brief life of Charles Darwin's daughter is also a family book as the author is Darwin's great-great-great-grandson. Darwin's great-great-granddaughter, the poet Ruth Padel, has also written a sequence of poems on Darwin.

A sombre reason may explain this absence of work on experts in human behaviour as parents. Many of their children led troubled lives; some were bitterly critical of their parents as parents; some put forward theories that opposed their ideas; some, like Sir Richard Bowlby, the son of John Bowlby, who devised attachment theory, believe the very idea of this book is probably 'prurient', the word Sir Richard used when we had a tense telephone exchange. Psychology books don't often qualify for that adjective.

Many psychologists and analysts were unconventional parents to say the least. The pioneering psychoanalyst Princess Marie Bonaparte, the great-grandniece of Napoleon and aunt of the Duke of Edinburgh, asked Freud if she should sleep with her son as her many lovers seemed unable to satisfy her. (Many of the princess' inadequate lovers were French politicians.) An Oedipal orgasm might be the answer, the princess thought. The usually conservative Freud advised her against breaking the incest taboo. The princess took the advice and, perhaps more remarkably, she did not insist on analysing her lad.

Freud and Melanie Klein both analysed their children. Today it would be quite unacceptable for a parent to do that, and even in the early days of analysis it was controversial. Freud kept the fact that he had analysed Anna a secret; Melanie Klein's analysis of her daughter Melitta was hardly a success as mother and daughter did not see each other for the last 20 years of Klein's life and, as I have said, Melitta celebrated the day her mother died.

There were less dramatic rows too. Natalie, the daughter of Carl Rogers, the founder of humanist psychotherapy, rebuked him for being insensitive, cruel to his wife and drinking so much vodka that he smelled from a distance. Adrian Laing had to rescue his drunken father from a police station. One psychologist, who asked me not to publish his name, explained that his distinguished psychologist grandfather cut himself off from part of his family. When my contact suggested his grandfather might like to see his new grandson, his grandfather said that would not be necessary. Needless to say that psychologist wrote a well-known book on children.

To understand the way great psychologists behaved as parents, I argue one has to try to understand their childhoods. Many psychologists have seen the value of explaining their background and contributed to the series *A History of Psychology in Autobiography*, for instance. Some said little about their early years but others recognized that the way they were brought up influenced the work they chose and how they behaved as parents too.

Each chapter, therefore, discusses the childhood of the psychologist or psychiatrist, their ideas on child development and parenting, and how they behaved as parents. Unless one were to write a three-volume Victorian novel, there is a limit to the characters one can study. I cover Darwin, Watson, Freud, Jung, Piaget, Bowlby, Melanie Klein, R.D. Laing, Skinner, Carl Rogers and Benjamin Spock, as he wrote the most influential book on parenting of the 1950s and 1960s.

Among those I have had to leave out are Niko Tinbergen, who shared the Nobel Prize for medicine in 1972. As he had a homely approach, I will give a very brief account of what he told me in an interview. It was then fashionable to extrapolate from ethology to human psychology, as Desmond Morris did in his bestseller, *The Naked Ape* (1967).

Tinbergen said:

> Of course in a minor, incidental way I could not help looking at my own children with the eyes of an ethologist. When one of my children began to yawn compulsively when our family doctor came to see her, he said, 'she seems to be very tired' and I had to explain to him that she was merely scared stiff – it is a very common 'displacement activity' such as scratching, or biting your nails when under slight stress.

Tinbergen offered another example:

> One of our children started biting his nails when he was still not quite a toddler. I remembered that female birds often eat anything hard and white when they have just laid eggs, and that my wife was a bad 'processor' of calcium, a defect that he might well have inherited, and (with the puzzled approval of our very research-minded doctor) we smuggled extra calcium into his diet. A wild gamble, but it paid off: the nail biting stopped promptly and never came back.

Tinbergen was less successful when he tried to apply ethological ideas to autistic children. He told me: 'as autistic children don't speak, understanding them must be based on expression and movement. These sorts of movement and expressions had been seen in animals. Many of these children live in perpetual conflict between hyper-anxiety and frustrated social longing.' Few specialists in the autism spectrum see much value in this approach now.

Between them, these 'experts' had 51 children so the subjects of this book did, as the Old Testament urged, 'prosper and multiply'. The beginning of each chapter will set out just who begat whom – and when.

The last few years have seen a tremendous amount of interest in parenting. As well as hundreds of self-help books, television programmes like *The Three Day Nanny* offer advice on how to do the best for one's children. Channel 4 also ran a series on how psychologists could help get children to sleep properly. There have been many others, so when, in the final chapter, I attempt some tentative conclusions, I also look at what parents today could learn from the experiences and expertise of great psychologists and psychiatrists.

Some of those discussed were fine writers, and perhaps the most engaging account of a childhood is Burrhus Skinner's in *Particulars of My Life*. Skinner noted that he was born into a stable home and that 'the first personal possession I remember was my Teddy Bear'. The children were sent to bed at eight o'clock and kissed both their parents until one night when the young Skinner kissed his mother but not his father. Mother told her son to kiss father but father said 'That's all right'. Skinner added that 'He understood his son had reached an age when boys did not kiss their fathers'.

Skinner's father was a fairly successful lawyer but his mother was 'in many ways the dominant member of the family'. She was often ready to point out the error of her husband's ways. 'I doubt whether he ever made a mistake that he did not report to her', their son wrote. She did console her husband sometimes but not much in one way. 'She was apparently frigid', Skinner wrote, basing this on conversations he had with E.R.W. Searle, an uninhibited lawyer who knew his parents well and gave him some inside information. Mother 'apparently gave my father very little sexual satisfaction', her son said. He and his brother slept next to his parents' room and the connecting door was usually left open. One night Skinner heard 'murmurs and muffled activity'. Then he heard his mother say 'Do you hate to quit?' He did not hear what his father replied. Searle once said that Skinner's father 'would be a better man if he went to see the chippies now and then'. The chippies were prostitutes, but Skinner was sure his father never did.

Skinner said of his frustrated father:

> life was to wear him down. He struggled to satisfy that craving for a sense of worth with which his mother had damned him but forty years later, he would throw himself on his bed, weeping and cry 'I am no good, I am no good'.

When he had daughters himself, Skinner did his best to instil in them a sense of self-worth. His daughter Deborah, sitting in her Hampstead garden, told me she remembered her father with great affection.

Obviously parents should be careful not to abuse the power they have over their children. There is some evidence for what seems to be a platitude. Young *et al.* (2011) found that children aged between 11 and 15 who claimed their parents were 'always emotionally neglectful and controlling' were more likely to have a psychiatric disorder four years later. Controlling is much to the point. If a parent is a psychologist, the dynamics are even more complicated because the parent has special knowledge too – and eventually her or his children will realize that.

I am very aware of these questions of power over children.

A very personal note

I come to this subject at a crisis in my life. I am a psychologist and the father of two children – one of whom died recently. My son Reuben was 38 years old. 'Death by misadventure', the coroner ruled. The death of my much-loved son made me question everything and also made it necessary to work and study. Denial, some might say. I wouldn't agree. I had planned this book before Reuben died – indeed we discussed it as he was a fine writer and editor – but writing it has an added sharpness for me now.

Soon after Reuben died, I accidently met Michael Eysenck, the son of Hans Eysenck, the controversial psychologist who did much work on intelligence and personality. Michael was kind. He told me that if one of his children had died it 'would have knocked all the stuffing out of me'. The phrase has remained with me. This book inevitably raises ethical issues. Is it right to study one's own children who have no choice in the matter when they are little? How objective can one be? Does being studied make a child feel 'exploited' when that child is older? Reuben sometimes complained that I had no right to use observations of him as a baby and a child in my book on *The Development of Play*. It did not fundamentally damage our relationship but I know he was never happy with that history.

I've toyed with writing this book for 20 years after meeting the three children of Jean Piaget in Lisbon in 1996 at a conference celebrating the centenary of his birth. Piaget was the most influential child psychologist of the twentieth century and his theories were largely based on the observations he and his wife, Valerie Chateney, made of their children. I have also interviewed two of Watson's children, Melitta Schmideberg, the daughter of Melanie Klein, Deborah Skinner Buzan and Adrian Laing. Dan Spock talked to me by telephone, as did Sir Richard Bowlby, though he refused to discuss his father in any detail. Anna Freud's last secretary, Gina Le Bon, gave me an interview and talked about Anna Freud's deep love for her father.

'Physician heal thyself' is a good motto. So is 'psychologist know thyself'. Goethe famously said 'If I knew myself, I'd run away', which makes it very odd that he was Freud's favourite writer as one aim of analysis is to allow us to know ourselves.

Old Abraham and his carving knife

Very few texts on parenting reveal how the Greeks, Romans and medieval thinkers saw this crucial human task, but some famous stories in the Old Testament focus on sons and fathers. To obey the Lord, Abraham was willing to sacrifice his son Isaac. After the prophet lay Isaac down on a rock and sharpened the filicide knife, the Lord relented and hey-presto-ed a convenient ram to be slaughtered instead of the boy. Few commentators dwell on the fact that the ram was then seasoned with sweet smelling spices 'pleasing to the Lord', so one presumes Abraham would have been willing to pepper and salt his son, either before or after having murdered him. Isaac seems to have forgiven his father remarkably easily. 'Sure Dad, the Lord comes first, I understand', we are supposed to believe he thought as they trekked down to the tents of Israel.

Isaac's son Jacob, on the other hand, was an indulgent father and would probably have told the Lord to get back on His cloud if He dared ask him to harm one hair of Joseph's head. Jacob's love for his youngest made Joseph's brothers seethe with jealousy. No one made them an Amazing Technicolour Dream Coat, so they sold the pesky youth into slavery in Egypt. Being a slave turned out to be a good career move for Joseph, however, as it gave him the chance to interpret the Pharaoh's dreams, thereby becoming the first psychoanalyst; he then rose to the position of Grand Vizier. As far as I can make out Joseph was the only 'psychologist' ever to achieve serious political power.

The Fifth Commandment states: 'Honour thy father and thy mother that thy days may be long'. Honour thy child? Jehovah doesn't seem to have thought of that. The Almighty was far too invested in being the Ur-dad to worry about what children needed from their parents. Jehovah, of course, did not just punish the children of Israel but lectured them on their inclination to sin, to worship false gods and, generally, to get everything wrong. Being a Jew, I can snip that it's no wonder Jews specialize in guilt.

Some Greek and Roman texts show that 2,000 years ago, parents had very recognizable feelings about their children. One text is the lost *Consolatio* of Cicero, which the great Roman lawyer and politician wrote after his daughter died. Cicero adored Tullia, and described her to his brother Quintus: 'How affectionate, how modest, how clever! The express image of my face, my speech, my very soul.' When she died suddenly in February 45 BC after giving birth to a son, Cicero was devastated. 'I have lost the one thing that bound me to life', he wrote to his friend Atticus.

Atticus told Cicero to visit so that he could comfort him. In Atticus' library, Cicero read everything Greek philosophers had written about overcoming grief, 'but my sorrow defeats all consolation'. Neither political business nor seeing friends helped as 'there was nothing I cared to do in the forum: I could not bear the sight of the senate-house; I thought – as was the fact – that I had lost all the fruits both of my industry and of fortune'. Through all the turmoils of his career, 'I had a refuge, one bosom where I could find repose, one in whose conversation and sweetness I could lay aside all anxieties and sorrows'.

Seeking works other than elegies for dead children, I asked Professor Mary Beard for help. She confirmed that the ancients did not write much about parenting, but directed me to one source, Plutarch's *Essays*. In one, Plutarch blamed fathers who put the education of their sons in the hands of flatterers. Schoolmasters, Plutarch advised, 'should be of blameless life, of pure character, and of great experience'. Socrates would shout: 'Men, what can you be thinking of, who move heaven and earth to make money, while you bestow next to no attention on the sons you are going to leave that money to?' Plutarch commented: 'I would add to this that such fathers act very similarly to a person who is very careful about his shoe but cares nothing about his foot.'

For me, Plutarch's most interesting views were on what we would now call pushy parents – and the problems they inflict on their children and themselves. 'While they are in too great a hurry to make their sons take the lead in everything, they lay too much work upon them, so that they faint under their tasks, and, being overburdened, are disinclined for learning', Plutarch wrote.

Fifteen centuries after Plutarch, the Renaissance brought a flurry of interesting writing on parenting. The Dutch polymath Erasmus came to England in 1499 to help educate eight-year-old Prince Henry, who became Henry VIII. Erasmus wrote *On the Rules of Etiquette for the Young*, *On the Order of Study* and *On the Education of Children*. He had no children himself but he did have some sense of the balance children need between love and discipline. 'We learn with great willingness from those we love', he said. He was also critical of bullying parents, noting that 'Parents themselves cannot properly bring up their children if they only make themselves feared'. Mothers should be affectionate but fathers had to get to know their offspring too.

Erasmus was keen on cleanliness. Children had to wash their faces every morning, though one should not encourage them to get obsessive because 'to repeat this exercise afterwards is nonsense'. They could wipe their nose with their fingers but not with a cap or a sleeve.

Erasmus might have his obsessions but he was an astute observer too, noting, or perhaps quilling, as writers then used quills, 'Nature has equipped children with a unique urge to imitate whatever they hear or say; they do this with great enthusiasm', but he did not think much of imitation as he added, 'as though they were monkeys and they are overjoyed if they think they have been successful'. We shall come to monkeys later.

Some 80 years later, the French philosopher Michel de Montaigne lambasted fathers who did not tell their sons they loved them because they feared admitting that would lose them authority. One of his friends lost his son and felt guilty that he had never told the boy he adored him.

A child should be encouraged to listen, Montaigne wrote,

> to have his eye and ear in every corner; for I find that the places of greatest honour are commonly seized upon by men that have least in them, and that the greatest fortunes are seldom accompanied with the ablest parts.

As an aristocrat who sat at the best tables, Montaigne heard many trivial conversations 'at the upper end of the chamber' while social inferiors discussed serious subjects below the salt. A peasant, a bricklayer, a cooper, might have something to teach. 'By observing the graces and manners of all he sees, he (the child) will create to himself an emulation of the good, and a contempt of the bad.'

Oddly the most eloquent pre-modern writer on fatherhood was a king of England, though the royals are not generally noted for their parental wisdom. James VI of Scotland and I of England (1566–1625) was supremely well educated. His family history included a drastic study only a royal would have dared. James' great-grandfather lodged two children with a mute woman on the Isle of Inchkeith to see whether or not they would spontaneously speak the language of the Bible. They did not, of course, start burbling Hebrew.

James' own childhood was traumatic. His mother, Mary Queen of Scots, fled to England after she was suspected of murdering her second husband. She had to leave her baby son behind in Scotland. Uneasy lies the head remotely connected to the crown. Three of James' four guardians were executed or murdered before he was 16. Mary herself was beheaded in 1587 by her cousin, Elizabeth I, who was fed up with Mary's constant plotting to seize the throne of England.

James was fortunate, though, in one of his tutors, George Buchanan, who provided stability and 'tough love'. Buchanan was willing to whip his royal charge if His Majesty did not pay attention to his lessons, a lesson James did not forget.

James married in 1589 and his first son, Henry, was born in 1594. James wrote a pamphlet for him as he felt it was his duty to advise the boy on how to be a king. It is powerful and often wise. He charged Henry 'in the presence of GOD, and by the fatherly authority I have over you, that ye keep it ever with you, as carefully, as Alexander did the Iliads of Homer'. If Henry ignored his advice, James protested, 'before that Great GOD, I had rather not be a Father, and childless, than be a Father of wicked children'. James emphasized Henry should learn from his own mistakes.

Henry should not imagine he had a licence to sin just because he was royal. A king should 'shine before their people, in all works of sanctification and righteousness'. James urged his son to read Scripture 'with a sanctified and chaste heart: and to pray to understand it properly'. Once every 24 hours,

> when ye are at greatest quiet, to call yourself to account of all your last day's actions, either wherein ye have committed things ye should not, or omitted the things ye should do, either in your Christian or Kingly calling.

Examining one's conscience and behaviour was vital. 'Censure your self as sharply, as if ye were your own enemy. For if ye judge your self, ye shall not be judged.'

James warned his son against fanatical priests, vain astrologers and necromancers. Henry should also 'take no heed to any of your dreams, for all prophecies, visions, and prophetic dreams are accomplished and ceased in Christ'. Freud could stuff his unconscious.

The king had to rule impartially, so James urged Henry to neither love the rich, nor pity the poor. In England he would often have to deal with the dishonest natives and their mania for novelties – especially tobacco, which James hated.

James revered his dead mother and reminded his son, 'ye know the command in God's law, Honour your Father and Mother'. The king should not let his parents 'be dishonoured by any; especially, since the example also touches yourself. For how can they love you, that hated them whom-of ye are come?' Servants had to be watched carefully. If the king could not ensure they obeyed him, why should the country obey him?

James' strict religious education made him a stern moralist. Before he married, his son

> must keep your body clean and unpolluted, till ye give it to your wife, whom-to only it belongeth. For how can ye justly crave to be joined with a pure virgin, if your body be polluted? Why should the one half be clean, and the other defiled?

Henry should avoid 'the idle company of dames, which are nothing else, but irritamenta libidinis'. Idle dames could make idle loins itch! James' own unhappy family was proof of the havoc twitchy and itchy loins could provoke; his grandfather's adulteries 'procured the ruin of his own Sovereign and sister'. For some reason James did not mention his great uncle, Henry the awful VIIIth.

The king then turned to the royal 'image'. People would always be watching the king and so his table manners must be impeccable. Gluttony made a bad impression, so majesty must not be seen scoffing anything exotic, such as boar stuffed with pomegranates. Henry should also not be 'effeminate in your clothes' and never wear 'long hair or nails, which are but excrements of nature'. The king could play card games, but not chess 'because it is over-wise and Philosophicke a folly'. Henry must 'play always fair, that ye come not in use of tricking and lying'.

Last, James urged Henry to remember his duty to God and to ensure that his deeds reflected 'the inward uprightness of your heart' and showed 'your virtuous disposition; and in respect of the greatness and weight of your burden, to be patient in hearing, keeping your heart free from preoccupation, ripe in concluding, and constant in your resolution'. James urged his son 'to digest ever your passion, before ye determine upon anything'. Henry should judge every man according to his own offence and not punish or blame the father for the son, nor the brother for the brother. He should never seek excuses to take revenge.

It was a wise and beautiful love letter. James, however, was destined to be as unlucky a parent as he had been a child. Henry died of a mysterious fever when he was 18; his father was inconsolable. James' second son, the less brilliant and less loved Charles, succeeded to the throne. His insecurities – James never wrote a pamphlet for him – made him stubborn, and that stubbornness helped provoke the English Civil War. Charles paid for his obstinacy with his head.

The fathers I have discussed did not study their children in any scientific sense. The sixteenth- and seventeenth-century thinkers who might have done so had one disadvantage: most were childless. Erasmus had no children and nor did Descartes, Spinoza, Leibniz, Hobbes, John Locke or, a century later, David Hume and Immanuel Kant. The only important philosopher of that time who did have children was Bishop Berkeley, who seems to have been a rather neurotic dad. When his son went to Oxford, the bishop took lodgings in the city himself to make sure the boy did not get into trouble as so many students did.

By contrast with the philosophers, great sixteenth- and seventeenth-century writers were a fecund lot. Shakespeare had a son, Hamnet, who died when he was ten in 1596, as well as two daughters. John Donne, the greatest English poet of the early sixteenth century, had 12 children. The French playwright Jean Racine had seven children; John Milton, the author of *Paradise Lost*, had five. The difference between the two groups is curious, and, as far as I can see, inexplicable.

The writers felt the loss of their children. Shakespeare's contemporary, the playwright Ben Jonson, lost a child and mourned in a fine poem.

On My First Sonne

Farewell, thou child of my right hand, and joy;
My sinne was too much hope of thee, lov'd boy
Seven yeeres thou wert lent to me, and I thee pay,
Exacted by thy fate, on the just day.
O, could I loose all father, now. For why
Will man lament the state he should envie?
To have so soone scap'd worlds, and fleshes rage,
And, if no other miserie, yet age
Rest in soft peace, and, ask'd, say here doth lye
Ben Jonson his best piece of poetrie.
For whose sake, hence-forth, all his vowes be such,
As what he loves may never like too much.

Good observers were not always philosophers or tutors. Lewis Jenkin was a royal servant who spent seven years with William, Duke of Gloucester, who was born on 24 July 1689 at Hampton Court. William was the son of Princess Anne, the daughter of James II.

William was 'a very weakly child' and few believed he would live long. His mother had had 12 miscarriages and not one of her four babies who were born survived long. William's first days were not easy as his wet nurse had too large a nipple, but a new nurse was found, and for the next six weeks, the baby thrived. 'All people now began to conceive hopes of the Duke living', Lewis wrote, 'when Lo he was taken with convulsion fits.' The prince's desperate mother summoned physicians from London, who recommended an age-old remedy: change the wet nurse. Mothers of young babies flocked to Hampton Court, hoping to become the tit royal. The infant duke was passed from breast to breast, testing each potential wet nurse.

The final choice was pure accident. The baby's father, Prince George of Denmark, walked through the room where the would-be wet nurses were lined up and took a fancy to the breast of Mrs Pack, the wife of a respectable Quaker from Kingston. Her presumably perky nipples inspired confidence. Mrs Pack was packed into bed with the ailing baby, 'who sucked well and mended that night'. Sadly, however, Mrs Pack was, according to Lewis, 'fitter to go to a pigsty than to a prince's bed' and tried to cash in on her sudden fame.

William did thrive but some illness caused 'an issue from his pole', according to Lewis. Some historians of medicine have assumed fluid was leaking from William's weirdly large head. Jack Dewhurst claims that the prince suffered a mild form of hydrocephalus, but that condition is usually associated with low intelligence. William was certainly not backward, however, and he grew up fairly normally, though his walking was never quite normal. William could not go up or down steps without help. Lewis was not sure whether this was a real infirmity or due to 'the overcare of the ladies about him' (the man could have been a therapist!). The issue came to a head one day when William's father believed the boy was shamming and, for the first time in his life, beat him with a birch rod. 'He was whipped again and went ever well after', Lewis noted.

The boy prince pluckily endured a succession of illnesses. In the spring of 1696, for example, his eyes swelled and became bloodshot. His mother sent for Dr John Radcliffe, who prescribed a horrid medicine, which William promptly spat out. Radcliffe then applied blisters to the boy's back, which made him scream in pain.

More happily, William became friends with George Lawrence, an enterprising boy who organized a troop of 20 boy soldiers; many were sons of the royal servants. William joined in the fun and organized a troop of his own. Anne and her husband were delighted their boy was bright and busy, but it was too good to last.

In June 1700, William suddenly became very ill. Four days after he first started running a fever, William died. Lewis noted the desperate sadness of his mother. William was just 11 years old.

Many psychologists and psychiatrists discussed here suffered tragedies. Darwin lost three of his children. Sophie was not the only person close to Freud to die an untimely death. Four of Freud's relatives committed suicide. Melanie Klein lost one of her sons and her daughter was sure her brother had killed himself. One of Watson's sons committed suicide soon after his father died and his daughter made a number of attempts on her life. R.D. Laing lost a daughter when she was in her twenties and one of his sons died in mysterious circumstances. As Bowlby said, 'children are so vulnerable'. The question is – are the children of great psychologists and psychiatrists especially vulnerable? And can we learn anything from their experiences?

Notes and references

At the end of each chapter, I outline the main sources of information for it, other works referred to and, sometimes, further reading. On Freud's visit to Bad Gastein, interview with Christian Ehrlater when I visited; on Freud as a father, Ernest Jones, *Sigmund Freud*, Basic Books (1953); Martin Freud, *Glory Reflected*, Angus and Robertson (1953); Hanns Sachs, *Freud, Master and Friend*, Ayer Co Publishing (1944); and Elisabeth Young Bruehl, *Anna Freud*, Yale University Press (2008).

The quotes from Niko Tinbergen come from the author's interview in D. Cohen, *Psychologists on Psychology*, Routledge (1977).

B.F. Skinner, *Particulars of My Life*, Jonathan Cape (1976), discussed his teddy bear, his mother, his father and their probably unhappy sex life.

On early studies of children:
Cicero, *Selected Writings*, Penguin (1993).
Erasmus, *On the Education of Children* (circa 1510), now available in a 1990 edition from Kliniksieck Publishers.
Erasmus, *A Handbook on Good Manners for Children* (circa 1510), also now available in a 1990 edition from Kliniksieck Publishers.
Montaigne, Michel de, *Essays*, Penguin (1993).
Plutarch, *Essays*, Penguin (1992).

On trying to be a good father:
James I, *Basilikon Doron*, EBBO (2011; originally published circa 1612).

On the unhappy pregnancies of Queen Anne:
Dewhurst, Jack, *Royal Confinements*, Weidenfeld & Nicolson (1980).
Jenkin, Lewis, *Memoir of Prince William*, Payne (1789).

Other references:
Keynes, Randal, *Annie's Box*, Fourth Estate (2001).
Kirschenbaum, H., *Carl Rogers*, PCCS Books (2010).
Laing, Adrian, *R.D. Laing*, HarperCollins (1997).
Laing, R.D., *The Divided Self*, Penguin (1961).

Morris, Desmond, *The Naked Ape*, Jonathan Cape (1967).
Murchison, C.A. (ed.), *A History of Psychology in Autobiography*, Clark University Press (1930).
Padel, Ruth, *Darwin: A Life in Poems*, Vintage (2001).
Winnicott, D.W., *Clinical Notes on Disorders of Childhood*, William Heinemann (1931).
Young, R., Lennie, S. and Minnis, H., Children's perceptions of parental emotional neglect and psychopathology. *J Child Psychology and Psychiatry*, 889–97 (2011).
Zweig, S., *Erasmus*, Cassell (1933).

2

CHARLES DARWIN

The first child psychologist

In her memoir, Charles Darwin's daughter, Henrietta noted:

> My father took an unusual delight in his babies and we have all a vivid memory of him as the most inspiriting of playfellows.... Many a time even during my father's working hours was a sick child tucked up on his sofa, to be quiet and safe and soothed by his presence.

Her father wrote in his autobiography: 'I have been most fortunate in my family and I must say to you my children that not one of you has ever given me a moment's anxiety except on the score of health.' This was a fond but true statement. As Darwin was the second most prolific of all the fathers I discuss, it is worth listing his 'brood', as he called it.

His first son, William Erasmus Darwin, was born on 27 December 1839. Anne Elisabeth, his first daughter, was born on 2 March 1841. Her early death ten years later destroyed Darwin's belief in Christianity. The third child also did not survive long: Mary Eleanor died when she was only 23 days old.

The next children were all more long-lived. On 25 September 1843, Darwin and his wife had a third daughter. Eighteen months later, George Howard Darwin was born. Henrietta edited her mother's letters and had them published in 1904. She lived to the age of 86. George became an astronomer and studied the evolution and origins of the solar system. He died in 1912.

Elisabeth Darwin was born on 8 July 1847 and died in 1926. She never married and had no children. Then Francis Darwin was born on 16 August 1848. He helped his father with his experiments and influenced Darwin's writing of 'The power of movement in plants' (1880). Like George, Francis was elected a Fellow of the Royal Society and then Professor of Botany at Cambridge. He died when he was 77 years old.

Leonard Darwin was born on 15 January 1850. He became chairman of the British Eugenics Society. After he died at the age of 93, a colleague wrote to Darwin's niece, Margaret Keynes, 'My very dear friend Leonard Darwin ... was surely the kindest and wisest man I ever knew'.

Horace Darwin was born on 13 May 1851. He founded the Cambridge Scientific Instrument Company. He was elected a Fellow of the Royal Society and knighted. He also died at the age of 77.

Emma Darwin gave birth to their tenth and last child, Charles Waring, on 6 December 1856. He died of scarlet fever when he was just 18 months old. His father wrote a loving memorial to his infant son.

Darwin's fame rests on the theory of evolution which he developed during and after a trip on the HMS *Beagle*. He also wrote on worms, climbing plants and a pioneering book on the expressions of the emotions in apes and children.

The Darwins were always writing. In 1838, when he was 29 years old, Charles Darwin wrote two notes. 'I have so much pleasure in direct observation', he said in one, contrasting natural observation with the work of geologists who tried to deduce the history of the earth from unmoving, unsmiling rock formations. Later in April, Darwin noted that his father, 'the Governor', said that 'if one has children, one's character is more flexible – one's feelings more lively'. Soon after writing these notes, Darwin decided to marry his cousin, Emma Wedgwood.

The couple would have ten children, one of whom Darwin would observe systematically. His study of his beloved first son, William, was the first proper longitudinal study of an infant. Darwin made scattered observations of his other children but they were not as methodical. Darwin was truly remarkable. He not only wrote *On the Origin of the Species* but was an astute child psychologist. He was also a loving father and had no inhibitions about expressing his feelings about his 'brood', as he sometimes called them. He wrote of 'the unspeakable tenderness of young children'. Being a good scientist, he wondered if one could observe one's own children objectively without being distracted by the love one felt for them, especially when a child was crying. Typically, Darwin mentioned this when he wrote to friends asking them to observe the shape of their children's mouths.

Darwin has been the subject of many biographies. An exceptionally interesting one is by John Bowlby, a fairly orthodox Freudian who developed attachment theory which stresses how vital it is for mothers to bond with their infants. Bowlby became convinced that Darwin suffered from anxiety and depression – and that this was both caused by, and contributed to, his gastric problems. It made him worry for his children. The great naturalist became depressed because his mother died when he was nine years old, Bowlby suggested. Bowlby's famous paper on 44 juvenile thieves argued that they suffered from maternal deprivation. Darwin was excellent proof of Bowlby's thesis, though no one has yet suggested he was also given to stealing things. To be less frivolous, Bowlby was a keen digger and also suggested the depression might have been aggravated because Darwin caught Chagas' disease while sailing on the *Beagle*. So-called kissing bugs spread the disease with their bites. The disease can cause fevers, headaches and swollen lymph nodes for decades.

In a recent book, Tim Berra ignores Bowlby and blames genetics. Inbreeding between the Darwin and Wedgwood families was the cause of Darwin's ill health. At least five of the 25 marriages in the Darwin–Wedgwood family were between close relatives. That explains why rather more of Darwin's children died than one would expect for Victorian families of his class, Berra argues. Darwin himself was concerned about inbreeding and lobbied in 1870 for questions about first-cousin marriages to be added to the following year's national census form.

From an utterly different point of view, Ruth Padel, who is Darwin's great-great-granddaughter, has written about him and his children; she understands, it seems to me, the connection between Darwin's love of his 'brood' and his observations. In her *Natural History of Babies*, Padel says eloquently that Darwin started 'to make notes on the expressions' the children made and that he looked for the first 'signs of each emotion'.

Darwin will observe all his ten children, Padel writes. For 16 years he will watch them playing, smiling, wondering 'at stirring tissue; at the human suddenly awake like painted bison'. Padel offers a fine image, seeing these babies or bison 'shaking their shaggy selves off a streaming wall'. She ends her poem with Darwin torn as he is observing one of his children crying. He wants to observe accurately, but 'sympathy with his grief spoiled all my observations'. More than any other observer, Darwin managed both to be scientific and warm, a rare feat.

Darwin and Emma settled in Upper Gower Street in central London. Their eldest son, William, was born on 27 December 1839 and became an immediate subject for scientific scrutiny, as well as being much loved. The Darwins saw more of their children than most of their class and time. The Victorian Mrs Beeton, in her *Book of Household Management*, gave precise instructions on how nannies should behave. A well-to-do household would leave most of the day-to-day care of children to the servants; if a father ever saw his offspring it would be for a few brief moments at the end of the day. Winston Churchill's parents, for example, were more typical of their time and class. As a child in the 1870s, Churchill saw very little of either his mother or his father. His nanny taught him reading, writing and arithmetic (his first reading book was called *Reading Without Tears*). Unsurprisingly, Churchill became very close to her, and called her 'Old Woom'. She was his confidante, nurse and mother substitute.

Darwin worked from home after his return from the voyage on the HMS *Beagle* so he was more present than many fathers. In his autobiography he wrote:

> There are I suspect very few fathers of five sons who could say this with entire truth. When you were very young it was my delight to play with all of you and I think with a sigh that such days can never return.

Soon after he was born William got the nickname Doddy. Darwin's detailed notes on William remained private until 1872 when a French historian, Hippolyte Taine, published a paper on how his baby girl learned language. Darwin then went back to notes he had composed 37 years earlier. He had been busy after all with

On the Origin of the Species which finally came out in 1859. That embroiled him in many controversies.

Darwin's notes mix observation and affection. I report them in some detail as they were pioneering as well as very thoughtful. In his paper Darwin does not always report his observations chronologically; I have taken the liberty of trying to do so for the sake of clarity.

'During the first seven days various reflex actions, namely sneezing, hiccupping, yawning, stretching, and of course sucking and screaming, were well performed by my infant', Darwin wrote. 'On the seventh day, I touched the naked sole of his foot with a bit of paper, and he jerked it away, curling at the same time his toes, like a much older child when tickled.' 'The perfection of these reflex movements', Darwin added, 'shows that the extreme imperfection of the voluntary ones is not due to the state of the muscles or of the coordinating centres, but to that of the seat of the will'. In other words, newborn infants were not able to will their actions.

There was one exception, perhaps. Darwin saw 'that a warm soft hand applied to his face excited a wish to suck', but he could not believe that a seven-day-old infant could have any associations with his mother's breast.

The baby's ability to focus his eyes interested Darwin too. William could fix his eyes on a candle as early as his ninth day. For the next 36 days, 'nothing else seemed thus to fix them; but on the 49th day his attention was attracted by a bright-coloured tassel'. Darwin was also surprised by how long it took William to follow an object with his eyes if that object was 'swinging at all rapidly'. William only managed that after he was eight months old.

The first sign of communication came young when William wrinkled his face to show that he wanted something. When 46 days old, he first made little noises without any meaning, Darwin suggested, to please himself, and these soon became varied. At almost the same time, Darwin saw the first 'Pleasurable Sensation'. One of his babies smiled at 45 days, a second infant at 46 days old. 'The smiles arose chiefly when looking at their mother, and were therefore probably of mental origin.' But sometimes there was no apparent reason for the smiles.

Darwin also wanted to see at what age William displayed emotions. The first sign of real anger came when William was about 70 days old. He frowned when he was given some rather cold milk and his father thought 'he looked like a grown-up person made cross from being compelled to do something which he did not like'. Blood gushed into his whole face and scalp, which seemed to Darwin proof the baby 'easily got into a violent passion. A small cause sufficed; thus, when a little over seven months old, he screamed with rage because a lemon slipped away and he could not seize it with his hands'.

Freud read Darwin avidly and the following observation may have influenced Freud in arguing that babies go through an oral stage. 'The movements of his limbs and body were for a long time vague and purposeless, and usually performed in a jerking manner', Darwin said, but there was one exception to this rule, namely, 'that from a very early period, certainly long before he was 40 days old, he could move his hands to his own mouth'. 'When 77 days old, William took the sucking bottle in his right hand, whether he was held on the left or right arm of his nurse, and he would not take it in his left hand' until a week later, although Darwin tried to make him do so. 'Yet this infant afterwards proved to be left-handed, the tendency being no doubt inherited – his grandfather, mother, and a brother having been or being left-handed.'

Between 80 and 90 days of age, William put all sorts of objects into his mouth, but he did so in an odd way because he often first touched his nose with the object and then dragged it down into his mouth.

> After grasping my finger and drawing it down into his mouth, his own hand prevented him from sucking it; but on the 114th day, after acting in this manner, he slipped his own hand down so that he could get the end of my finger into his mouth. This action was repeated several times, and evidently was not a chance but a rational one.

William's hands and arms were much more under his control than his legs and the rest of his body.

A month later, at 120 days, William often looked intently at his own hands and other objects close to him,

> and in doing so the eyes were turned much inwards, so that he often squinted frightfully. In a fortnight after this time (i.e. 132 days old) I observed that if an object was brought as near to his face as his own hands were, he tried to seize it, but often failed; and he did not try to do so in regard to more distant objects. I think there can be little doubt that the convergence of his eyes gave him the clue and excited him to move his arms.

Darwin's observations allowed him to identify some crucial stages in child development, like the moment an infant sees herself or himself in the mirror and knows 'it's me'.

When William was 'four and a half months old', Darwin wrote:

> he repeatedly smiled at my image and his own in a mirror, and no doubt mistook them for real objects; but he showed sense in being evidently surprised at my voice coming from behind him. Like all infants he much enjoyed thus looking at himself, and in less than two months perfectly understood that it was an image; for if I made quite silently any odd grimace, he would suddenly turn round to look at me. He was, however, puzzled at the age of seven months, when being out of doors he saw me on the inside of a large plate-glass window, and seemed in doubt whether or not it was an image.

One of Darwin's daughters was much slower 'and seemed quite perplexed at the image of a person in a mirror approaching her from behind'. Darwin tried this with apes, but, 'far from taking pleasure in looking at themselves they got angry and would look no more'.

Over a century after Darwin observed William, Gordon Gallup, a psychologist at the State University of New York, put a mirror into the cage of a chimpanzee.

At first the chimp reacted as if the reflection was another individual but, over time, it learned that this was its own reflection. Next Gallup anesthetized the chimpanzee and painted a red mark on its eyebrow and another over its ear. When the anaesthesia wore off, the chimp failed to show any interest in the marks until it caught sight of itself in the mirror. Then the chimp began to act like children who know that they are looking at themselves in the mirror, and began to touch its own eyebrow and ear, while watching its image in the mirror. The chimp was self-aware, Gallup argued, and knew the reflection it was looking at was of itself. Orangutans, gorillas, elephants and dolphins also recognize themselves in mirrors, according to Diana Reiss in *The Dolphin in the Mirror* (2012). She argues it takes 'sophisticated integration of information about yourself and your own movements and what you're seeing in front of you in that glass'.

Fear came younger than self-recognition – at around four months. Darwin often made

> strange and loud noises, which were all taken as excellent jokes, but at this period I one day made a loud snoring noise which I had never done before; he (William) instantly looked grave and then burst out crying. Two or three days afterwards, I made through forgetfulness the same noise with the same result. About the same time (viz. on the 137th day) I approached with my back towards him and then stood motionless; he looked very grave and much surprised, and would soon have cried, had I not turned round; then his face instantly relaxed into a smile.

Darwin did not think William recognized anyone until he was nearly four months old but then he started to do so routinely. 'When nearly five months old, he plainly showed his wish to go to his nurse.' William, Darwin believed, showed empathy (though Darwin did not call it that) at six months and 11 days 'by his melancholy face, when his nurse pretended to cry'. But he did not spontaneously exhibit affection by overt acts until a little above a year old, namely, by kissing several times his nurse 'who had been absent for a short time'.

One of the enduring themes in child development studies is when children start to play peekaboo. Darwin did that with his children often.

> When 110 days old he (William) was exceedingly amused by a pinafore being thrown over his face and then suddenly withdrawn; and so he was when I suddenly uncovered my own face and approached his. He then uttered a little noise which was an incipient laugh. Here surprise was the chief cause of the amusement, as is the case to a large extent with the wit of grown-up persons.

Darwin added: 'I was at first surprised at humour being appreciated by an infant only a little above three months old, but we should remember how very early puppies and kittens begin to play.' He saw an incipient laugh on the 113th day of William's life but much earlier in another child. Many early psychologists studied smiling and laughing in children precisely because their own children were their subjects.

When he was five-and-a-half months old, William uttered an articulate sound, 'da', but without any meaning attached to it. A little later, on 7 June 1840, Darwin wrote to his cousin W.D. Fox that William was 'a prodigy of beauty & intellect. He is so charming that I cannot pretend to any modesty'. Darwin added that he had not 'the smallest conception that there was so much in a five month baby'. When a little over a year old, he used gestures to explain his wishes; 'to give a simple instance, he picked up a bit of paper and giving it to me pointed to the fire, as he had often seen and liked to see paper burnt'.

William was not always charming, even to his adoring father. When he was 11 months old, 'if a wrong plaything was given to him, he would push it away and beat it'. Darwin presumed that the beating was 'an instinctive sign of anger, like the snapping of the jaws by a young crocodile just out of the egg'.

As intriguing as the question of when children recognize themselves is the question of when they begin to associate ideas; William managed this at five months. 'As soon as his hat and cloak were put on', Darwin recorded, William

> was very cross if he was not immediately taken out of doors. When exactly seven months old, he made the great step of associating his nurse with her name, so that if I called it out he would look round for her.

During the next four months, William developed this skill:

> when asked for a kiss he would protrude his lips and keep still, – would shake his head and say in a scolding voice 'Ah' to the coal-box or a little spilt water, &c., which he had been taught to consider as dirty.

Darwin noted that Taine's daughter was older when she started to associate ideas.

> When a few days over nine months, William learnt spontaneously that a hand or other object causing a shadow to fall on the wall in front of him was to be looked for behind. Whilst under a year old, it was sufficient to repeat two or three times at intervals any short sentence to fix firmly in his mind some associated idea.
>
> The facility with which associated ideas due to instruction and others spontaneously arising were acquired, seemed to me by far the most strongly marked of all the distinctions between the mind of an infant and that of the cleverest full-grown dog that I have ever known.

Weirdly, Darwin then contrasted the mind of an infant with that of a pike, described by Professor Möbius, who was a Victorian expert on oysters and ran a large aquarium. For three months, Möbius' daft pike 'dashed and stunned himself against a glass partition which separated him from some minnows'. The pike was then placed in the aquarium with the minnows, but 'in a persistent and senseless manner he would not attack them!'

Nearly 30 years ago, Reissland (1988) showed that newborn babies imitate actions such as the sticking out of the tongue literally hours after they were born. Darwin never recorded William imitating an action so young but the baby was four months old when his father thought that he tried to imitate sounds. Darwin was not totally sure, as he admitted, 'but I may have deceived myself, for I was not thoroughly convinced that he did so until he was ten months old'. Then Darwin thought William began 'to try to imitate sounds, as he certainly did at a considerably later period'.

At the age of 11-and-a-half months, however, William could imitate all sorts of actions, such as shaking his head and saying 'Ah' to any dirty object, or carefully and slowly putting his forefinger in the middle of the palm of his other hand, to the childish rhyme of 'Pat it and pat it and mark it with T'. Darwin, the fond father, was amused to see his son looking pleased 'after successfully performing any such accomplishment'.

> At exactly the age of one year, William made the great step of inventing a word for food, namely mum, but what led him to it I did not discover. And now instead of beginning to cry when he was hungry, he used this word in a demonstrative manner or as a verb, implying 'Give me food'. This word therefore corresponds with ham as used by M. Taine's infant at the later age of 14 months. But he (William) also used mum as a substantive of wide signification; thus he called sugar 'shu-mum', and a little later after he had learned the word 'black', he called liquorice black-shu-mum, – black-sugar-food.

On 1 July 1841, when William was just over 18 months, Darwin wrote to Emma (whom he addressed as his dear 'Titty'): 'Doddy's reception of me was quite affecting. He sat on my knee for nearly a quarter of an hour gave me some sweet kisses and sniggered and looked at my face and pointing told everyone I was papa.' Darwin clearly was not with Emma at that moment as their first born asked where was mama 'and he repeated your name in so low and plaintive a tone, I declare it almost made me burst out crying'. Darwin ended: 'Dear old Doddy, one could write about him forever.'

Doddy's health, however, was a concern over the next few months. He had stomach problems and a persistent cough. Darwin's father, a well-known doctor, blamed the stomach aches on the fact that Doddy was being given half a cup of cream every morning. 'Nothing could be more injurious', Darwin reported his father saying. A little later Darwin found the child's shoes were wet and that there was no water by his bedside. 'I tell you all these disagreeableness that you may feel the same necessity that I do of our own selves looking and not trusting anything about our children to others.' In not relying too much on servants to help with the children, the Darwins were radical.

On 25 January, Darwin wrote that 'our little boy is a noble fat little fellow. And my Father has christened him Sir Tunberry Clumsy'. Clumsy was a character in Vanbrugh's comedy *The Relapse* and in Sheridan's less well known play *A Trip to Scarborough*.

Five days after his son had suffered the stomach aches, Darwin was unusually critical of Doddy. 'I fear he is a coward. A frog jumped near him … and (he) screamed with horror at the dangerous monster.' Darwin had to kiss him to deal with 'the open mouth bellowing'. Darwin finally solved the crisis by throwing a stick at the frog.

On 22 February 1842, when his son was 22 months old, Darwin wrote to his sister Susan Darwin:

> Poor Doddy lamented a good deal over Emma's going; he has got such a wise way of comforting himself on all occasions. If anything is refused him, as going with Emma, he says in a cheerful tone 'go in a geegee tomorro' – and if that is refused 'go some day' and if that is refused, he says 'go when Doddy big man'.

A month later Darwin wrote to Emma about playing at tussling with his son. On 9 May, he added that he hoped Doddy's temper was better. He agreed with Emma that calomel was worth trying, presumably because their son was teething, and ended with a reference to their new daughter, saying 'I long to kiss Annie's botty wotty'. By October, William was much better, Darwin was relieved to write.

Babies are not totally perfect. One unpleasant emotion William showed was jealousy. One incident occurred when Darwin fondled a large doll, and when he weighed little Annie, 'he being then 15½ months old'. Unfortunately Darwin did not detail the responses which convinced him his son was jealous. As so often, William's behaviour reminded Darwin of animals, for he pointed out dogs too were often jealous.

In October 1843, Darwin moaned that he hated the idea that Annie was not a 'good little soul … bless her little Botty'. He added that absence made him 'very much in love with his three little chickens'. By then they had a third child, Henrietta. Two months later, Darwin wrote that Emma had started to put two little combs in Annie's hair 'and it makes her look quite a beauty'. His little daughter was 'as good as gold except that she has most days an uncomfortable about five o'clock in the Evening when she is very difficult to appease'.

William could, of course, be naughty. 'When two years and three months old, William used to throw books or sticks, &c., at anyone who offended him.' Darwin's other sons did the same but not his daughters, which made him think 'that a tendency to throw objects is inherited by boys'.

William remained the main subject of Darwin's observations, but he was not especially dexterous,

> for when he was 2 years and 4 months old, he held pencils, pens, and other objects far less neatly and efficiently than did his sister who was then only 14 months old, and who showed great inherent aptitude in *handling anything*.

Children also threw tantrums. William's reactions showed how intensely children suffer from undefined fears. Darwin took William, when the child was two-and-a-quarter years old, to London Zoo. His son enjoyed looking at familiar animals such as deer, antelopes and all the birds, even ostriches, but the larger animals in cages frightened him. William often said afterwards that he wished to go again, but not to see 'beasts in houses'. Darwin suggested 'the vague but very real fears of children, which are quite independent of experience, are the inherited effects of real dangers and abject superstitions during ancient savage times'.

Three months after he had married Emma, the couple spent three weeks alone at Maer. During this period Darwin wrote a long note about the development of morality. David Hume had suggested that sympathy with another person was the origin of all moral feelings. Hume did not observe animals, of course, but Darwin argued that human beings have

> parental, conjugal and social instincts and perhaps others ... these instincts consist of a feeling of love or benevolence to the object in question. Without regarding their origin we see in other animals they consist in such active sympathy that the individual forgets itself and aids and defends and acts for others at his own expense.

Baby William gave Darwin the opportunity. 'The first sign of moral sense was noticed at the age of nearly 13 months', Darwin noted. 'I said "Doddy won't give poor papa a kiss, – naughty Doddy".' Darwin thought these words 'made him feel slightly uncomfortable; and at last when I had returned to my chair, he protruded his lips as a sign that he was ready to kiss me'. But William then shook his hand in an angry manner until Darwin received his kiss. It became a routine over the next few days, 'the reconciliation seemed to give him so much satisfaction, that several times afterwards he pretended to be angry and slapped me, and then insisted on giving me a kiss'.

Another example of 'moral' behaviour impressed Darwin. 'When 2 years and 3 months old, William gave his last bit of gingerbread to his little sister, and then cried out with high self-approbation "Oh kind Doddy, kind Doddy".' Two months later, he became extremely sensitive to ridicule, and often thought people who were laughing and talking together were laughing at him.

> A little later (2 years and 7½ months old) I met him coming out of the dining room with his eyes unnaturally bright, and an odd unnatural or affected manner, so that I went into the room to see who was there, and found that he had been taking pounded sugar, which he had been told not to do. As he had never been in any way punished, his odd manner certainly was not due to fear, and I suppose it was pleasurable excitement struggling with conscience.

Darwin believed the genesis of sympathy lay 'in a very slight change in association' whereby a person observing another's action would feel part of that pleasure or pain. If one followed a social instinct that would give lasting pleasure but giving in to personal appetites would give pleasure but that pleasure would fade.

A fortnight after William struggled with his conscience over the sugar, Darwin recorded his son being deceitful for the first time. He noticed William eyeing his pinafore, which he had carefully rolled up, and told his father to go away. Much intrigued, Darwin wanted to see what was in the pinafore, 'notwithstanding that he said there was nothing and repeatedly commanded me to "go away"'. The tell-tale pinafore turned out to be 'stained with pickle-juice; so that here was carefully planned deceit'.

Darwin was also struck by the following:

> An infant understands to a certain extent, and as I believe at a very early period, the meaning or feelings of those who tend him, by the expression of their features. There can hardly be a doubt about this with respect to smiling; and it seemed to me that the infant whose biography I have here given understood a compassionate expression at a little over five months old.

Darwin then repeated the fact that William had shown sympathy with his nurse by pretending to cry when she seemed upset; he was just over six months old.

Emotional intelligence came young to William too.

> When pleased after performing some new accomplishment, being then almost a year old, he evidently studied the expression of those around him. It was probably due to differences of expression and not merely of the form of the features that certain faces clearly pleased him much more than others, even at so early an age as a little over six months. Before he was a year old, he understood intonations and gestures, as well as several words and short sentences. He understood one word, namely, his nurse's name, exactly five months before he invented his first word mum; and this is what might have been expected, as we know that the lower animals easily learn to understand spoken words.

Darwin did not publish his observations on his daughter Annie for reasons which will become clear. She was born in Gower Street on 2 March 1841, two years after William; another descendant, Randal Keynes, in *Annie's Box* describes some aspects of Annie's life.

When she was nearly three, she and William were allowed to cut pictures out of *Punch* and *The Illustrated London News*. A few months later, Darwin saw his daughter looking at a print of a girl weeping at her mother's grave. 'I heard Willy say "You are crying". Annie burst out laughing and said, "No I aren't. It is only water coming out of my eyes."' When the children were a little older, the Darwins hired a tutor to teach them how to write in an elegant hand. Annie's handwriting, however, was often tilted and her spelling was less than perfect.

The Darwins were caring and careful parents but they suffered, as did many Victorian parents, as three of their ten children died young. Annie became seriously ill when she was ten years old. Darwin took her to Malvern to see Dr Gully. She was not in a critical condition and he left her in Gully's hands while he went to London.

He had to return on 17 April 1851 because Annie had become dangerously ill. 'You would not recognise her at all with her poor, hard, sharp pinched features', Darwin wrote to his wife. Gully told Darwin he was not sure Annie would last the night. Darwin flung himself on the sofa in an agony of grief. But she did last the night. For the next five days, Darwin wrote each day to Emma. One day he wrote: 'I can't sit still but am constantly up and down.' On Monday there was hope as Annie seemed better, 'but I must not hope too much.' Then she vomited a bright green fluid and the moment of hope would prove a cruel illusion.

Annie died peacefully around noon on Wednesday, 23 April. Darwin was grateful that they at least had a daguerreotype of her taken two years earlier.

Annie's death left both her parents endlessly anxious about the health of their children. Darwin wrote that most melancholy of works, a memorial to a dead child. It is worth quoting at length because it says so much about her father's love for her. He called her 'our poor child'.

> Her dear face now rises before me, as she used sometimes to come running down stairs with a stolen pinch of snuff for me, her whole form radiant with the pleasure of giving pleasure. Even when playing with her cousins when her joyousness almost passed into boisterousness, a single glance of my eye, not of displeasure (for I thank God I hardly ever cast one on her,) but of want of sympathy would for some minutes alter her whole countenance. This sensitiveness to the least blame, made her most easy to manage & very good: she hardly ever required to be found fault with, & was never punished in any way whatever. Her sensitiveness appeared extremely early in life, & showed itself in crying bitterly over any story at all melancholy; or on parting with Emma even for the shortest interval. Once when she was very young she exclaimed 'Oh Mamma, what should we do, if you were to die'.

Darwin adored her – and appreciated her. Annie was very affectionate.

> When quite a Baby, this showed itself in never being easy without touching Emma, when in bed with her, & quite lately she would when poorly fondle for any length of time one of Emma's arms. When very unwell, Emma lying down beside her, seemed to soothe her in a manner quite different from what it would have done to any of our other children. So again, she would at almost any time spend half-an-hour in arranging my hair, 'making it' as she called it 'beautiful', or in smoothing, the poor dear darling, my collar or cuffs, in short in fondling me.

She liked being kissed.

> Occasionally she had a pretty coquettish manner towards me; the memory of which is charming: she often used exaggerated language, & when I quizzed her by exaggerating what she had said, how clearly can I now see the little toss of the head & exclamation of 'Oh Papa what a shame of you'.

> She cordially admired the younger children; how often have I heard her emphatically declare 'what a little duck, Betty is, is not she?'

Annie loved names and words, Darwin wrote, looked them up them in dictionaries and

> also she would take a strange interest in comparing word by word two editions of the same book; and again she would spend hours in comparing the colours of any objects with a book of mine, in which all colours are arranged & named.

Darwin admired his daughter's courage as she coped with her last illness, writing:

> her conduct in simple truth was angelic; she never once complained; never became fretful; was ever considerate of others; & was thankful in the most gentle, pathetic manner for everything done for her. When so exhausted that she could hardly speak, she praised everything that was given her, & said some tea 'was beautifully good.' When I gave her some water, she said 'I quite thank you'; & these, I believe were the last precious words ever addressed by her dear lips to me.
>
> We have lost the joy of the Household, and the solace of our old age: she must have known how we loved her; oh that she could now know how deeply, how tenderly we do still & shall ever love her dear joyous face. Blessings on her.

After Annie died, Darwin still walked to church with his family every Sunday but he did not go inside – ever. Decades later, his son Francis noted that talking of Annie would still make Darwin cry when he was an old man. In the last year of his life, Darwin consoled the botanist Joseph Hooker, who had just lost a brother. Darwin contrasted the death of someone young and someone old. 'Death', he told Hooker, 'when there is a bright future ahead is grief never to be wholly obliterated'. He never could bear to visit Annie's grave because it would bring back such vivid memories. Annie's death had been 'a sudden and dreadful wrench' while one knew that the death of a father was always 'drawing slowly nearer'.

Three weeks after Annie died, Emma gave birth to a son. She hoped that caring for a newborn child might ease her pain but it did not. Instead both she and Darwin imagined how much pleasure Annie might have got from the new baby they called Horace. Emma had her religion as consolation; she believed she and Annie would meet again after death, but Darwin did not have that solace. For him work was the best way to cope and he did that. After Annie's death, he worked on his two volumes on barnacles. He let the children watch him often as he worked, their presence being comforting. When one of his sons visited a neighbour, the boy asked 'where does your father do his barnacles?' His friend was understandably mystified.

After Horace, Darwin and Emma had a daughter, Mary Eleanor, who died when she was not even a month old. A year and two days after Mary's birth, another daughter, Henrietta, was born who would write a touching memoir of her parents. Darwin always enjoyed his children and their company as a few incidents reveal.

One letter records four-year-old Francis offering his father a nut and then half a nut. Leonard boasted when he was five that he was an extraordinary grass finder as he offered his sister a blade of grass at dinner. The family was playful, far more playful than Darwin's own family had been, a blessing he attributed to Emma's influence.

Darwin, however, was eternally anxious about the health of his children and whether they had inherited his tendency to be sick. In late August 1857 Leonard fell seriously ill and Darwin became convinced they would lose another child. 'It makes life very bitter', he wrote to Hooker. But after ten days the boy recovered. 'A man ought to be bachelor', Darwin added, because then he would not have to suffer such agonies of anxiety over the children he loved.

A year later six children in the village where they lived died of scarlet fever. Henrietta fell ill and the family went at once to the Isle of Wight to make sure Henrietta got better. After ten horrible days, she did.

The last death the couple had to endure was of their youngest, Charles, who suffered from Down's Syndrome and died on 28 June 1858 when he was 18 months old. Henrietta said: 'Both my father and mother were infinitely tender towards him but when he died in the summer of 1858 after their first sorrow they could only feel thankful.'

Darwin liked working with his children. Francis helped with his father's work on *Climbing Plants*. As they lived in Kent, which was famous for its hops, the question to ponder when drinking beer was, how does a hop find a support and grow on it? Darwin and Francis cultivated different hop species under glass plates and noted the position of the tip. They discovered that the shoot of a young hop sprouts round all points of the compass. They studied other climbing plants and found out they gyrated until they latched on to a support, but even hops showed some 'intelligence' and could alter their growth to avoid obstacles.

Darwin also worked with Horace on worms. Father and son discovered that worms, like plants, can make their way round obstacles; one section of the book had the heading 'Mental Qualities'. In a less than wonderful pun they noted that 'There is little to be said on this head'. Worms might be low on 'the scale of organisation but possess some degree of intelligence'.

Darwin also let his children witness some of his anxieties. In 1865, for example, Leonard, who was then in his teens, realised how distressed his father was when they were in the garden. Darwin turned away from his son as if he could not bear to speak. Leonard wrote:

> Then suddenly there shot through my mind the conviction that he wished he were no longer alive. Must there not have been a strained and weary expression on his face to have produced in these circumstances such an effect on a boy's mind.

Darwin fretted about how the children would manage to make a living, just like Freud would do about his children 50 years later. Darwin would have less cause to do so, however. George became an astronomer and, eventually, Plumian Professor of Astronomy and Experimental Philosophy at Cambridge University. Francis edited his father's *Autobiography* and became a botanist specializing in plant physiology. He influenced Darwin's 'The power of movement in plants' (1880).

When Horace went to Cambridge, Darwin wrote him a lovely letter which revealed much of his own way of approaching scientific thinking:

> I have been speculating last night what makes a man a discoverer of undiscovered things; and a most perplexing problem it is. Many men who are very clever – much cleverer than the discoverers – never originate anything. As far as I can conjecture the art consists in habitually searching the causes and meaning of everything which occurs. This implies sharp observation and requires as much knowledge as possible of the subject investigated.

Horace became an engineer and founded the Cambridge Scientific Instrument Company. He was the Mayor of Cambridge from 1896 to 1897, and was made a Fellow of the Royal Society in 1903.

One final scene shows how close to their father the 'brood' stayed. In 1880, two years before he died, Darwin's children surprised him in his study. They had a present for him, a fur coat. Francis wrote to Henrietta: 'You will see from father's delightful letter how much pleased he was.' Darwin wrote to the children thanking them and added 'The coat, however warm will never warm my body as much as your dear affection has warmed my heart'.

In her memoir, Henrietta wrote touchingly of her father's last illness.

> At the end of the month (January 1882) my father's health relapsed. All February and March this state continued and he did not dare walk far from the house for fear of the heart pain seizing him. I have however happy memories of his sitting with my mother in the orchard.

By 13 March Darwin was near the end. He rallied in April, however, and on the 17th, Emma wrote: 'Good day, a little work, out in the orchard twice.' The next day, she wrote 'Fatal attack at 12'. But Darwin rallied yet again over the next two days and recovered enough to tell Henrietta '"You are the best of dear nurses". He passed away peacefully at half past three on April 19th'. It was a calm end to an intellectually stormy life. Emma wrote to her son Leo: 'I will tell you that the entire love and veneration of all you dear sons for your Father is one of my chief blessings and binds us together more than ever.'

Darwin's funeral was a state occasion at Westminster Abbey. The pall bearers included two dukes, an earl, the queen's printer and three men who had supported Darwin's theory of evolution, Joseph Hooker, Thomas Huxley and Alfred Russell Wallace. His publication of a paper in 1859 finally pushed Darwin to publish *On the Origin of the Species*.

It is a pity that Darwin did not publish his observations of William far earlier because they might well have spurred other early 'psychologists' to study babies in some detail. It is worth too contrasting the precision of his notes with the work of

James Sully, a theologian who became a psychologist after studying with Helmholtz and du Bois Redmond who also taught Freud. In the 1890s, Sully published two books on children. Children feared animals and the dark, and Sully added, a shade dramatically, 'Children sometimes appear to feel a repugnance to a black sheep or other animal just because they dislike black objects, though the feeling may not amount to fear properly so called'. Sully thought that 'the mere bigness of an animal, aided by the uncanny look which often comes from an apparent distortion of the familiar human face, may account for some of these early fears'.

Birds could also be frightening because when children saw them peck, these 'movements readily appear to a child's mind a kind of attack'. Sully claimed this explained why pigs once frightened a two-year-old boy when he saw them sucking ... 'he thought they were biting their mother'.

Sully added that 'Alarming animals, generally black, as that significant expression *bête noire* shows, are frequently the dread of these solitary hours in the dark room'. He cited as an example of how frightening 'these nightmare fears may be in the case of nervous children, like Charles Lamb'. Lamb's family had a history of insanity and, as a child, he was plagued by nightmares, many of which featured an aunt who appeared as a witch.

Freud was born three years before Darwin published *On the Origin of the Species*. Freud, however, only ever observed one child, who is known in the literature as Little Hans. In the light of that, I look first at one of the most immediate successors to Darwin, one of the most influential psychologists of the twentieth century – John B. Watson – who did observe children, and not just his own. Watson believed that psychology should be useful and that its insights should allow people to improve their lives. He also believed he owed it to his children to try to bring them up according to his theories.

Notes and references

Much of the material in this chapter comes from Darwin's pioneering 'A biographical sketch of an infant', *Mind*, vol. 2, 285–95 (1877). He polished and published these in response to an article by the French historian, Hippolyte Taine: 'Lingual development in babyhood', *Popular Science Monthly*, vol. 9 (1876).

Of the many biographies of Darwin and his family, the most useful for this study have been:
Berra, T., *Darwin and His Children*, Oxford University Press (2013).
Bowlby, J., *Charles Darwin*, Hutchinson (1990).
Darwin, Henrietta (ed.), *Emma Darwin, a Memoir*, John Murray (1915).

The other relevant works by Darwin himself are, of course, first:
Darwin, C., *On the Origin of the Species*, John Murray (1859).
Darwin, C., *The Correspondence of Charles Darwin*, vol. 2, edited by Frederick Burkhardt and Sydney Smith, Cambridge University Press (1988).

Darwin, C., *Autobiographies of Charles Darwin*, Penguin (1991; originally published in 1880).

Darwin, C. and Darwin, F., *The Movements and Habits of Climbing Plants*, Quill Pen Press (2010; originally published by Appleton in 1880).

Darwin, C. and Darwin, H., *The Formation of Vegetable Mould Through the Action of Worms*, Echo Press (2007; originally published by John Murray in 1881).

Other references:

Gallup, Gordon, Keenan, Julian and Falk, Dean, *The Face in the Mirror*, Harper Perennial (2004).

Padel, R. (2010) *Darwin: A Life In Poems*, Vintage (2010).

Reiss, D., *The Dolphin in the Mirror*, Mariner (2012).

Reissland, N., Neonatal imitation in the first hour of life: observations in rural Nepal. *Developmental Psychology*, vol. 24, 464–9 (1988).

Sully, James, *Children's Ways*, Appleton (1917).

3
JOHN B. WATSON
A behaviourist's tragedies

John Broadus Watson boasted he could fashion any child into a lawyer, a doctor or a thief.

When I wrote a biography of Watson, I interviewed his two surviving children – Polly Hartley, his eldest daughter by his first marriage, and James, his youngest son by his second wife, Rosalie Rayner. Twenty years after their father died both had strong feelings and mixed memories.

Watson came to his views early in his career. His own childhood was far from ideal. He was born in Greenville, South Carolina in 1878, which was described as 'a village of 20,000 souls'. Souls was apt because Greenville was a gospel village. In 1825, the Baptist Theological College was set up there. Watson's mother, Emma, was a devout Baptist. His father, however, was a confirmed sinner – and proud of it. Pickens drank to excess, chased women and finally ran away to live with a Native American woman. His 13-year-old son was devastated and began being 'somewhat insubordinate at school'. Cheeking teachers was the least of it. Watson and a friend, Joe Leech, boxed each other when their teachers were not looking. School over, the lads would cause mayhem on their way home; they often engaged in the charming Southern pastime of 'nigger fighting'. Watson only got into serious trouble, though, when he fired a gun in the middle of Greenville. Somehow he escaped jail, however.

Watson never explained how, during the next two years, he calmed down, but he did so and became an excellent student. Then, he somehow persuaded the president of the local university, Furman, to accept him. Watson buckled down to his books and fellow students nicknamed him 'Swats', which he hated. After Pickens left, the family was poor so Watson had to take on many odd jobs to pay for his education. He grumbled but he worked; the wild teenager had taken the first steps to becoming a respectable academic – for the next 20 years at least. His troubled childhood left its mark, though. Watson was often insecure. He slept always with a night light on, for example, and was frightened of thunderstorms. The irrational fears of psychologists deserve a study perhaps.

Watson was 21 when he got his degree from Furman. He wanted to leave Greenville but his mother was desperately ill. To make a living, Watson taught in a local school. There he began the work which would make him one of the key psychologists of the twentieth century. At the Batesburg Institute, he kept 'a house of rats', partly to amuse the children and partly because he liked observing and training the animals.

When his mother died in July 1900, Watson was free to pursue his studies. He persuaded the ever pliable president of Furman to write glowing letters of recommendation to two top universities, Princeton and the University of Chicago. Both were willing to accept him as a graduate student; Watson chose Chicago. A month after his mother died, Watson left Greenville with just $50 in his pocket. He never went back.

Watson's doctoral dissertation, *Animal Education* (1903), analysed the relationship between brain and the development of behaviour, mainly learning, in rats. This research would influence his views on children – and the way he eventually brought up his own.

Watson was always good with his hands and built a series of 'puzzle boxes' for the rats. One box had hidden entrances, which the baby rats had to find to reach food. The rat had to pull a string to open a latch to get at the food. Later he made a more elaborate contraption, a plank the rats had to walk. At a certain point on the plank, their weight counterbalanced the latch and sprang open the door so they could reach the food. Young rats – those who were 30 days old – mastered these tasks quicker than rats who were 75 days old, Watson found.

Learning was not an even process. One rat took 12 minutes the first time before he 'realized' he needed to pull the string to open the latch. The second time the same rat got the solution in 12 minutes again, but then he solved the problem in three minutes, in eight minutes, in two minutes, then in three minutes again. After that, there was a sudden burst of insight as the rat took 0.35 minutes, 0.33, 0.16, 0.08, 0.108 minutes to spring the latch. Watson had made an important discovery about learning; the process was jagged. Rats reached their peak of performance between 23 and 27 days, he also discovered. 'It is a pleasure to watch them', he wrote, 'they fly from place to place trying everything'.

Watson became the youngest person to obtain a doctorate at Chicago. There, he wrote 35 years later in a brief autobiographical note, 'I first began a tentative formulation of my later point of view'. In 1902, however, the formulation was not just tentative but private and triggered considerable anxiety. As he was completing his doctorate, Watson had some kind of breakdown. Studying the rats led him to believe psychology had to be an objective science which relied on observation, and nothing but observation. People should be observed just like rats. His fellow psychologists, however, believed one had to use introspection to understand the human mind. And rats were not rat-ional enough to introspect. At the time introspection was not about understanding your feelings but trying to pin down the 'atoms of the mind', the basic elements of thinking. Psychologists were trying to imitate physicists in their search for these atoms. Watson knew his ideas conflicted with everyone else in the field, and that made him very nervous.

The breakdown was also the result of rejection. Watson proposed to a young woman who refused him. He soon found another love though. One student in his laboratory, Mary Ickes, came from a wealthy and rather grand family. Her brother, Harold Ickes, would become Franklin D. Roosevelt's Secretary of State. Ickes saw Watson as an adventurer who was not good enough for his sister. When he realized Mary was keen on the psychologist, he sent her away to Altoona in Pennsylvania.

Watson was not going to be put off so easily, however; he followed Mary and proposed to her, though he only had a modest salary of $600. She accepted him despite her family's objections. Their first son, John, was born in 1904 and their daughter, Polly, two years later. The children were fun to be with and to watch grow up, but Watson did not observe them in any formal way.

Two years after Polly was born, Watson moved from Chicago to Johns Hopkins and became professor of psychology when he was only 28 years old. The next 12 years were very productive – and that owed something to his stable marriage. Their daughter Polly told me that her parents hardly ever quarrelled, or at least that they took care to do so when they were alone. Polly, who would lead a troubled life herself, was not happy, however. Her mother was not particularly demonstrative and neither she nor her father tended to go in for much hugging and kissing. When Polly was a child it seemed to her just to be their natural style; it was not then a philosophy of parenting based on Watson's theories.

By 1913 Watson had done significant work on many aspects of animal behaviour and had started to study a few human behaviours which included studies of how accurately people typed and shot with bows and arrows when they were drunk. Watson, however, had seen that psychologists kept on contradicting each other when they discussed their introspections. These contradictions, Watson argued, made it impractical to rely on dreams, memories and associations to understand why we do what we do. Look at the behaviour instead, he insisted. The paper that established him as a major figure, 'Psychology as the behaviourist views it', argued that psychology had 'failed signally … during the fifty-odd years of its existence as an experimental discipline to make its place in the world as an undisputed natural science'. He blamed the fact that there was

> something esoteric in its methods. If you fail to reproduce my findings, it is not due to some fault in your apparatus or in the control of your stimulus, but it is due to the fact that your introspection is untrained.

Psychology should abandon introspection and rely on the observation of behaviour. The idea was so controversial that Watson did not send a draft of his paper to any of his friends because he was worried they might try to persuade him to play down his views. In the end, the paper was largely well-received.

In February 1916, Watson decided to focus on the study of children. His plan was strikingly simple, but it had never been tried before. He would observe 40 children from birth onwards in a nursery. He had hardly started, though, when America joined the First World War. As one of America's leading psychologists, Watson was asked to visit American troops in Europe to help craft educational materials to stop the GIs sleeping with French girls and getting VD. The Pentagon feared for its privates' 'privates'.

Before he sailed for Europe, Watson kissed his 11-year-old daughter, Polly, which surprised her as he had not done that for years. James, his youngest son, also claimed his father never kissed him.

Watson hated the military and, after less than a year, he was back at Johns Hopkins and determined to continue his work on children. He soon found out that William Darwin had perhaps not been as much of a prodigy as his fond father had imagined. William had not fixated with two eyes on an object until he was nine days old, but in Baltimore, one 14-hour-old baby could coordinate his eye movements to stare at a light right in front of him; three hours later, the baby could turn his head and stare at a light 20 degrees to his right or left. Babies were smarter than psychology gave them credit for.

Watson also wanted to see how tiny babies responded to threats. Did they make 'defence movements'? His experiment was comically crude. The experimenter, almost certainly Watson, pinched the baby's nose. One outraged four-day-old put his hand up at once and pushed back at the aggressive psychologist's fingers. Pinching the babies' knees also upset them. These tiny infants could coordinate their muscles well enough to try to protect themselves. Impressive, Watson concluded.

Watson also observed smiles, that most powerful of signals a baby can give. He saw one four-day-old baby smiling. Other babies smiled on the seventh or eighth day, usually when stroked gently or tickled lightly. Babies often held out their arms to be held, asking for love. Love led to a disturbing thought. There seemed to be no immediate bond between a mother and a child. The fact that the mother stroked and embraced the child created the love, it seemed. Watson came to believe that most mothers became almost addicted to hugging and kissing their offspring – and that it might not be too healthy as it might foster incestuous impulses.

By 1919, Watson's marriage was in crisis. Mary, his wife, feared he was having an affair. She and Watson were invited to dine with a local couple, the Rayners. Their daughter Rosalie, Mary suspected, was in love with her husband. Mary was cunning as a rat, a comparison that is perhaps justified, given her husband's work. She pretended to feel unwell and went to lie down in Rosalie's bedroom. The moment she was alone, Mary searched all the cupboards and discovered passionate letters Watson had written.

The history of Johns Hopkins exacerbated the crisis. Mark Baldwin, Watson's predecessor as professor of psychology, had been sacked in 1908 after he had been discovered in what was then called 'a negro brothel'. A respectable university could not afford a second sexual scandal. Watson's daughter Polly told me her father realized he risked losing his job and tried to persuade Mary to go to Switzerland for two years so that there would no scandal and he might cling on to his position. Mary felt too angry and betrayed, and her brother Harold Ickes encouraged her to be uncompromising. She refused to go abroad. In the end, Watson had to resign before he was sacked.

Watson wrote later that every cell in his body belonged to Rosalie. Polly told me she believed Rosalie was the only person to whom her father gave himself heart and soul. She added she would never have described Rosalie that way in 1920 because the divorce was such a shattering experience for her.

The divorce was also a shattering experience for Watson. It cost him his job and all his money. He left for New York and had to live in a friend's flat. Nearly all his colleagues who had admired his work now shunned him. The only man to offer practical help was Stanley Resor who ran the advertising agency J. Walter Thompson. He offered Watson work but insisted the famous professor start at the bottom as a travelling salesman. That was the American way. The man who had been drafted in by the Pentagon to devise education programmes for GIs now had to go from shop to shop selling goods like Yuban Coffee. Doing that, Watson discovered he could increase sales massively if he got shops to place his products by the till so customers picked them up as they were paying. Working for J. Walter Thompson was the end of his career as an academic psychologist, but Watson did not want to abandon the research he had started on children.

After he went to J. Walter Thompson, Watson also wanted to pursue child psychology but he could not juggle two jobs. So Rosalie introduced him to a friend of hers, Mary Cover Jones, a young psychologist from Vassar, who could observe children every day. Watson persuaded the Laura Spellman Rockefeller Foundation to finance her. Jones would watch the infants at the Manhattan Day Nursery and carry on the work Watson had started at Johns Hopkins. He went faithfully to the nursery every Saturday and tried to squeeze an hour or two during the week to visit, in between helping devise campaigns for Pond's Cold Cream, Camel cigarettes and railway companies.

Only one aspect of Watson's work with children is much remembered now – his work on Little Albert and how infants could be conditioned to fear. These studies started tamely; Watson showed three babies a pigeon, a rabbit and a black cat; in every case the seemingly fearless baby tried to touch the animal. When one baby was 172 days old, a stranger held her and took her into a darkened room where she could not see her mother. 'Pshaw', the baby seems to have said, 'Can't scare me'.

Children were not naturally afraid of animals but rather curious, Watson concluded. Their over-protective parents taught them fear, a view that would affect his attitude to his own children.

Little Albert has become one of the most controversial infants in psychology. Watson and Rayner showed the nine-month-old boy a white rat and other furry objects. Albert enjoyed playing with them until, one day, Watson made a loud sound behind the baby's head. Albert screamed and was obviously very scared. The stimulus produced a lasting response as Watson and Rayner showed Albert animals and furry toys many times without making any noise, let alone a terrifying one. It did not help. Albert still recoiled in terror; a little animal that had been a source of joy and curiosity now triggered fear.

The experiment has been the source of much controversy. Years later Little Albert was identified as Douglas Merritte, the son of a wet nurse who worked at a hospital on the Hopkins campus. But historical detective work has shown there was a complication. Douglas died at the age of six of hydrocephalus. Did that mean he had reacted to the rats and noise the way a normal baby would? If Albert was abnormal, one could not extrapolate from his experience to that of all children, which was precisely what Watson wanted to do.

Watson and Rosalie's first child, Bill, was born on 21 November 1921. Watson liked having a baby around again. He told the one psychologist who had been supportive during his divorce crisis, E.B. Titchener, that having a baby made him feel young again and that he was sorry he had to go to work every day; he would rather stay at home and watch Billy grow up day by day. But Rosalie was a psychologist too and so she made many of the day-to-day observations. The parallel with Piaget and his wife is, we shall see, striking.

One of the first things Rosalie realized was that singing could quieten the baby and, which was typical of the couple, that suggested an experiment. They tried to see what would happen if Bill listened to music while his movements were hampered. Rosalie restrained Bill's head, hands and feet while someone played the Victrola. Billy raged for all the soothing music.

Next, when Bill was three months old, the Watsons tried to condition his bowel movements. 'I thought I had succeeded in conditioning bowels but it was a false observation', Rosalie wrote. In fact, Bill was often constipated and had to be given laxatives.

Later in February Bill was using his hands forcefully. They no longer 'waved at random on each side of the body. They seem more stable to work towards each other'. At 110 days Bill could reach out to objects; by May, when he was six months old, he had some skills. He could take a doll or a toy rabbit and swing it. The Watsons' notes show their child was becoming more curious – and that reminded Watson of the young rats he had studied back in 1902.

By April Bill was also beginning to make sounds. He was cooing, laughing out loud and saying 'Ah'. Once Rosalie noticed her son saying 'Da' and she repeated it back to him. She and Watson also tried to condition him to say 'Dada' – frustratingly no details of how were given – but by June they still had not had much success.

On one occasion Rosalie had to leave her son for a few days but when she got back the baby did not recognize her. She said she had to recondition him but does not actually specify what that involved.

Watson had definite – and by present-day standards sometimes questionable – ideas. When Bill was eight months old his parents were going to a party and Watson left the room first. Rosalie tip-toed away through the back door, hoping her baby son would not realize she had left. But Bill was not to be fooled and began to howl. Watson was amused but he also disapproved; he did not want his son to be so dependent.

Bill was starting to say 'Boo Boo' or 'Goo Goo' on a regular basis but his parents wanted to him to burble 'Dada'. It was only on 24 June that he managed to do that although initially it did not refer to his father but to his bottle. The notes on Bill then seem to come to an end for some 18 months.

Watson wanted to understand what had happened to Little Albert, and Mary Cover Jones focused on fears – and what could be done to cure children of them. As usual it required furry animals. One child at the nursery was a five-year-old girl who was terrified of rabbits. They read her Beatrix Potter stories; they explained rabbits were nice creatures; they got her to make unthreatening rabbits out of plasticine. Slowly, they managed to get her to say that she did like rabbits, but the next time she saw the rabbits, she still howled with fear.

A second child, Peter, was a bright three-year-old boy who was frightened of rabbits and white rats, fur coats, feathers, cotton wool, frogs, fish and mechanical toys; they all scared him – sometimes silly. When he saw a two-year-old girl pick up a rat and play with it, Peter screamed and fell flat on his back. Watson was by now sure that the way to de-condition fear was by gradual exposure to the stimulus that provoked it. Watson persuaded the nursery to give Peter his lunch while the rabbit was displayed in a wire cage. Day by day, the cage got closer. Finally Peter did eat with one hand and play with the rabbit with the other. Watson's technique is now known as desensitization and used with some success in the treatment of some phobias.

Watson and Rosalie hoped to bring their own children up free of such fears. In an amusing article, 'I am the mother of the behaviourist's sons', Rosalie admitted she was a little too affectionate to always stick to her husband's rules. 'In some respects I bow to the great wisdom in the science of behaviorism, and in others I am rebellious', she wrote.

> I secretly wish that on the score of [the children's] affections, they will be a little weak when they grow up, that they will have a tear in their eyes for the poetry and drama of life and a throb for romance ... I like being merry and gay and having the giggles. The behaviorists think giggling is a sign of maladjustment.

Billy did not disappoint his mother, in fact, as he was so fond of her he would cry when she went out. Watson might adore Rosalie but she remained his devoted student and kept to his stringent rules.

Billy also developed a terror of goldfish, but his father exposed him to goldfish just as Peter had been exposed to rabbits. The goldfish phobia disappeared. Watson had less success, Rosalie noted, 'with nail biting. Our older son bites his nails which is a very bad symptom in a behaviourist's family'. They tried pasting glue over his fingers, sending him to bed with gloves on. But no ploy worked.

Watson was the first person who tried to devise an objective test for two of Freud's key ideas – the Oedipus Complex and sibling rivalry. Neither of these tests required methodological subtlety, according to Watson. If an infant boy saw his father 'violently kiss' his mother, would the child become livid with jealousy? The test was child's play. Watson kissed his second wife Rosalie passionately and waited to see if their 11-month-old son, Billy, would howl. If he howled, the Oedipus Complex would have been shown to be true. Baby Billy did not howl when he was just under a year old, but when he was a year older, he had become perfectly Oedipal – and tried to hit his father.

Sibling rivalry was not going to challenge Watson's experimental imagination either. Did a toddler attack a new baby? Yes or no. Freud himself had arrived at the idea of sibling rivalry during his self-analysis which started in 1896. He discovered that 40 years earlier, when his parents had a second son, baby Julius, he had not merely been jealous (unconsciously, of course) but wanted the baby dead. The two-year-old Freud did not do his brother any harm by sticking pins in his arms or resorting to any other kind of violence. (In fact Julius was sickly and died when he was eight months old.)

Watson's notes suggest testing began when Billy was 11 months old. He and Rosalie decided to see what happened if they were physically affectionate. 'When father and mother embraced violently, the youngster could not be made to keep his eyes on his parents.' Billy was not the least interested, but it was very different if his parents shouted at one another and, especially, if they seemed to fight; then, the noise and angry faces made Billy whimper and cry, as if he were afraid. It was not until Billy was two that he behaved as Freud's theories suggested he should. Then, if Rosalie embraced Watson, their son would begin to attack his father. When Billy was two years and nine months old, he would say on Sundays 'you going to office, Dada', which would mean he could have his mother all to himself. Oedipus was surfacing.

When Billy was two years old, his parents had their second child, Jimmy. When Rosalie came back from hospital after two weeks, Billy's nurse kept him in his room. Then he was brought to see his mother who was feeding the baby at the breast. Sibling rivalry would suggest Billy foam at the mouth or stick pins, if he had any pins, into the new arrival. Billy did nothing of the sort; he leaned against his mother's knees and said 'How do Mama'. He did not try to kiss her and, for about half a minute, he did not appear to notice the baby. Then he saw Jimmy and said 'Little Baby', took the baby's hands, patted them together and said 'that baby that baby'. The nurse then took the baby from Rosalie which upset Billy who said 'Mama take baby'. Watson had, arguably, shown the Oedipus Complex was real but that Freud's notions of sibling rivalry were flawed. Billy seemed rather fond of the new arrival, often cooed 'little baby' and took his brother's hands.

A second child did not make Rosalie a better behaviourist mother. Though she agreed with her husband's views, she was not as strict as he was. Sometimes she could not resist 'kissing her two little pieces of protoplasm'. The protoplasms loved it, of course.

Watson soon became worried that mothers kissing their children would stimulate the Oedipus Complex, while if a father hugged his boys they were likely to become effeminate. As the boys grew older, their parents tried to deal with problems in a supremely rational way. They often discussed problems round the dinner table. The children could speak freely but we do not know if the children understood the issues.

Watson recorded one later instance of jealousy. When Billy was three, a nurse said, 'You are a naughty boy. Jimmie is a nice boy – I love him'. The Watsons sacked the nurse who had tried to control Billy's behaviour in such a crude way.

As the children grew up, Watson had a rather different anxiety; he did not want his sons to become too dependent on each other. They shouldn't hug, either, so Billy had to shake hands with Jimmy when they were going to bed.

Toilet training remained a concern. As soon as the children could toddle, Watson insisted they go to the bathroom at eight o'clock and 'take care of the matter themselves'. The boys then had to go back to their parents and report; the adults were not so obsessed as to insist on inspecting the toilet before it was flushed. Their policy was to trust their children. According to their second son, this admirable idea was a little naive as both he and his brother lied about what they managed to produce.

The observations allowed the Watsons to list what made their boys cry. These included, which is no surprise, having to sit on the toilet as well as being left alone in a room and watching the adult leave. Other actions that made the boys cry were failing to get a child to play, being dressed, being undressed and being bathed. Many of these reactions were rage responses brought on by the fact of having their movements hampered, Watson and Rayner claimed.

The constant observations led Watson to conclude that his children cried most often between nine and 11 in the morning. Tiredness seemed to be part of the problem, so Watson suggested the children have a rest before lunch. Again irritatingly the notes do not tell us if it worked.

In one way Watson and Rosalie were extremely progressive. They never felt their children should not see them embracing. Billy saw his mother naked and was taught the proper words for his genitals. Once he said that his mother had big black breasts and he had little white ones.

Though he was no longer a professor, Watson was much in demand as an expert. He wrote on child behaviour in popular magazines like *Harper's*, *McCalls* and *Cosmopolitan*, and gave many talks on the radio which made him a national figure. In 1928, he and Rosalie published *Psychological Care of Infant and Child*, when Billy was seven and Jimmy was five. The book became a best-seller and was highly influential. It argued that bringing up a child requires discipline on the part of the parent. Parents had to be much tougher with themselves. They should not look on children as toys created for their own pleasure. Children had the right to expect that their parents would prepare them for the modern world rather than mollycoddle them to gratify their own egos.

Fathers had to restrain the appalling behaviour of mothers, Watson argued. Mothers were too soft and kept on smothering the baby with hugs and kisses. Most mothers, Watson said, were guilty of '*psychological* murder . . . I know hundreds who want to possess their children's souls'. Watson outraged 1920s women's groups, complaining 'kissing the baby to death is just about as popular a sport as it has ever been'. Once when he and his wife went on a drive with friends, he noticed one mother kissed her baby 32 times. Watson shocked the Mothers' Union even more by suggesting that all this kissing 'is at bottom a sex seeking response'.

Fathers had to protect babies from such smother love but, unfortunately, many were more obsessed with getting their children to obey them. 'Most fathers should be punished for the idiotic parental duty dogma they try to instil in their young.' The dogma was that children owed their parents. 'Children don't owe their parents anything', Watson countered. Watson also warned of the dangers of corporal punishment and what he saw as silly Victorian fears about masturbation.

We have seen that Watson had cause to be bitter about his own childhood and, as he became a national figure, his father, who had abandoned him and his mother, started to turn up at his Manhattan office. Did remorseful Dad want to see his son? Not really. He just hoped to touch him for a few dollars – which Pickens used to get pickled. Father was not the only one asking for a hand-out, as it turned out. Watson's first son by Mary Ickes, John, was 28 years old and finding it hard to make a living. He too tried to wheedle loans which were rarely, if ever, repaid.

For Watson, a wise parent was detached, not punitive. 'In many ways I adored him as an individual', Jimmy said in an interview in *The Journal of the History of the Behavioural Sciences* in 1987. His father was bright, witty and reflective. 'But he was also conversely unresponsive, emotionally uncommunicative, unable to express and cope with any feelings of emotion of his own and determined unwittingly to deprive my brother and me of any kind of emotional foundation', Jimmy told me. He also remembered there were no toys in the bathroom and no toys to cuddle. A clear legacy of their father's past which had left him with a dread of the dark, the boys were never allowed any night lights.

Jimmy told me he thought his father was influenced by Freud. A child who was touched too much by his mother might fall in love with her and Freud suggested being too close to one's mother might make a man homosexual. So Watson also kept his physical distance – and wanted Rosalie to do so too.

'Watsonism has become gospel and catechism in the nurseries and drawing rooms of America', the philosopher Mortimer Adler despaired in 1928. The philosopher Bertrand Russell differed, claiming that Watson ignored the fact that some children, like Mozart, were born with exceptional abilities. No one conditioned Mozart into being a great composer or Picasso into being a great artist. But Watson was right about the dangers of excessive mother love and Russell thought the advice was 'wholesome' for most parents. He finished his review by saying that no man had made such an important contribution to our knowledge of ourselves since Aristotle.

The press was often fulsome too. The *Atlantic Monthly* said the Watsons' book was 'a godsend to parents'. Many of Watson's old colleagues, however, thought he had demeaned himself – and psychology – by writing like an agony aunt.

Watson also believed in teaching his sons physical skills, so they learned how to swim, how to box and how to skate. Every weekend they went off to camps so they could sleep as soundly in tents as in their bedrooms.

Rosalie did not follow these rules naturally, though. She was, her son James told me, 'very much a fun person'. In the interview he gave ten years after he had talked to me, Jimmy said he did not remember Rosalie 'bootlegging affection for her children'. She loved playing with her sons, and sometimes helped the boys tie their father's pyjamas in knots. They were even allowed to smear themselves with blue nail polish which they thought was great fun. 'I would like to feel that our sons are a little more part and parcel of our home.... I think lots of people are forgetting in this epoch of scientific rationalization what fun a home can be', Rosalie added.

As Watson was famous, the boys became celebrity children and models of modern children. *The World* pictured them riding bicycles and said: 'They are free from fear and temper tantrums. They are happy children.' Once Billy got lost in a snowstorm which led to a flurry of articles.

As the boys got older, Watson thought again they could talk about problems with their parents. A well-run family sat down and discussed what we now call 'issues'. Children could talk about difficult matters sensibly. Despite this emphasis on honesty in the Watson household, Jimmy only discovered that his father still always slept with a light on much later.

Dividing life between his work as a vice president of J. Walter Thompson and his family made it difficult for Watson to do, even to talk, serious psychology. His daughter Polly told me she remembered Watson's old colleague Karl Lashley, who was famous for his work on memory in animals, coming to dinner once. The two men talked deep into the night, something Watson relished because he rarely got the chance to discuss such topics now.

In 1931 the Watsons moved to Westport. With the help of Billy and Jimmy, he built a garage and then set about building a barn with a gothic vaulted room. This building is stunningly beautiful. Watson also made a motorized trolley on which one could wheel hamburgers to hungry guests. Watson taught his sons to ride and shoot and hunt, good masculine skills. He liked to do carpentry with his boys, which Jimmy felt was his most natural way of communicating with them. Very male! 'I respected my father as a man but not as a father really', he told me.

Jimmy did not remember his father ever showing anger either verbally or physically. Nevertheless, he felt he needed to please his father by working hard both at school and on the farm. His father paid him ten cents an hour. Watson's relationship with Billy was more difficult. 'Billy tended to goof off and shirk his duties round the animals. Dad chided him about it but was never terribly critical. He also got on Billy because Billy didn't work very hard in school.' Billy's school career was indeed erratic.

Despite wanting to please his father, Jimmy could be difficult. He quarrelled with Leslie Hohlman, a gay psychiatrist who visited the family with a number of boyfriends. It is odd that Watson, who was so afraid his boys might be gay, entertained Hohlman, who once turned up with a naval officer. The sailor and the shrink shared the master bedroom, which Jimmy found 'stunning', given his father's views on homosexuality. Jimmy did not like Hohlman who tried to force him to eat foods he did not like. Once Jimmy took this dislike to extremes and vomited in Hohlman's face.

Relations with Watson's first son John remained troubled. When he got married, Rosalie went to the wedding but Watson stayed away, complaining John was 'an improvident young puppy' who could not earn his own living. But Watson did not give up on him. When John was 30, his father lobbied Cornell University to accept him as a student. John, however, was typically feckless and did not last long as a student.

Their fairly placid, happy life in Westport would not last forever. In the summer of 1936, Rosalie caught dysentery and became desperately ill. Watson went to be with her in hospital every day. Jimmy went to see her a number of times and told me he was terrified by how grey his mother looked. In a final attempt to help, Watson gave Rosalie a blood transfusion. Billy and Jimmy were sent off to camp to spare them the distress of seeing their mother in danger of her life. When they came back their mother had died. Jimmy recalled his father putting his arms round him and Billy. Watson was crying. 'Somehow we will get through this', he told his sons. The rules of behaviourism had little to offer in such a crisis. Watson, in grief, did not really provide his children with the fathering they now desperately needed.

Jimmy felt his father was very confused by Rosalie's death. Billy had already started to go to boarding school and, not long after her death, Jimmy was sent to board too. 'I felt very cut off from Dad', he said. He was asked to leave the first school he went to because of his difficult behaviour, but his father did not comfort him. Instead he arranged for him to go to live with a former teacher and his wife who were very helpful to him. As I could not interview Billy, it is hard to be sure about how the trauma affected him but he finally went to Harvard and on to Columbia where he qualified as a doctor. Then, he chose to specialize in psychiatry, which at first pleased Watson who said he would have studied that, if he had been able to afford medical school. But Watson did not find Billy's professional choices easy. Jimmy believed that 'Dad had lots of difficulties with Billy's psychiatric orientation'. Watson was upset that his son decided to train as a Freudian psychoanalyst as psychoanalysis hardly focused on behaviour. The rift was not just theoretical. To become an analyst Billy had to have a training analysis which explored his memories and the problems of the way his parents had brought him up. Billy blamed many of his own difficulties on behaviourism. Analysis made him aware of his own feelings about his childhood, his brother said, 'and that's a process that's not designed to make Dad dance through the streets'. The analysis did not cure Billy of his persistent depression.

When the Second World War broke out in 1939, Jimmy, much to his father's alarm, joined the Air Force. He rang his father every Sunday evening to reassure him he was well.

After he had gone to work in advertising, psychologists ignored Watson. B.F. Skinner, who became the leading behaviourist of the 1930s and 1940s, never met Watson, for example, because by then Watson was a forgotten, almost historical figure. In 1956, a paper by Gustav Bergmann reminded the profession of Watson's contribution. Belatedly the American Psychological Association awarded Watson its gold medal. Jimmy, Billy and Watson's secretary, Ruth Lieb, came with him to

New York for the presentation. Ruth Lieb told me Watson said he would not go to the ceremony because he no longer had handmade shirts or shoes. Jimmy told me his father said it was because he had become so fat. So Watson, Jimmy and Ruth Lieb stayed behind in the hotel while Billy went to collect the gold medal on his father's behalf.

A year after he had been awarded the gold medal he was ambivalent about, Watson died. It was perhaps lucky he did so as, four years later, Billy committed suicide.

Billy's suicide was far from the last tragedy in the family. Watson's only daughter, Polly Hartley, also made a number of suicide attempts, though when I met her in 1978, she did not mention them or blame her father for her problems. She had a daughter who has, however, been strident. 'My household, as I was growing up, was a house of hidden shame', Marietta Hartley said. She felt her grandfather had always been ashamed of having been a farm boy of very modest means who happened to make good. Her mother, she said, was plagued by feelings of her own powerlessness, her inability to stop either of her parents from drinking, or later, to manage her terrible depressions. In her 1990 autobiography, *Breaking the Silence*, Marietta Hartley claimed that Watson's practical application of his theories caused all the distress. It would be fair to say, however, that Watson's theories were only one of a number of factors. Polly married an artist, a successful ad agency executive who was also an alcoholic. He committed suicide in the family's Brentwood apartment while Marietta and her mother were in the next room. Marietta then married a pathologically jealous man who beat her up frequently.

The ironies of Watson's life are terrible. He was a brilliant man who clearly tried hard to be a good father. Of his four children, John had to fight with drink, Polly made many suicide attempts and Billy committed suicide. Only Jimmy had an apparently happy life. As a psychologist he worked mainly in industry, including a long spell on an island in the Bering Sea at a fish cannery.

Freud, as we shall, seems to have been luckier or wiser as a father, even though his behaviour towards his daughter Anna was at times outrageous.

Notes and references

I have relied a good deal on my own biography of Watson, *John B Watson, the Founder of Behaviourism*, Routledge (1979), and my interviews with two of his children. His granddaughter had a very critical view of him as a failed family man (Marietta Hartley, *Breaking the Silence*, Putnam (1990)). Whereas Freud and Darwin have had many biographers, Watson has had to make do with only two so far. The second is K.W. Buckley, *Mechanical Man: John Broadus Watson and the Beginnings of Behaviorism*, Guilford Press (1989).

Other references:
Bergmann, G., The contribution of John B Watson. *Psychological Review*, vol. 63, 265–76 (1956).

Harrell, W. and Harrison, R., John B. Watson remembered: an interview with James B. Watson. *Journal of the History of the Behavioral Sciences*, vol. 23, 137–52 (1998).
Jones, M.C., The elimination of children's fears. *Journal of Experimental Psychology*, vol. 7, 383–90 (1924a).
Jones, M.C., A laboratory study of fear: the case of Peter. *Pedagogical Seminary*, vol. 31, 308–15 (1924b).
Rayner, R., I am the mother of the behaviourist's sons. *McCalls Magazine*, December (1930).
Todd, James T. and Morris, E.K. (eds), *Modern Perspectives on John B. Watson and Classical Behaviorism*, Greenwood Press (1994).
Watson, J.B., *Animal Education*, University of Chicago Press (1903).
Watson, J.B., Psychology as the behaviourist views it. *Psychological Review*, vol XX, 158–77 (1913).
Watson, J.B. and Rayner, R., *Psychological Care of Infant and Child*, W.W. Norton (1927).

4

SIGMUND FREUD

The man who analysed his daughter in secret

By the age of 40 Sigmund Freud was a perfectly mature man, according to his devoted biographer, Ernest Jones. Before he started writing, Jones assured Freud he was quite mature enough himself to be free of any danger of hero worshipping the founder of psychoanalysis. Ironically, Freud made many of his most famous breakthroughs immediately after he was 40. He began his self-analysis, which led him to conclude that dreams are wish fulfilments, and he began to develop the technique of free association which was essential to analysis. Freud's *On the Interpretation of Dreams* was published in 1899. When Jones said that he would not hero worship Freud, it was wishful thinking.

Freud wrote that he had been fortunate in his wife and his children. In many ways that was true, but the sentence compressed, even repressed, a complex story – and one which psychoanalysts have not been eager to examine; even a perfectly mature man may have hidden flaws. Some of these flaws affected his children.

When his children were small, Freud was most frank with Wilhelm Fliess, an eccentric doctor who believed most psychological problems were due to the nose. In the endless letters he wrote to Fliess, Freud also often expressed his fears for his children's health, sometimes with good reason.

Freud's eldest son, Martin, wrote *Glory Reflected*, a book that gives many details about the holidays the Freud family took and a glowing account of what it was like to have Freud as a father. Freud's daughter, Anna, guarded her father's privacy to the day she died. There is also some material in the memoirs that one of Freud's sisters, Anna, wrote, *Eine Wienerin in New York*, and in those of the family housekeeper, Paula Fichtl. There are many biographies of Freud but no one has written a book on Freud and his children as Berra has written on Darwin's children, perhaps because many of the Freud papers in the Library of Congress are embargoed, some until 2057, some in perpetuity. These include correspondence relating to the Bernays family, with whom Freud was doubly linked by marriage. He married Martha Bernays, while his sister

Anna married Martha's brother, Eli. Papers relating to Anna Freud are restricted in perpetuity. It is not impossible to speculate on the reasons. Anna Freud has been dead for over 30 years so the speculation is not impertinent.

Freud called his daughter 'Anna Antigone', because she was so devoted to him, he said. As Freud 'invented' or discovered the Oedipus Complex, calling his daughter Antigone was hardly neutral. In Greek mythology, Antigone was the daughter of Oedipus and Jocasta, the couple who committed incest without either knowing it. Jocasta handed her baby son to a shepherd when Oedipus was born because the oracle foretold the child would kill his father and marry his mother. The shepherd was to leave the baby exposed on a rock to ensure the mite did not survive, but he was not given to infant murder. Oedipus lived, grew up and, as socially mobility was fluid in ancient Greece, the son of the shepherd became a prince in Corinth. Eventually he set out for Thebes and quarrelled with King Laius, not knowing the man was actually his father, when they met 'where three roads meet'. In what could be described as an ancient road rage incident, Oedipus then killed him.

Oedipus hurried to Thebes and married Jocasta, Laius' widow, without any idea that she was his mother. The marriage was happy and produced four children including Antigone. When Oedipus discovered Jocasta was actually his mother, he fled his city, leaving it to his sons who killed each other as each wanted to be sole ruler. In Sophocles' tragedies, *Oedipus at Colonus* and *Antigone*, their uncle Creon grabbed the throne. Creon declared Antigone's brother, Polynices, a traitor and that his body must be left outside the city to rot and be eaten by animals. Traitors did not deserve a proper burial.

Antigone decided to bury her brother by herself, however; Creon's guards captured her. Creon locked Antigone in a tomb where she was left to die.

Given Antigone's fate, it was surely strange for Freud to call his daughter after her. He said he gave her the fond nickname because she had sacrificed much for him, but Antigone sacrificed her life, not for her father, but for her brother. This is a provocative thought but it could be argued that calling Anna Antigone reflected one of Freud's perhaps unconscious wishes – to commit incest with his daughter.

Understanding Freud as a father requires understanding his own childhood – and its contradictions. Months after he was born in 1856, his mother Amalie became pregnant again. She and her husband adored their new baby but the sickly Julius died when he was eight months old. Forty years later, during his self-analysis which led to his 'discovery' of psychoanalysis, Freud found he had been delighted when his little brother died as he did not want to compete with another male child. By the time Amalie's second son, Alexander, was born, Freud was ten and his position in the family was beyond challenge. He was admired for his intelligence. His sister Anna complained that the clever son was given a room all of his own so he could study in peace. Freud wrote that his mother's love made him feel like a conquistador.

There was very public adversity, however, too. When Freud was ten, his family was disgraced. His uncle, Josef, was found guilty of forging Russian banknotes and sentenced to ten years in prison. Freud had just started going to secondary school. His friends and their families read about the trial in the Viennese papers. Freud's father's hair turned grey from grief. For the rest of his life, Freud was haunted by Uncle Josef; he recorded nine dreams about him in *On The Interpretation of Dreams*. One involved a telling pun, as it included the words '*für Onkel*' which literally means 'for uncle'. In English there is no hidden meaning but, in German, *furunkel* means a carbuncle or sore. His uncle was certainly that. Uncle Josef somewhat miraculously was released after serving only a few years in jail.

In 1873, at the age of 17, Freud went to Vienna University. He was a gifted student but got into trouble with the authorities; he often did not report for military service and was arrested once at least. This wild streak became more intense when, in 1884, on Walpurgisnacht, 30 April, Freud first took cocaine. In German folklore Walpurgisnacht is the night that witches meet on a high mountain brewing up potions to give them the stamina they need for orgies, consorting with devils and trying out new broomsticks. Freud chose the date deliberately.

Studying the effects of cocaine would, Freud believed, make his name as a scientist, but he came to depend on it and used the drug for nearly 20 years. Anna was around six years old when Freud stopped using the drug. Ernest Jones, his official biographer, either did not know for how long Freud was a cocaine user or concealed it. We do not know how much Freud told Anna about his cocaine use. It seems reasonable to assume that he did not reveal the part it played when he wooed his future wife, Martha Bernays.

When Freud first saw Martha in 1882, she was peeling an apple. She was petite, attractive, intelligent and rather reserved. He pursued her avidly; she responded quickly. A few days after they met, she squeezed his hand under a table.

Martha's rather snobbish mother, Emmeline, did not approve of any such engagement, however. Jacob, Freud's father, was a failed businessman. Freud might be a doctor, but he had virtually no patients and kept on having to borrow money. Martha's family, on the other hand, was distinguished. Her uncle, Jacob Bernays, had been one of the leading Biblical scholars of the mid-nineteenth century.

Appearances were deceptive, however. The Bernays family had its share of scandals too. Like Uncle Josef, Martha's father, Berman Bernays, had been sent to jail, in his case for embezzlement. When Sigmund met Martha, the forger's nephew fell in love with the embezzler's daughter. Given her husband's fate, Emmeline wanted Martha to marry a man who could offer her financial security.

Emmeline would have been outraged if she had ever discovered one letter Freud wrote to her daughter. Martha was a respectable Jewish virgin, but Freud advised her to try cocaine, flirting:

> Woe to you, my Princess, when I come. I will kiss you quite red and feed you till you are plump. And if you are forward you shall see who is the stronger, a gentle little girl who doesn't eat enough or a big wild man who has cocaine in his body.

Finally, after a four-year engagement, Martha and Freud were married in 1886. Their first daughter, Mathilde, was born the year after; in the next eight years, they had five more children. When his children were young, Freud was struggling to establish himself, as well as being a regular user of cocaine. He was a man of his time and left the business of bringing up the children largely to his wife, to her sister Minna who came to live with them after her fiancé died, and to a nurse called Josefine. Josefine was dedicated to the children but quite often teased by Freud's sons. One of them, Martin, told her he refused to take baths because Eskimos went months without bathing. Josefine replied she could not care less what other children did. If Freud ever bathed his children, no one remembered it. He was an occasional parent except during the two to three months of the summer holidays.

Martin wrote: 'My father as I knew him was very like any other affectionate father in Vienna although I wonder whether or not he studied me in a psychoanalytic light.' If he did, his father did not say so. Martin offered one telling anecdote. His mother hired a wet nurse who was even less useful than the nurses provided for the baby William before the dreadful Mrs Pack appeared. Martin's wet nurse had no milk at all. Talk about a bad breast! The dry wet nurse was sacked.

Martin also revealed that while he was writing *On the Interpretation of Dreams*, Freud did ask his children to tell him their dreams, which they did with some enthusiasm. I analysed the dreams recorded in *On the Interpretation of Dreams* for an earlier book and calculated that Freud analysed 144 dreams. Twenty-seven per cent of these were his own but none appeared to have been dreamed by a child, let alone his children. The omission is strange given his children told him their dreams.

Freud developed a complicated theory about the stages of childhood based largely on the memories of his adult patients. The first stage was the oral stage; then came the anal stage; then the genital stage where boys first developed the Oedipus Complex and girls the parallel Electra Complex. In their unconscious, small boys want to kill their fathers so they can sleep with their mothers, Freud argued. Young girls are also jealous, hate their mother and want their father's undivided attention. By the time boys and girls are three or four, they have learned the rules of family life well enough to 'know' these desires are forbidden as well as being unrealistic. So children repress these 'bad' desires, but the repression devours so much psychic energy that all memories of early childhood are repressed. That is why we remember so little of the first years of our lives, a phenomenon Freud called childhood amnesia.

The only child Freud ever saw as a patient was the five-year-old son of Freud's friend and relative, Max Graf. Graf took Little Hans to Freud when the boy developed severe agoraphobia. Hans would not leave his house because he was afraid a horse would bite him. The horse reminded Hans of his father, Freud said, basing this on nothing more than the fact Max Graf had a moustache and wore glasses. These made Graf look like a horse, Freud decided. (No wonder the surrealists made Freud their patron saint!) Little Hans' fear, that a horse might bite him, was a desperate compromise to solve his Oedipal conflict. Freud arrived at this insight as follows. Hans loved his father but his father was also a rival for his mother's love. Such thoughts were forbidden, Little Hans knew unconsciously, so the lad was a stew of guilt, repressions and terror. The lid would blow off his inner kettle any moment. As a result the child developed acute castration anxiety.

Little Hans could avoid horses by refusing to go out into the street, but the real monster, Dad, wielding the imaginary castrating knife, was at home. In a sleight of the unconscious mind, his fear of horses let Little Hans ward off the greater anxiety, that his father would cut off his penis. One can only wonder that in the Bible, Abraham's son Isaac did not develop a galaxy of phobias after his father had shown himself all too willing to roast him for the Lord.

Freud almost never offered advice to parents on the basis of his theories, but the question that has hardly been asked, let alone answered, is how did Freud deal with the Oedipus and Electra Complexes in his own children? That question is most acute when it comes to his last child, Anna, who was born in 1895.

Freud believed Anna brought him luck. When she was just two months old, he wrote to Fliess: 'We like to think the baby has brought a doubling of my practice.' In his letters, Freud mentioned the children only a few times. When Freud's sister, Rosa, was married, for example, he told Fliess that Sophie was the star of the occasion and that 'the loveliest part of the wedding by the way was our Sopherl with curled hair and a wealth of forget me nots on her head'. Little Anna never struck her father as beautiful but 'cheeky'. She was a clever little girl and in *On The Interpretation of Dreams*, Freud recorded that when she was 19 months old 'little Anna only hallucinates forbidden objects', which in this case seem to have been strawberries. A year and a bit later, Freud was proud that his small daughter had described a small Roman statuette he bought as 'an old child'. Quite a good description for a child who was not quite three years old, papa thought.

Freud was not always present, however, when Anna did something noteworthy. Later he wrote to Fliess: 'Recently I was told that little Anna said on Tante Minna's birthday; "on birthdays I am usually rather good".' Freud's phrase 'I was told' is telling; he obviously was not there when little Anna made the remark. He was writing *On The Interpretation* when Anna was a toddler and had even less time than usual for his family. In September 1897 and 1898 Freud and his wife even went on holiday to Italy alone, leaving the children in the care of Minna and the admirable Josefine.

His father, Martin wrote, worked endlessly, sometimes 16 hours a day. So it is not surprising that Freud was perhaps at his best as a father when he took his children rambling during the summer holidays.

Until 1909, when he was 13, Martin spent these holidays with his parents. In *Glory Reflected*, he records where they went and noted 'hardly a day passed without father taking us for walks in the forest'. Freud taught his children simple rules when climbing mountain pathways. One should keep a fair distance between oneself and the person ahead; one should not talk; one should not stop often to rest; and one should be careful not to loosen stones which might endanger people lower down the slopes.

Freud often told jokes while he walked and Martin remembered one. The devil's grandmother apparently got annoyed while she was flying over Vienna and tipped pots and pans 'of devilish design' over the city – crockery that turned into chimneys. Martin also remembered that he wrote some poems when he was young and, to his delight, his father sent these to some of his friends.

The walks let Freud enjoy two simple pleasures, Alpine flowers and mushrooms. Freud would spend some time scouting to find an area blessed with interesting fungi. He led his children like a 'small band' as they looked out for interesting specimens; they played as if they were 'chasing some flighty and elusive game; and there was always competition to decide who was the best hunter. Father always won', Martin recorded. Father also knew which mushrooms were poisonous. His children never got food poisoning. Of mushrooms, Martin said: 'We found them exciting and exhilarating, enjoying them not less than many enjoyed tennis, golf, shooting and other fashionable and expensive sports.'

Anna Freud told her friend Lou Andreas Salomé years later that they had to roll up the bags they brought with them 'so that the mushrooms would not notice'. When Freud found a mushroom he would cover it fast with his hat 'as though it were a butterfly'. The child who found the best mushroom got a florin.

Freud was surprisingly nimble during these expeditions. Martin even records his father doing a back somersault which made his children laugh. Freud was 40 at the time. Martin also said his father had a free heart – remarkable given his pessimism about human nature. One of the influences on Freud was the philosopher Schopenhauer who was so gloomy he spent a considerable part of his life alone in his room where, one presumes, nothing could get at him.

In 1899 the family went to Berchtesgaden, the small town which would later be Hitler's retreat. There four-year-old Anna made an impression. 'Little Anna', Freud wrote, 'is positively beautified by naughtiness. The boys are already civilized members of society, able to appreciate things. Martin is a comical creature, sensitive and yet good natured in his personal relationships'. His fond father recorded Martin asking when they passed a small cave: 'Is Herr Dragon at home?' 'Only Frau Dragon', his father replied. Martin got into the spirit of it and told Frau Dragon that they would call again bringing sweets. Freud, the theorist of sibling jealousy, was pleased that his children 'get on very well without any signs of jealousy'.

Martin remembered two crises during these holidays. Once when he and his brother Oliver were fishing, some men watched them from the road. The boys 'were shocked and considerably surprised when the men began abusing us shouting that we were Israelites – which was true – and that we were stealing fish – which was untrue – and being very offensive indeed'.

The boys went home with fewer fish than usual and told their father. Freud became 'very serious for a few moments, remarking that kind of thing could happen to us again and that we should be prepared for it'. That was far from the end of it, however. Freud had to go to a nearby town that afternoon and his sons rowed him across the river. The men who had abused them earlier – and a few women too – blocked the way. In his own childhood Freud had been with his father when a man threw his father's hat in the gutter and called him a dirty Jew. Freud's father meekly picked up his hat; one did not get into a fight with anti-Semites. Freud was not intimidated as his father had been. He jumped out of the boat and, Martin added, 'commanded me in so an angry voice to stay where I was that I dared not disobey. My mild mannered father had never spoken to me in anything but kindly tones'.

That upset Martin, but he took an oar from the boat, 'swung it over my shoulder and stood by ready to join any battle that might develop'.

The battle was short-lived, for who could withstand the analyst in all his fury? Freud, 'swinging his stick charged the hostile crowd which gave way before him'. Martin records an incident much later which shows what Freud always said – that, though he did not believe in God, he belonged to the tribe of Jews.

On the last holiday he took with his parents, Martin found his father leaning against a rock and his face turned purple red. Freud could not speak and pointed to his rucksack. 'I guessed he was indicating the bottle of Chianti I carried', Martin said. For once Freud drank straight from the bottle, removed his tie and unbuttoned his collar. The fastidious Freud 'did not however go so far as to remove his jacket'. They had to abandon the walk.

Martin never, however, had the intense relationship with his father that Anna had. For her, papa was everything. She was never that close to her mother. She did not get along with her brothers either and her relationship with her sister Sophie was especially fraught, Sophie being the more conventionally attractive child. She had beauty while Anna had brains. Freud once spoke of Anna's 'age-old jealousy of Sophie'. But Freud appreciated Anna's fierce intelligence, even though she was troubled – and seems confident enough of her father's love to tell him what troubled her.

As a teenager, Anna complained to Freud that 'unreasonable thoughts and feelings plagued her'. She was sent to health farms to rest. Though she did not shine at school, Anna started reading her father's work when she was 15. It was a compliment to her intelligence that he allowed her to do this.

By the time Anna was 18, Sophie was getting married and Freud believed Anna might be upset because she was jealous of Sophie's future husband who had managed to win Sophie's love quickly. Anna had always felt 'excluded' from Sophie's love. Anna was astonished and replied to her father that she was 'indifferent about Max', Sophie's husband-to-be. The exchange between father and daughter was both touching and mature. 'It is not really nice to say it', Anna went on, 'but I am glad Sophie is getting married because the unending quarrel between us was horrible for me'. Anna obviously felt her father was judging her because she pleaded, 'I would like very much to be reasonable or at least to become a reasonable person'. She sent her father many greetings and a kiss and asked him to write to her soon. 'I will become more reasonable if you will help me', she said in the last line of her letter.

In 1913, soon after Sophie's wedding, Anna went to England to improve her English. Freud asked Ernest Jones to look after her, but Jones did rather more; he began to court her. Freud was livid for good and bad reasons. Jones was something of a Don Juan and had lost two hospital jobs after female patients had complained about inappropriate intimacies. He was not likely to make an ideal husband, but Freud would probably not have been happy if his beloved Shakespeare himself wooed his daughter with sonnets. Anna was 'still far away from sexual longings', Freud told Jones. Freud had a keen sense of irony, but he was too close to Anna to see any irony in the fact that the analyst who argued that children were sexual beings was protesting that his daughter was too young to have sexual feelings. Freud told Jones he and Anna had agreed 'that she should not consider marriage or the preliminaries before she gets 2 or 3 years older'. He added he did not expect her to 'break the treaty'.

For once Jones did not meekly accept what Freud said. He shot back that Anna 'will surely be a remarkable woman later on, provided that her sexual repression does not injure her. She is of course tremendously bound to you'. Anna stayed cool towards Jones. His predictions, it could be argued, were all too true.

During the First World War, Anna stayed at home with her parents. She had passed the examinations to be a teacher and, as Austrians were impoverished during the war, the family needed her income. Her brothers had to join the Austrian Army. Martin explained that his father forbade him to join the cavalry and insisted he join the artillery. Freud wrote to him, warning him that he was a little too inclined to see war as some kind of sport. The war allowed Martin to fulfil a childhood dream, however, that of leading a troop on horseback, which Martin did even though he was in the artillery. In *Glory Reflected*, Martin recalled that his father claimed a man would never be truly happy until he had fulfilled one of these childish dreams.

In matters domestic, however, Freud did not rule. When Anna wanted to change her bedroom, Freud said it was fine with him but that hardly counted as any domestic decision was up to Martha. Anna was a qualified teacher and 20 at the time.

Anna's dreams were less martial than Martin's – and more complicated. Sometime during the war, she had decided she too wanted to be an analyst so she had to undergo a training analysis. Freud would not let her see any of his colleagues because he worried they would learn too much about his family, a family that had had many secrets. Apart from the fact that Uncle Josef had been jailed, Freud's half-brother Emanuel died in somewhat mysterious circumstances when he fell out of a train, and a niece had killed herself as had a cousin. So Freud would analyse Anna himself, but keep the fact secret, even from her mother. In autumn 1918, Freud had few patients so he could see Anna during the day. He only told his close friend Sándor Ferenczi that 'Anna's analysis will be very elegant'. No one else knew of it then, it seems.

The bizarre nature of a parent acting as his child's analyst is clear when one considers the dynamics of psychoanalysis. The patient has to confront complex feelings with their roots in her or his childhood. According to Freud, the analyst 'becomes' the parent to whom the child can say anything that troubled her or him, fishing all kinds of desires from her unconscious mind for the neutral analyst to help her understand. But if the analyst is one of the patient's parents, the dynamic would seem to be fatally compromised.

Biographers have tried to winkle out the details of Anna's analysis and it is reasonable to suppose that some of the papers in the Library of Congress that are restricted in perpetuity concern that. In her biography, Elisabeth Young Bruehl stresses the fact that Anna felt she had no experience of loving but does not stress that this was probably just what papa wanted, given the way he had brushed the priapic Ernest Jones away. Paul Roazen, the distinguished historian of analysis, suggests the analysis had a peculiar problem; there were unspoken conflicts between Anna and her father and 'Anna may have been more afraid of her father than either of them knew'. While her father's motives may have been 'the very best medically and humanly the situation was bizarre'. Freud would have been 'invading the privacy of her soul; he added new transference emotions to their relationship, without the possibility of ever really dissolving them'. Taking his daughter into analysis undoubtedly gratified an Oedipal tie on his part, Roazen judged, but for her, 'the analysis helped to limit the possibilities for personal gratification, although she had a role in her father's life as well as her eventual leadership of the movement, which constituted a rich exchange'. Then Roazen softened, for he was talking about the father of psychoanalysis, after all. 'Perhaps only by normal standards was her relationship to such a father a tragic one.' One can debate whether tragic was a fair adjective. Anna inherited much of Freud's 'empire'.

With all the documents that are embargoed, it is impossible to be precise about the sequence of events in the relationship between Anna Freud and her father from 1918 when her analysis started to 1924 when she presented her paper, 'On beating fantasies', to the Viennese Psychoanalytic Society. It is clear, though, that the already close relationship between the two became even closer, and even more entangled. The evidence lies in three published papers. Two were written by Freud himself, 'A child is being beaten' and 'The psychogenesis of a case of homosexuality in a woman' – and one by Anna.

In 'Psychogenesis of a case of homosexuality in a woman', Freud (1920) argued, an 18-year-old homosexual girl was the victim of 'constitutional factors'. He then suggested that this girl's case was not a classic one for psychoanalysis because the girl did not suffer from a divided personality. In fact, Freud said, his patient did not suffer at all from her attraction to other women, even though she did have beating fantasies.

A surprising number of analytic patients, as it happened, had such beating fantasies. Freud suggested this 'beating fantasy' was very pleasurable. It was, as Anna explained in her own paper, 'discharged in an act of pleasurable autoerotic gratification'. In other words the fantasy led to masturbation. The tangle is worth trying to untangle. A daughter, who her father nicknames Antigone, who is a child of incest, is building on her father's paper about a daughter who fantasizes about committing incest and being beaten. Incest is taboo so fantasies involving it deserve punishment.

Freud said in his 1920 paper:

> In two of my four female cases an elaborate superstructure of daydreams, which was of great significance for the life of the person concerned, had grown up over the masochistic beating fantasy. The function of this superstructure was to make possible a feeling of satisfied excitation, even though the masturbatory act was abstained from.
>
> (p. 190)

This makes one wonder whether Anna told him her fantasies ended in masturbation. Freud highlighted one girl and one daydream, which

> was formed by a girl of about fifteen, whose fantasy life, in spite of its abundance, had never come into conflict with reality. The origin, evolution, and termination of this daydream could be established with certainty, and its derivation from dependence on a beating fantasy of long standing were proved in a rather thoroughgoing analysis.

The thoroughgoing analysis was, it is plausible to argue, his own of Anna.

Which female patient aged 15, or close to that age, was Freud treating around the end of the First World War? As a result of painstaking work by many historians, we know something about most of Freud's significant female patients. It was nearly 25 years since he had seen Fanny Moser and it seems unlikely he would write about her so long after he had treated her. Dora was 38 years old by 1920 and had not seen Freud for many years; Emma Eckstein rejected analysis after Freud and Breuer nearly killed her when Breuer forgot to remove her dressings after surgery. Anna von Lieben, or Cacilie M, was Freud's patient from 1887 to 1895. She was in her late thirties when Freud saw her, again long before this period. Another of Freud's patients, Lucy R, might seem more plausible in terms of the time she saw him, but the details of her case were different. Lucy R was besotted with her employer after his wife died and ended up marrying him. In his detailed account, Freud never mentions anything resembling a beating fantasy.

Not one of these patients could have been around 15 when they consulted Freud. The reasonable conclusion is that his daughter Anna was the daydreamer who fantasized incest – and incest with her father – and eventually admitted it to herself and to him. That would be perfectly normal during an analysis if the analyst did not happen to be your father. One could argue that to write of this even anonymously was very brave of both Anna and her father.

In her own paper Anna wrote that the daydreamer felt guilty because 'of her repressed strivings for her father'. She stressed this was due to

> the autoerotic gratification which regularly occurred at its termination. For a number of years, therefore, the little girl made ever-renewed but ever-failing attempts to separate the one from the other, i.e., to retain the fantasy as a source of pleasure and, at the same time, to give up the sexual gratification which could not be reconciled with the demands of her ego.

In other words, Anna fantasized about sleeping with her father but felt guilty about it, a tangle indeed.

The patient stopped trying to

> separate the beating fantasy from the autoerotic gratification; the prohibition spread and now extended also to the content of the fantasy. Each break-through which now could occur only after a prolonged struggle in which strong forces

opposed the temptation was followed by violent self-reproaches, pangs of conscience, and temporary depressed moods. The pleasure derived from the fantasy was more and more confined to a single pleasurable moment.

But that moment of pleasure was 'embedded in unpleasure' – a telling word, 'embedded', when dealing with incest. The German is *einbetten* and it too is very literal, as *ein bett* is a bed.

To deal with her problems, the girl started to imagine 'nice stories' quite different from the beating fantasies. The nice stories, of course, did not end with any masturbation because that would not have been 'nice'.

Anna wrote in 1924, some years after her own analysis had started: 'The daydreamer herself was quite unaware of any connection between the nice stories and the beating fantasy, and at that time would most certainly and without any hesitation have denied it.' If from time to time the beating fantasy recurred it 'had to be punished by a temporary renunciation of the nice stories'.

When she was 15 the girl found a storybook which captured her imagination. The story was of a 15-year-old noble youth (i.e. the age of the daydreamer) who was captured by a knight and held prisoner in his castle. The knight nearly killed the youth but always stopped short. Then the fury of the torturer was 'transformed into pity and benevolence – that is to say, at the climax of each scene – the excitement resolves itself into a feeling of happiness'.

If one looked at the fantasies and daydreams, Anna said,

> we are surprised by their monotony, though the daydreamer herself never noticed it either in the course of fantasying or in talking about them in her analysis. Yet she was otherwise by no means an unintelligent girl and was in fact quite critical and exacting in the choice of her reading material.

Just like Anna Freud was, in fact ...

The stories always turned on

> antagonism between a strong and a weak person; a misdeed – mostly unintentional – on the part of the weak one which puts him at the other's mercy ...; a slowly mounting anxiety, often depicted by exquisitely appropriate means, until the tension becomes almost unendurable; and finally, as the pleasurable climax, the solution of the conflict, the pardoning of the sinner, reconciliation, and, for a moment, complete harmony between the former antagonists.

The daydreamer never imagined a dark truth, Anna Freud argued, that both fictions involved strong and weak persons. She added a telling phrase, saying these two characters 'oppose each other as adults and children'. Just like her and her father did but, it could be argued, pretended they did not. She went on to argue that the 'difference between the two rests in their solution, which in the fantasy is brought about by beating, and in the daydream by forgiveness and reconciliation'.

According to Freud his daydreaming patient never actually masturbated but, in Anna's account, the 'patient' (who I have suggested was herself) did. Anna then used her father's theories to cap her case history. Freud argued the beating fantasy is a substitute for an incestuous love scene that was distorted by repression and regression. The beating fantasy represented a return of the repressed while the nice stories represented its sublimation. 'In the beating fantasy the direct sexual drives are satisfied', Anna wrote, while 'in the nice stories the aim-inhibited drives, as Freud calls them, find gratification'. If a child develops 'normally', 'the originally undivided current of love becomes separated into repressed sensual strivings (here expressed in the beating fantasy) and into a sublimated affectionate tie (represented by the nice stories)'.

In both stories, the end is 'a friendship between a strong and a weak person, an adult and a boy, or, as many daydreams express it, between a superior and an inferior being'. But the boy was a mask, it seems. Anna wrote:

> The sublimation of sensual love into tender friendship is of course greatly facilitated by the fact that already in the early stages of the beating fantasy the girl abandoned the difference of the sexes and is invariably represented as a boy.

In her teenage years Anna tried writing stories – and so did the anonymous patient who produced 'an absorbing short story' which started with a noble youth being taken prisoner and tortured, and ended with his refusal to escape. The youth decided to stay as a result of 'positive feelings for the knight'.

Anna's paper often reads like a counterpoint to her father's papers. He noted that his female patient had 'an elaborate superstructure of day-dreams, which had grown up over the masochistic beating-phantasy ... [one] which almost rose to the level of a work of art'. He would not be the first father to admire his daughter's work.

What is striking is that it seems we are reading two accounts of the same case which it seems likely was the analysis of Anna Freud by her father. I am well aware that this is a speculation but Anna's feelings and fantasies about her father would have had to be at the centre of the analysis. It says much about the way Freud lived that there seems to have been no risk of his wife interrupting them. When father and daughter were working in his study, mother stayed in the kitchen or in their living room. Martha did not know what was going on.

Despite conspiring together to keep all this secret, father and daughter do not seem to have agreed on how successful the analysis was. In a letter to Lou Andreas Salomé in 1922, Anna said:

> With me, everything became so problematic because of two basic faults: from a discontent or insatiability with myself that makes me look for affection from others, and then from actually sticking with the others once I have found them. [The first] is just what you and *Papa* cannot understand.

Freud, on the other hand, believed he had understood his daughter perfectly, but he admitted how much he depended on Anna. In a letter to Lou Andreas Salomé in 1922, he said:

I have felt sorry for her for quite some time now, because she is still living at home with us old folks &, but yet, on the other hand, if she really had left us, I would have felt diminished, like what is happening to me now, for example, almost as if I had to give up smoking.

Anna was not the only one of his children Freud analysed. His son Oliver had an obsessional neurosis which his father tried to cure. 'It is particularly hard for me to [be] objective in this case', Freud wrote to Max Eitington, a rich analyst who had helped Freud financially during the war. He added that Oliver had been 'my pride and my secret hope for a long time until his anal masochistic organisation appeared clearly.... I suffer very much with feelings of helplessness'. Oliver's relationship with his father remained difficult and he emigrated to the United States with his wife. Oliver had a successful career as a civil engineer.

During Anna's analysis, Freud had to face a terrible tragedy. In 1920 his daughter Sophie died. Freud was 64 years old and his letters (mainly unpublished so far) speak about the agony he felt. Anna never spoke about how she felt when her sister and rival died. It is uncanny that, just as Freud had seen his brother Julius die, Anna saw her sister die. It was far from the last tragedy. After Sophie died, Freud became very attached to her two-year-old son, Heinele. He was devastated when the boy died in 1923.

Soon Freud would have to deal with the problem of Anna's previously non-existent love life. In 1925, Dorothy Burlingham, whose grandfather, Charles Tiffany, founded the high society jewellers, Tiffany & Co., came to him for analysis. She was unhappy in her marriage. She and Anna became friends, close friends and life partners. When I asked Anna Freud's last secretary, Gina Le Bon, whether the two women were lovers, she replied 'Does it matter?' They were discreet if they were. In his biography of Anna, Robert Coles, the distinguished psychiatrist, merely says the relationship between the two women was 'complex'. With a splendid disregard of boundaries, Freud analysed Anna, Dorothy and, for good measure, Dorothy's husband.

Homosexuality was no crime, though it was no great advantage either, Freud said later to a woman who wanted him to 'cure' her son of homosexuality. One of many intriguing questions is whether the father knew Anna was a lesbian, if indeed she was a practising one. Young Bruehl is sure that Anna remained chaste all her life. His daughter's renunciation of sex makes one ask if Freud was secretly, or even unconsciously, pleased because no man would ever be able to replace her beloved papa? There is no evidence Freud hoped to convert Anna to heterosexuality.

Just before he turned 70, Freud became physically dependent on Anna. After he stopped using cocaine around 1902, Freud smoked ever more heavily – and he developed cancer of the jaw. Anna had to take on many nursing chores. After an operation on his jaw, Freud had to wear a prosthesis in his mouth. It hurt, but without it, he could not speak or eat properly. A small antiseptic room was set up in the apartment so that Anna could take it out, clean it and put it back every day. It was an intimate task and neither Freud nor Anna would have missed the symbolism. Anna inserts her fingers and an object in her father's mouth. We do not know what Martha thought of that but Anna protected her right to perform this task for her father. 'I would not leave him now under any circumstances', Anna said.

Despite the analysis and despite her triumph in being the one who fitted the prothesis, Anna could still get jealous of both her mother and Aunt Minna. They fought over who should accompany Freud on trips even when Anna was in her mid-thirties. In 1929, she managed to make sure that she accompanied her father to Berlin. 'At first mama wanted to go in my place but I did not want that at all.' She was honest in her jealousies and later confessed to Max Eitington that she was troubled by jealousy of all the women who came to her father for training analyses. This distinguished group included Helene Deutsch, Joan Riviere and Princess Marie Bonaparte.

Anna was recognized as a brilliant child therapist by the end of the 1920s. She managed this both because of her relationship with her father, and despite it. They loved, respected and depended on each other. Freud had reasons to feel guilty towards her but when, in 1935, the Italian analyst Eduardo Weiss asked Freud whether or not he should analyse his own son, Freud admitted he had analysed Anna and said 'Concerning the analysis of your hopeful son, that is certainly a ticklish business.... With (my) own daughter I succeeded well'.

Freud's relationship with his sons was less intense, though he was concerned about their ability to earn a living. Like Anna, Martin was still living at home when he was well into his thirties. In 1934, 25 years after Martin had met the anti-Semites by the river bank, he ran into a battle between Jewish students and Austrians. In the 1930s, riots were frequent in Vienna. The Jewish students were fighting back. Martin said: 'The idea that Jews might abandon meekness as a defence against humiliating attacks was new and attractive to me.' A few days later he went to Kadimah, a Jewish organization. His father, as usual, had to pass through Martin's bedroom in order to reach the bedroom that Martha and he shared. Martin was for once glad to be woken up.

Ernst Freud became an architect and set up his practice in Berlin in 1920 where a large number of his clients were doctors. In 1933, when Hitler became Chancellor of Germany, Ernst left Berlin for London where he settled in St John's Wood. He later edited an edition of about 200 of his father's letters; he left out anything which might damage Freud's reputation.

On his eightieth birthday on 6 May 1936, when he was in much pain, Freud praised Anna to Lou Andreas Salomé. He quoted Mephistopheles in Goethe's *Faust*:

> In the end we depend
> On the creatures we made.

Again he praised Anna, writing to Lou Andreas Salomé: 'It was very wise to have made her.'

Anna became director of the Vienna Psychoanalytical Training Institute and, in 1937, started a nursery school for poor children. Dorothy Burlingham and a wealthy friend, Edith Jackson, provided the money. The nursery was experimental. Children were allowed to choose their own food and organize their own play. Though some of their parents had been reduced to begging, Anna and Burlingham were very struck

> by the fact that they brought the children to us, not because we fed and clothed them and kept them for the length of the day, but because 'they learned so much', i.e. they learned to move freely, to eat independently, to speak, to express their preferences, To our own surprise the parents valued this beyond everything.

When the Nazis marched into Vienna in 1938, Freud refused to leave the city. The nursery soon had to close as it was a Jewish enterprise. The Nazi takeover changed life dramatically for Freud and his children.

The day after the Nazis marched into Vienna, Martin Freud went to his office to do something for his father. 'I knew I must destroy documents of great importance.' He had invested money abroad for his clients which 'had been perfectly legal under lenient Austrian laws but I knew it would be a crime in the eyes of the dollar hungry Nazis'. He had to protect his clients, 'including my father', by destroying any evidence of these transactions.

But before Martin could destroy the documents, a gang of Nazi sympathizers strutted into his office. A haggard-looking man pressed a pistol against Martin's head. 'Why not shoot him and be finished with him?' he shouted. Martin was saved by the arrival of Ernest Jones who told them he was British, not a Jew. He decided that the most sensible step was to get a Nazi of some seniority to deal with the situation. Jones also went to tell Anna Freud what was going on.

Within minutes a young blonde District Commissioner arrived. This officer 'radiated an authority which had an immediate effect on the rabble which had been tormenting me for so long', Martin noted. The Commissioner was even polite and allowed his sister, Anna, to join him. She had been waiting outside.

Anna and Martin went back to their parents' apartment to find a number of Gestapo men had arrived. Martha Freud was calm. She told them that in her house they did not let guests stand up while they waited so would they please sit down. She then graciously told the Gestapo that they had some cash in the house.

'Help yourselves, gentlemen', Martha said. The cash came to the not small sum of 6,000 schillings. Freud then walked into the room looking worried but said nothing. The 'gentlemen of the S.S' took the money and, bizarrely, provided a formal receipt.

As the Nazis took the 6,000 schillings, Freud said to his wife: 'Dear me, I have never taken so much for a single visit.'

The Gestapo confiscated the passports of all the family – and left.

Anna Freud then had a conversation with her father when they seemed to have no chance of escape.

'Wouldn't it be better if we all killed ourselves', she asked.

Freud was adamant. 'Why? Because they would like us to', Freud replied. He had no intention of giving them the pleasure.

Anna only allowed her father's doctor, Max Schur, to report this dialogue in *Freud: Living and Dying* 34 years later.

On Tuesday, 22 March, the Gestapo marched into 19 Berggasse again and arrested Anna Freud. When he heard, Max Schur came at once. He knew Freud would be distraught. Freud was terrified he would never see Anna again. The usually calm therapist paced up and down, smoking one cigar after another.

Anna did not go unprepared to meet the Gestapo. She was frightened she would be tortured and had persuaded Schur to give her two tablets of Veronal to swallow as a last resort.

In the apartment at Berggasse, Schur did not manage to calm his patient. Freud continued to pace up and down, lighting one cigar after another. Paula Fichtl and Dorothy Burlingham both wrote that it was obviously the worst day of his life.

The Gestapo made Anna wait for hours and then put a clever question to ruffle her. She was asked what it meant to be a member of an international organization. The Gestapo men told her they had information about a conspiracy of Jewish ex-soldiers who were about to terrorize Vienna. Anna explained the only international organization she belonged to was the International Psychoanalytic Association which did not have guns hidden under the analytic couches. But it was hard for her to stay calm. Somehow though, Anna was allowed to leave the Hotel Metropole by the end of the evening.

Freud was relieved beyond words when Anna finally returned home safely late on 22 March. Max Schur said that for once Freud showed his true feelings and wept.

Anna's arrest was the turning point. Freud finally decided to leave Vienna, though he knew he did not have long to live. In the three months before they left, Anna had to report constantly to the police and be polite to Nazi officials as she negotiated exit visas for her father and family. Freud wrote that he knew how deftly she managed this. The family finally left Vienna in May 1938. They were helped by a Nazi, Anton Sauerwald, who made most of the arrangements, including the transportation of most of Freud's books and furniture to London.

Freud would live until September 1939. When he had appointed him as his doctor, he had made a deal with Schur that Schur would give him morphine when it no longer made any sense to live. When he died Anna was at his bedside.

Martin's *Glory Reflected* omits a crucial episode. He could not stomach the fact that his father and the family had been helped to escape Vienna by a Nazi. When Sauerwald was arrested as a war criminal in 1945, neither he nor Anna did anything to help him. It was only after Sauerwald had been in jail for nearly two years that Anna said their father would have wanted them to be just and help the man who had helped them. Against Martin's wishes, she finally wrote the letter to the authorities that Sauerwald had been asking her to write for two years.

By the end of the 1960s, 30 years after Freud died, Anna Freud was famous as one of the leading child analysts in the world. According to her secretary, Gina Le Bon, Anna did not forgive the Nazis or Germany. 'Miss Freud would not have a Mercedes but drove a Volvo rather and she was a very bad driver as opposed to Miss Burlingham.' Another striking detail Gina Le Bon gave me is that when Anna Freud discovered that the IBM typewriters were being made in Germany, she would not have one.

Darwin was both born into a dynasty and married into one when he married Emma Wedgwood. Freud founded one. Though only one of his children became world-famous, two of his grandchildren did. One of them was the great painter Lucian Freud; another, Lucian's brother Clement, became an MP. Freud's nephew Edward Bernays worked for Woodrow Wilson and is also reckoned to have founded the art or science of public relations. Does that mean Freud was a good father? He was certainly unlucky in some aspects of his life. In studying his escape from Vienna, I established that, as well as his daughter and his grandson who died so young, eight of his relatives either killed themselves or died in mysterious circumstances.

To end on a happier note, Clement Freud told a lovely anecdote about travelling to China as part of a parliamentary mission during the Cultural Revolution. The young Freud went with the young Winston Churchill, then the Conservative MP for Stretford.

On the last day the Minister for Information asked Clement Freud if there was anything at all he would like to ask. He said:

> Yes. Everything you do, you do with extreme care and precision.... Now I am in your country with a colleague, than whom I am older, have been in parliament longer, have held higher positions in our respective political parties: we are both staying at the Peking Palace Hotel and his suite is bigger than mine. Why?

The very embarrassed Minister replied: 'It is because Mr Churchill had a famous grandfather.'

'It is the only time that I have been out-grandfathered', Clement Freud wrote. Freud would have enjoyed that quip too, I venture to suggest.

There were some similarities – and many differences – between Freud and the man who for a few years he called his Crown Prince, Carl Gustav Jung, as fathers.

Notes and references

The Library of Congress holds the archives of Sigmund Freud and Anna Freud, some of which are still embargoed. Anna Freud's last secretary, Gina Le Bon, gave me an interview. The recollections of Freud as a father mainly come from his son

Martin's *Glory Reflected*. Elisabeth Young Bruehl, *Anna Freud*, Yale University Press (2008) gives an excellent portrait of his devoted daughter. Robert Coles, *Anna Freud: The Dream of Psychoanalysis*, Da Capo Press (1993) and Paul Roazen, *Freud and His Followers*, Da Capo Press (1992) tease out the tensions that arose from the fact that Freud analysed his daughter. Freud wrote about that to the Italian analyst Eduardo Weiss and contributed an introduction to Weiss' *Elements of Psychoanalysis* (1931). Freud's short introduction is in the Standard edition of the *Collected Works*, vol. xxi, published by the Hogarth Press (1961).

Two other works offering material on his children are: Anna Freud Bernays, *Eine Wienerin in New York*, Aufbau Verlag (2005) – she published her memoir long after her brother's death; D. Berthelsen, *La Famille de Freud au jour le jour; souvenirs de Paula Fichtl*, Presses Universitaires de France (1991).

Much interesting material from the Freud family can be found in:
Freud, Anna, On beating fantasies, *Int. J of Psychoanalysis*, vol. 4, 89–102 (1923).
Freud, Clement, *Freud Ego*, BBC Books (2001). It has been alleged that Clement Freud almost certainly abused some young girls sexually. His family responded in a very dignified way – and apologised.

Freud's relevant works are:
Freud, S., *On the Interpretation of Dreams*, Standard edition, vols 4–5, Hogarth Press (1899).
Freud, S., A child is being beaten, first published in *Int. Zeitung für Psychoanalyse*, vol. 5, 151–72 (1919).
Freud, S., Über die Psychogenese eines Falles von weiblicher Homosexualität, *Internationale Zeitschrift für Psychoanalyse*, vol. VI, 1–24 (1920). Translated as The psychogenesis of a case of homosexuality in a woman, in the Standard edition (1974), vol. xviii, 147–72 (1924).
Freud, S., *Letters of Sigmund Freud, 1873–1939*, edited by Ernst Freud, Hogarth Press (1961).

Other references:
Cohen, D., *The Escape of Sigmund Freud*, Robson Press (2010).
Cohen, D., *Freud on Coke*, Cutting Edge (2011).
Jones, Ernest, *Sigmund Freud*, Basic Books (1953). This remains the standard text.
Schur, Max, *Freud: Living and Dying*, Chatto & Windus (1972).

5
CARL JUNG
The archetypal prick, a provocative title

In a paper he published in 1917, Jung wrote: 'The latest investigations show the predominant influence of the father's character in a family often lasting for centuries. The mother seems to play a less important part.' Jung could be a loving father but he rarely let his children stand in the way of his own pleasure. This chapter is provocatively called 'the archetypal prick' since Jung made much of archetypes. They were part of the collective unconscious which he argued contained humankind's old histories, mysteries, wishes and fears.

Laurens van der Post wrote a 'hardly show one wart' biography of Jung, and J.D.F. Jones called his biography of van der Post *The Storyteller* because his subject told so many lies. Nevertheless, van der Fib became close to Prince Charles. In 1974 the Prince and van der Post went to Kenya, repeating a trip Jung made 50 years earlier. Jung was in search of ancient wisdom and, as he generally was, the true nature of his self. Prince Charles had similar ambitions.

Edzard Ernst, once professor of complementary medicine at the University of Exeter, has written that 'Van der Post wanted to awake Charles' young intuitive mind and attune it to the ideas of Carl Jung's "collective unconscious" which allegedly unites us all through a common vital force'. Ernst believes this belief in vitalism has made Prince Charles enthuse so much about alternative medicine, as 'virtually every form of the otherwise highly diverse range of alternative therapies is based on the assumption that some sort of vital force or energy exists'.

Van der Post became a godfather to Prince William. When Princess Diana was depressed, Charles turned to him to find a therapist for her. Van der Post recommended a Jungian, of course. Princess Diana sensibly abandoned this attempt by her husband to control her therapy and, eventually, was treated by Susie Orbach, author of *Fat is a Feminist Issue*. In one way, it's surprising Jungian ideas did not seduce Princess Diana as she took to astrology, some aspects of spiritualism and colonic irrigation.

Many Nazis were also oddly fascinated by the occult, and the novelist Thomas Mann once said that Jung was always 'half a Nazi'. Jung certainly more than shared the casual anti-Semitism of his day. Jews were different from other people and even needed to be dressed differently, Jung barbed, because otherwise 'we mistook them for people like ourselves'. He did not just do little to help Jewish analysts after Hitler took power, but helped Hermann Goring's cousin, Matthias, take over the Berlin Psychoanalytic Society in 1936.

There was at least one Jew, though, with whom Jung was careful. When he and Freud worked together, Jung hid his views about Jews. If Jung had been frank with him, it is unlikely Freud would have decided to call Jung his 'son and heir' or his Crown Prince. Jung was also not frank about his love life. He had an affair with an American woman he met in Paris, slept with a number of his students and finally lived in a *ménage à trois*. This chapter examines in some detail his relationships with Sabina Spielrein and Toni Wolff as these affected his children deeply when they were young; all of them loved and respected their mother and felt their father was cruel to her at times.

As a Jew and being little inclined to mysticism, I tend to see Jung critically. But Jung himself had difficult parents and a far from serene childhood, and, despite the problems his infidelities caused his children, he seems to have been a good enough father *sometimes*. The phrase a good enough father is inspired by the work of the English psychoanalyst D.W. Winnicott, whose ideas of the good enough mother were discussed in the introduction.

As it happens Winnicott reviewed the most personal book Jung wrote, *Memories, Dreams, Reflections*. 'Jung in describing himself gives us a picture of childhood schizophrenia', Winnicott said, 'and at the same time his personality displays a strength of a kind which enabled him to heal himself'. Winnicott worried that readers of *The International Journal of Psychoanalysis* might think he thought Jung insane, so he added: 'I must ask the reader at this stage to understand that I am not running Jung down by labelling him "a recovered case of infantile psychosis".'

Carl Gustav Jung was born in 1875, the son of an ambitious mother who made a disastrous marriage, she felt. Jung's father, Paul, never reached a position of any importance in the Swiss Reformed Church and, worse, wavered in his faith. Jung's mother, however, came from a distinguished line; her father, Johann, taught Hebrew and the Old Testament in a theological seminary.

After his first wife died, Johann kept a special chair in his study for her ghost; the ghost didn't just haunt him, or let him fiddle with her ectoplasm, but held conversations with her ex every week. His second wife, Augusta, was not delighted. There is an unexpected connection with Noel Coward. In *Blithe Spirit*, Coward's hero is pestered by the ghost of his first wife. She can't bear the fact that he's re-married so she arranges the death of her successor. Both women then decide they miss their husband too much and conjure up a car crash so that he dies and joins them in the afterlife. The three will live in a *ménage à trois* for eternity. Jung did much the same for some 40 years.

Obsession with the supernatural marked Jung's childhood. His mother sat behind his father while he was writing his sermons so she could scare away any ghosts who were hovering around. Emilie Jung was formidable and dominated her son's childhood. But she was also unstable. When Carl was three years old her depressions were so crippling, that Emilie had to be sent to an asylum in Basle. Some authors say for three years, but Jung wrote it was just a matter of months. An elderly aunt took care of him. Bereft, the infant Jung developed eczema. 'I was deeply troubled by my mother's being away. From then on I always felt mistrustful when the word "love" was spoken', Jung wrote. It affected his views of women. 'The feeling I associated with "woman" was for a long time that of innate unreliability, Father on the other hand meant reliability but powerlessness.'

Emilie Jung always seemed 'the stronger of the two' of his parents. Her son compared her to one of those 'seers who is a strange animal, like a priestess in a bear's cave'. Much of the time she 'held all the conventional opinions' she had to have as the wife of a minister, 'but then her unconscious personality would put in an appearance'. This unconscious personality was fierce, bizarre and

> emerged only now and then but each time it was unexpected and frightening. She would speak as if talking to a stranger but what she said was aimed at me and usually struck me to my being so that I was stunned into silence.

Jung tried to cope with his mother's moods by devising rituals that would give him some control; many centred on fires he lit in the garden of their house. At other times, he would sit on a stone in the garden and wonder 'Am I the one who is sitting on the stone or am I the stone on which he is sitting?' He also made a totem; he carved a tiny mannequin out of the end of his wooden ruler and placed it in his pencil case. He added tiny sheets of paper with messages inscribed on them in his own secret language. This gave him a feeling of security, he wrote later.

Jung wrote later that he too

> was two persons. One was the son of my parents who went to school and was less intelligent, attentive, hardworking, decent and clean than many other boys. The other was grown up – old in fact – sceptical, mistrustful, remote from the world of men but close to nature ... and above all close to the night, to dreams and to whatever God worked directly in him.

His parents did not communicate well and so Jung's relationship with his mother become perhaps too adult too young.

> My mother usually assumed I was mentally far beyond my age and she would talk to me like to a grown up. It was plain to see that she was telling me everything she could not say to my father for she early made me her confidant and confided her troubles to me.

His mother turned to him because she was so disappointed in her husband. Tactfully, Jung removed a sentence from the first draft of *Memories* which stressed that Emilie only stopped having breakdowns when her husband died.

When he went to school Jung soon showed a talent for self-dramatization. In his first year at the Humanistisches Gymnasium in Basle, another boy pushed him to the ground. Jung was unconscious briefly but remembered thinking 'now you won't have to go to school any more'. He then fainted a number of times to avoid going to school or doing homework. The fainting, Jung wrote later, 'was when I learned what a neurosis is'. Freud also fainted a number of times. The early psychoanalysts usually kept smelling salts close by.

In 1895 Jung went to Basle University to study medicine, and then went to work under Eugene Bleuler, one of the leading psychiatrists of the day. Bleuler thought well of his student and allowed him to present an unorthodox doctoral thesis which let Jung 'pursue his profound curiosity about occult and spiritualistic matters'. Jung discussed the case of S.W., who was really his cousin Helene Preiswerk. She had visions and hallucinations at séances which Jung attended with his mother. There is some controversy about when these séances took place. In his thesis Jung said they took place between 1899 and 1900, when Helene was 15 and he was 24. One of her other relatives claims, however, that Jung helped organize these sessions as early as 1895, when Helene was 11 years old and he was a 19-year-old first-year medical student. One wonders why he was not accurate about the dates.

In 1900 Jung read Freud's *On the Interpretation of Dreams*, but sensed he could not appreciate it yet. Freud was, after all, 20 years older. Three years later Jung went back to the book; by then he had flourished under Bleuler and become Oberartzt, literally 'top doctor' or clinical director, of the Burgholzi. Jung was deeply impressed by Freud's work but he still did not contact him.

On 14 February 1903, Jung married Emma Rauschenbach, the rich daughter of a rich family of Swiss industrialists. The couple honeymooned on Lake Como, and then went to Madeira and the Canary Islands. In a rather ungallant account, Jung revealed later that he and Emma spent much of the honeymoon arguing about how husbands and wives should divide their money. She, of course, had money while he only had a modest salary. When Jung came back to work, he flaunted the new wealth that came from his wife. He bought expensive clothes and arranged for a personal chef to cook his meals at the hospital. He was far too grand now to use the canteen.

When Emma was pregnant with their first child, she soon realized her husband was an indefatigable womanizer. One could only respond to a dominating mother, like Emilie was, Jung wrote later, 'either by becoming a homosexual or a Don Juan'. He could justify why it was all his mother's fault which makes it important to recall Jung's saying; 'The feeling I associated with "woman" was for a long time that of innate unreliability', he wrote. In fact sad Emma put up with absences and infidelities, not to mention brooding silences at dinner. She was as reliable a wife as a man could wish for. Unreliable was, in fact, a good adjective for her husband.

Their first child was born on 26 December 1904. Agathe would suffer badly from the tensions Jung provoked by his unfaithfulness. Becoming a father did not stop him having intense affairs with at least two of his students – Esther Aptekmann and Sabina

Spielrein. Spielrein (which ironically means clean play in German) was a talented Russian and the 'please spank me' heroine of the film *A Dangerous Method*.

'Please spank me' is frivolous but beating fantasies seem to have been common among the early analysts and their patients. Spielrein told Jung her father had often beaten her, and that she was troubled by fantasies of being beaten. Jung's superior, Bleuler, insisted she have no contact with her father and her brothers. Her eventual erotic encounters with Jung included times when Spielrein was beaten or fantasized she was being beaten. Some Jungians have even suggested that since she was beaten by her father, if Jung beat her it was a way of working through her issues. (There is an interesting question, though this book is not the place to discuss it in detail. A few years later, did Freud discuss Spielrein with Anna Freud? Did he tell her Spielrein had been beaten and did that influence both women in their discussions of beating fantasies?)

At least Jung did help Spielrein get better. She applied to medical school at the Burgholzi and, by now more than a little in love, became Jung's assistant in his laboratory.

Despite all his occult dabblings, Jung realized Freud's ideas needed some empirical backing. Some of the first psychologists like Wilhelm Wundt, who founded a laboratory in Leipzig in 1879, had given subjects word association tests. Typically, they studied the first response a subject made to a neutral word like 'chair' and how long that took. Jung saw such an approach could also probe the unconscious if, instead of neutral words, one used emotionally laden ones. Spielrein became one of his first subjects. Though she was now well, she persuaded Bleuler to let her live in the hospital for six months. If she was on the premises, she could help Jung more. One wonders if she ate in the hospital canteen, or did Jung let her share the meals his chef cooked, as well as letting her share his bed?

Jung put together a list of 100 words which ranged from the neutral, like 'plum', 'paint' and 'cow', to ones with more emotional associations, like 'quarrel', 'anxiety' and 'false'. Jung chose the words 'in such a manner as to strike easily almost all complexes of practical occurrence'. Among the not so random words he would ask patients to associate to were 'to beat' and 'to kiss'. Jung did not publish what Spielrein's individual responses to those two 'stimuli' were, though both were part of what she called the 'poetry' between them.

Jung told his subjects to 'Answer as quickly as possible the first word that occurs to your mind. This instruction is so simple that it can easily be followed by anybody'. But – and this was Jung's important discovery – what happened was far from simple. How long it took someone to respond, giving the first word that came into their head, varied. To the word *long* it took one subject 0.6 seconds to reply *short*; to the word *head* it took 0.9 seconds to reply *foot*. One subject, however, took 0.35 seconds to give an association to the word *voyage*, 0.22 seconds to *sin* and a staggering half a second to say *money* in response to *rich*. Sometimes subjects became flustered and said 'I don't know', or laughed defensively. This was not a question of 'intellectual difficulties', as the subjects were 'very intelligent persons of fluent speech', said Jung. 'The explanation lies rather in the emotions.'

When a subject took unusually long to respond, it was because something 'impeded' his or her response, 'that is, the adaptation to the stimulus word is disturbed'. Jung argued that 'we are dealing with something morbid in the psyche – with something which is either temporary or persistently pathological, that is, we are dealing with a psychoneurosis, with a functional disturbance of the mind'.

Working intensely with Spielrein on word associations left plenty of time for more physical associations. It gave Jung a perfect excuse to explain to his wife why he was not at home, why he was a little distracted and did not have much time for his two daughters. He and Emma's second daughter, Gret, was born on 8 February 1906.

The word association tests took an interesting turn when a nurse claimed she had been robbed of 70 francs. Jung seized the moment. All six nurses on the ward had to take the test, which he refined so he could play detective. Instead of the normal words, 'I selected the name of the robbed nurse, plus the following words: cupboard, door, open, key, yesterday, banknote, gold, 70, 50, 20, money, watch, pocketbook, chain, silver, to hide, fur, dark reddish, leather, centimes, stencil, receipt'. He also used words 'which had a special affective value: theft, to take, to steal, suspicion, blame, court, police, to lie, to fear, to discover, to arrest, innocent'. Sherlock Jung found the culprit. Jung deserves to be called the father of the lie detector test.

Jung was tempted not to mention Freud when he submitted *Studies in Word Association* for publication, as scientists were so hostile to psychoanalysis. 'The devil whispered to me' that it would be wise to say nothing about Freud, but then 'I heard the voice of my second personality; If you do a thing like that, as if you had no knowledge of Freud, it would be a piece of trickery. You cannot build your life upon a lie'.

In 1906 Jung sent the paper to Freud, who sent Jung a collection of his essays in return. They agreed on many issues. Among much else, both believed that beneath the conscious mind, there is another realm of the psyche, which both called the unconscious; both believed also that analysing dreams offered some way into that unconscious. Like new lovers, they did not harp on the differences. Jung even revealed one of his dreams in a letter which Freud interpreted as prophesying 'the failure of a marriage for money'. It has been argued that was the truth about Jung's marriage to Emma.

By 1908 certainly Freud was aware that Jung was hardly a model family man as Jung was sleeping with Spielrein, who had developed a fantasy of having his child. Their boy would be given the heroic name of Siegfried. In her diaries, she described her passionate encounters with Jung as 'poetry'. They might be poetry for her, but they were a bit on the side as usual for him. After five months he confessed to Spielrein he had had similar relationships before and needed 'tempestuous, ever-changing love in my life'. How else could he cope with the fact that women were innately unreliable?

The impact on his marriage – and his children – would be dramatic. At her wits' end, Jung's wife told Spielrein's mother what had been happening in an anonymous letter. Her mother wrote to Jung and got an astonishing reply: 'I moved from being her doctor to being her friend when I ceased to push my feelings into the background.' He then lectured:

> You do understand of course that a man and a girl cannot possibly indefinitely have friendly feelings with one another without the likelihood that something more may enter the relationship ... no one can prevent two friends doing what they like.

Zurich was not actually a capital of adultery in 1906, in fact. Jung added that he had never, as a doctor would have done, charged any fee. Paying the doctor established the boundaries. If Mrs Spielrein wanted him to treat her daughter as a patient, 'you should pay me a fee as a suitable recompense for my trouble'. Then he would never touch Sabina again. Jung even suggested ten francs an hour would be an appropriate sum.

In return or perhaps in revenge, Spielrein wrote to Freud, making it clear that she and Jung had been lovers. 'In the end the unavoidable happened ... it reached the point where he could no longer stand it and wanted "poetry". I could not and did not want to resist, for many reasons.' At the time Freud saw Jung as his 'Crown Prince' who had the advantage of not being a Jew. Freud was always worried psychoanalysis would be perceived as too Jewish. So he turned a blind eye to Jung's total disregard of medical ethics.

Spielrein's fantasy of having a child with Jung was to be disappointed. In 1908, Emma became pregnant with their third child – and this provoked tension and anxiety in his two children. Jung asked his four-year-old daughter what she would do if she had a little brother. 'Kill him', she replied in a perfect outburst of sibling rivalry. Emma and Jung's third child, Franz, was born on 1 December 1908. Jung wrote to Freud saying how delighted he was and that he felt at peace, 'just like a peasant', now that he had a son.

There was more to Agathe's feelings than sibling rivalry. Franz's birth traumatized her and she asked if her mother really had to die. When Jung asked her why she thought that, she said she thought mothers must die after giving birth. They became angels and then were reborn again. Jung first explained to her that a mother is like a soil and a father like a gardener who plants a seed. The euphemisms didn't wash and, finally, he told his daughter the truth about sexual intercourse. That was very frank for the period but knowing the facts of life troubled Agathe. In the next months, she had many disturbing dreams about childbirth and sex. She also had night terrors which reminded Jung of his own childhood. The little girl also worried about volcanoes and earthquakes. Jung tried to calm her by showing her books which had pictures of earthquakes and volcanoes in distant countries, far away from geologically placid Switzerland.

To help in this crisis, Jung turned to his mother and invited her to come and live nearby. Needless to say Emilie came trailing her ghosts and scared her grandchildren with tales of the supernatural, though she also seems to have provided some comfort to them.

Jung was probably quite happy that he had an impeccable reason to leave all this turmoil. Soon after Franz was born, he and Freud sailed to the United States to attend the twentieth-anniversary celebrations of Clark University. Freud had been invited to give lectures. Jung insisted he had not been invited to accompany Freud but independently, as the Americans recognized the importance of his work on word association. Both men saw the invitation as a mark of the fact that psychoanalysis was now internationally successful.

Freud never wrote about what happened during their transatlantic journey but there were incidents that were crucial to the history of psychoanalysis. The account we have comes from Jung's *Memories* only, a fact which has not been commented much, though it does mean we only have one side of the story. According to Jung, Freud refused to tell the Crown Prince his own dreams in detail, which Jung resented; he had told Freud his dreams in full cinemascope. Freud, Jung wrote, told him he had to keep details back to preserve his own authority. The perfectly mature man and the great mystic squabbled rather like children who squeal 'You can't have mine'. After that rebuff, Jung started to argue, in private at first, that Freud emphasized sex far too much as a cause of neuroses. That was ironic as by the time they met Freud's libido had been 'subdued' (to use his own words) while Jung's was bubbling along, hormones at full throttle.

The men sailed across the Atlantic leaving their wives and families behind. It was left to Emma to deal with the family and the children's everyday problems. In a tribute to her mother, Helene Jung said Emma was always there for her children.

For all their differences, as fathers, there were some similarities between the two men. Like Freud, Jung too sometimes took his family on walking expeditions in the mountains. He also liked sailing and treated himself to a two-masted yacht with red sails. It had a cabin large enough for three children to sleep in. Agathe and her sister Gret remembered what their father called their North Pole journeys. When it was foggy, Franz had to blow on the ship's horn every two minutes. Jung often told his children to 'annoy the wind' by making loud noises with the oars. On board he liked cooking in the open and the children had to hold an umbrella over him. Once he spent seven hours cooking a pike they had caught. It all sounds very jolly. There were two – maybe even more – sides to Jung.

Freud was a Jew who did not believe in God; he emphasized the primal importance of sexuality as the cause of neuroses. Jung was influenced and, arguably, besotted by the spiritual. For seven years he had deferred to Freud but, by 1913, Jung decided he could no longer work with him. As the split loomed, Jung experienced a horrible 'confrontation with the unconscious'. He worried he was 'menaced by a psychosis' or was 'doing a schizophrenia'. But though he might be more fragile, Jung had no intention of being bested and decided that this descent into madness was a gift. In private, he induced hallucinations, or 'active imaginations'. We do not know how these affected his children. He eventually refined this material into *The Red Book* which he refused to publish while he was alive. (Psychoanalysts certainly like to cosy up to their secrets.)

After the end of 1913, Freud and Jung never spoke again and never even exchanged a letter. Freud blasted Jung in letters and one paper. He wrote that he had promoted Jung as the first president of the International Psychoanalytic Society, which 'turned out to have been a most unfortunate step'. In 'On the history of the psychoanalytic movement', Freud quoted critics like Ernest Jones who had said Jung's ideas were 'as obscure, unintelligible and confused as to make it difficult to take up any position on it'.

The break with Freud made Jung turn for support to Emma who gave him unstinting comfort. Jung acknowledged in his *Memories*, saying 'the practical and moral support my dear wife gave me at this difficult time is remembered with gratitude'. Support seems to have included marital erotic encounters as their last child, Helene, was born in March 1914.

Emma accepted her husband's ways and moods, as did their children. It was not an era when couples divorced easily, though Emma did threaten it once. The family usually ate together when Jung was not away, and he liked his food. At dinner, Jung also seemed to have two personalities. At times he was very outgoing, telling stories which 'enthralled his family', but at other times he was silent and brooding.

Gratitude to his wife for her support when he broke with Freud did not make Jung faithful. In 1913, he took on a new patient who, like Sabina Spielrein had done, soon became a lover. Yet again the impact on his children would be huge.

Toni Wolff came from an old and rich Zurich family and was highly intelligent. Her father had just died and she was inconsolable. Jung made little progress in helping his young new patient – Wolff was 21 – until he hit on a link between her grief and some Greek myths. Wolff was entranced.

Two weeks after Emma gave birth to Helene, Jung showed just how unreliable he was. He and Wolff went on a two-week holiday together, leaving Emma to look after the baby while his own mother cared for the older children.

Emma wrote that the children were angered by the appearance of Wolff in their lives. They minded what they saw as an affront to their mother – and often expressed anger at their father, which gave Emma some comfort. Jung and Wolff were intimately connected for the rest of their lives; he called her his 'other wife' and sometimes showed up at professional receptions with a wife on each arm. Emma accepted the permanent emotional triangle. Jung organized the living arrangements to suit himself nicely. He lived with his wife at their home at Kusnacht and established Wolff in a tower he built nearby at Bollingen, a tower which the Jung family still own.

Later, Jung explained that it was not just a question of women being unreliable as per ever, but more complex. 'Back then I was in the midst of the anima problem', the word 'anima' being his term for the inner personality and also the feminine element in a male personality. He added: 'What could you expect from me? The anima bit me on the forehead and would not let go.' It bit him on a different part of his anatomy too, one might snipe.

Jung was mercurial and could also be an enchanting father. He would sometimes take his family hiking on Sunday and Franz remembered the summer of 1914 with some affection. The family went to stay with Emma's mother and played Indians against the English.

> Father was the leader. He wore a Canadian mountie's hat and a pair of cowboy boots from his visit to America with Freud. He looked like a sheriff. We built teepees and huts big enough to sleep in, and each side had a horse. We would light fires and burn down each other's teepees.

Jung even overcame his fear of snakes while he was with his children and killed an adder. Jung explained his interest in childhood games by saying he was counting on his unconscious to cure him and that required going back to his own childhood.

In her touching tribute to her mother, Helene said that: 'She shared her husband's interests and was always there as a sounding board.... No subject was not discussed with her. In reality she left the final decisions but not without having told us what she thought.' Emma had to be there for her children because Jung was so often absent.

Jung allowed his children some freedom as they grew up. He let Franz decide his attitude to Christianity and, when the boy did not want to go to Sunday school, that was fine. Jung wanted his children to choose the kind of education they wanted freely. Only one of their four daughters, however, finished secondary education – Gret who became interested in one of her father's pet subjects, astrology.

The interest in the supernatural also affected Agathe. In 1923, she told Jung she sensed the presence of corpses on the site of the tower at Bollingen. Her father thought she had inherited psychic powers from her grandmother and excavated. He found a skeleton which proved to be a French soldier who had been killed in 1799 when the Austrian Army blew up a bridge.

The children saw less of their father in the 1920s. Apart from the time he spent with Wolff, Jung travelled to India, to the American southwest and to Kenya. In every instance, in today's jargon, Jung was looking for his true self. That self had little to do with his children, it seems.

In 1924, Jung visited the Pueblo Indian chief, Ochwiay Biano, who complained: 'The whites always want something; they are always uneasy and restless. We do not know what they want. We do not understand them. We think they are mad.' 'Why is that?' asked Jung. 'They say they think with their heads.' Jung was surprised and asked Biano what he thought with. 'We think here', the chief replied, indicating his heart. Jung added that:

> What we from our point of view call colonialization, missions to the heathen, spread of civilization, etc., has another face – the face of a bird of prey seeking with cruel intentness for distant quarry – a face worthy of a race of pirates and highwaymen.

'The Americans want to stamp out our religion', Biano said,

> Why can they not let us alone? What we do, we do not only for ourselves but for the Americans also. Yes, we do it for the whole world.... If we did not do it, what would become of the world? If we were to cease practicing our religion, in ten years the sun would no longer rise.

Jung did not question this extraordinary claim. Christians believed rituals and prayers influenced God, Jung wrote. 'Why should that not also be true of so-called "savages" who felt they had a living relationship with Creation?'

In 1925, Jung continued his travels in search of self and went to Kenya where he loved the landscape, the gazelles and the warthog grazing, 'moving forward like slow rivers'. This 'stillness of eternal being' inspired Jung. But the dastardly British were ruining it all; a medicine man Jung met complained: 'In the old days, the medicine man had dreams, and knew whether there is war or sickness or whether rain comes and where the herds should be driven.' But since the whites were in Africa, the medicine man said, no one had dreams any more. 'Dreams are no longer necessary because now the English know everything', he explained. I can only wonder what Prince Charles, prince of the dream-destroying Britons, thought of that when he and Van der Post safari-ed in search of meaning.

Exposure to Indians and Africans did not make Jung abandon his view that Jews were 'others'. In 1927 he wrote:

> To accept the conclusions of a Jewish psychology as generally valid is a quite unforgiveable mistake. None of us would think of applying Chinese or Indian psychology to ourselves. The cheap allegation of anti-Semitism that has been levelled at me on the basis of this criticism is about as intelligent as attacking me for being prejudiced against the Chinese.

Jung's children tolerated and, it would seem, forgave their father's behaviour to their mother. Franz went to medical school but decided to become an architect. He lived in Kusnacht and had four children. Gret married a childhood sweetheart even though her family at one point tried to prevent the marriage on the grounds that the Jungs were too disturbed for proper people to deal with. Marianna, his fourth child, supervised the publishing of her father's work. Helene, the youngest, became a needlework expert and also worked on a subject that her father had often written about – the symbolism of icons.

During the Second World War, oddly like Freud, Jung refused to flee to the United States. His whole family lived in or around Kusnacht.

On 30 May 1961, when the family was having tea together, Jung collapsed. He was taken to his room but grew weaker. His daughter Marianne came to stay and helped Ruth, Franz's wife. Jung slept for the last few days of his life but he rallied and, on the last night of his life, recovered consciousness and asked Ruth to fetch a very good bottle of wine from the cellar. He drank with her and his son. Two of his children were with him the next afternoon. He sat in bed trying to talk but they could not understand him. They got some flannel, moistened it with camomile and let him suck from it. Suddenly Franz said 'Don't bother Ruth, it's too late'. That night there was a thunderstorm – and another one during his funeral. His daughter had the last word. 'That's father grumbling', she said.

Franz inherited Kusnacht. His son inherited it in turn. Visitors are allowed in from time to time to visit what Jungs admirers treat as a shrine.

After Jung's death his family battled over what could be included in *Memories, Dreams, Reflections*, the autobiography he wanted published posthumously. This account of his life mentions his wife only once and his children not at all. The family also condemned a biography by Deirdre Bair as an insult and threatened to sue her German publisher for invasion of privacy. To avoid a costly trial the publishers added a list of 40 family grievances in the German-language edition. It is perhaps the first book to include a hostile review within its pages.

The next subject provoked as much hostility as Jung – and from many of the same people. Freud disliked her, Anna Freud was jealous of her and her own daughter did not have a good word to say about her.

Notes and references

Bair, D., *Carl Jung*, Little Brown (2003). This is an excellent biography.

Relevant works by Jung himself:
Jung, Carl, *Studies in Word Association*, Heinemann (1918).
Jung, Carl, *Memories, Dreams, Reflections*, Fontana (1995).
Jung, Carl and Sghamdasani, S., *The Red Book*, W.W. Norton (2012).

On Jung's family:
Clark-Stern E., *Out of the Shadows*, Genoa Press (2015).
Gaudissart, Imelda, *Love and Sacrifice: The Life of Emma Jung*, Chiron (2008).
Jung, Helene, *La vierge au donateur*, Courtot Press (1923).

Other references:
Covington, C. and Wharton, B. (eds), *Sabina Spielrein, Forgotten Pioneer*, Routledge (2010).
Coward, Noel, *Blithe Spirit*, Samuel French (1941).
Ernst, Edzard, On Prince Charles' 65th birthday, published 14 November 2013 on his website and resuming themes covered in an interview in *The Guardian* on 30 July 2011.
Freud, S., *On the Interpretation of Dreams*, published in Standard edition, vols 4–5 (1899) and by Vintage (2001).
Freud, S., *On the History of the Psychoanalytic Movement*, translation by A.A. Brill, Nervous and Mental Disease Monograph Series (No. 25) (1917).
Hofstadter, G.B., *Jung's Struggle with Freud*, Chiron (1994).
Jones, J.D.F., *The Storyteller*, Scribners (1997) provides a critical account of Laurens van der Post. I interviewed the author for my film *The Madness of Prince Charles* (2005), now available from Canny Store and on Amazon.
Orbach, Susie, *Fat is a Feminist Issue*, Arrow (2006).
Winnicott, D.W., Review of Jung's *Memories*, *International J of Psychoanalysis*, 450–5 (1964).

6

MELANIE KLEIN AND HER DAUGHTER

'Some analysts seem to assume as a matter of course that analysed parents are also the best parents. This is definitely not the case', wrote Melitta Schmideberg, the daughter of Melanie Klein, in 1937. The famous analyst mother gave as good as she got. After Melitta had attacked her ideas, Klein wrote 'And there is one very obvious fact which should not be mentioned nor even hinted at by any of us'. Then, of course, mama spat it out: 'and that is Melitta's illness'. Her illness was never defined precisely but daughter was more than a neurone short of normality, Klein implied.

Klein was clearly a woman who inspired intense loyalty – and intense hatred. Anna Freud hated her and their feud plagued the British Psychoanalytic Society for decades. When the Freuds escaped to London in 1938, Klein sent a letter of welcome to the 'master'. Anna made sure she never got a reply, let alone an invitation to visit them in Hampstead. This rebuff was small by comparison with Melitta's. When Klein died in 1960, her daughter refused to attend the funeral – and wore red shoes to celebrate. Jews – and the Kleins were that – are supposed to tear something they wear when someone dies because the death of a relative is a tear in the fabric of the universe.

Unlike almost all the early analysts, Melanie Klein was not a doctor. She was born in 1882, in Vienna. Her father, Dr Moriz Reizes, was meant to become a rabbi but he lost his faith in God and, after a number of vicissitudes, became 'a medical consultant in a music hall', according to Julia Kristeva in her boisterous study of Klein. Moriz's profession wobbles from author to author; another biography claims he was a mediocre dentist (perhaps he pulled teeth in between comedy routines). It is not surprising Kristeva was left a little confused. Klein never published an autobiography but left various fragments which have been collated by Sayers and Forrester only recently (2012). In one Klein explains the family was hard up until miraculously they won a prize on the lottery, but even after that it seems his father continued in show business. Klein wrote:

> My father, at the time preceeding [*sic*] this favourable change, became attached to a kind of music hall, called an Orpheum, as a doctor. He had to be present at the performances, which was very boring for him and a sacrifice, because he wanted to be with his family, but a help financially.

Before the lottery win, Klein's mother chose to open a shop which Kristeva thinks was very unsuitable for the wife of a doctor; Libussa offered the public pets and plants, and the pets included reptiles. In one of the fragments of the autobiography, Klein says her mother hated the reptiles. Seeing her mother handle snakes, Kristeva suggests, may help explain Klein's fantasies of the mother's body teeming with foul 'bad objects'. The bad breast may have been a distortion of the jaws of a snake.

The family had tragic problems to deal with when Klein was four; her eldest sister Sidonie died of tuberculosis. 'I remember that I felt my mother needed me all the more now that Sidonie was gone.' Sidonie's death was only the first of many tragedies. Klein's brother Emmanuel died of a heart condition in his twenties. Hanna Segal argued these deaths left Klein with a legacy of depression.

Depression did not hold Klein back, though. She went to Vienna University to study medicine, but before she finished her studies, she met one of her brother's friends, Arthur Stephen Klein. He dazzled her and they married the day after Klein celebrated her twenty-first birthday. Klein's mother Libussa did not think her daughter was ready to marry as she suffered from depressive exhaustion, irritability and was 'an emotional cripple'. To help, Libussa moved in with the couple, but help she didn't.

Though her marriage was not happy, the Kleins had three children and they, Klein wrote, gave her real happiness. Melitta was born in 1904, Hans in 1907 and Eric in 1914. Libussa did little for her daughter's marriage as she 'tried to create situations in which husband and wife saw little of each other'. Arthur started to suffer from 'nerves' and stomach troubles. Melitta usually took her mother's side when her parents quarrelled.

In her autobiographical fragments, Klein painted a far more glowing picture of her mother:

> My relation to my mother has been one of the great standbys of my life. I loved her deeply, admired her beauty, her intellect, her deep wish for knowledge, no doubt with some of the envy which exists in every daughter.

Klein's husband was an engineer and when he went to work in Budapest in 1910, he took his family with him. Hungary was a turning point as Klein met one of Freud's closest associates, Sándor Ferenczi. He soon agreed to take her on as an analytic patient and apprentice. Klein read Freud voraciously.

Beginning to study psychoanalysis prompted Klein to try her hand at writing. She composed some 30 poems and four short stories. Some suggest that Arthur, with his nerves and gastric problems, was a dismal lover as they express a longing for sexual satisfaction. After the 1914–18 war, Klein became close friends with

Klara Vago and, according to Kristeva, they had a 'relationship'. Klein wrote an affectionate poem to Klara. The family in which Klein's three children grew up – a powerful grandmother, a dissatisfied mother and a father with nerves and indigestion – was riddled with frustrations. Frustration and envy would become key themes for Klein.

One of the paradoxes of psychoanalysis was that it saw the crucial importance of childhood, but toddlers could hardly lie on a couch and discuss their dreams and free associations. Anna Freud would write later that she felt children under the age of seven could not be treated directly as they were too young to manage the formalities of analysis. Klein was a mother, however, and had daily experience of children. She believed one did not have to try to talk to children to explore their unconscious. Crucially children played – and their play was the way they revealed their anxieties and conflicts.

Klein developed her insight into a technique. For children 'the road royal to the unconscious' was through toys, games, mucking about in the sandpit. The analyst would treat the child with paper, crayons, string, a ball and small cups in a room that had at least a sink with taps. To make sure the child's imagination could roam freely, these figures had to be almost fuzzy. Fire engines and toy trains suggested too obvious games. Like a playful parent, the analyst would play different parts – a monster, an elephant, a buzzing bee. Very naturally, Klein used her children as 'guinea pigs' to test and develop her ideas.

In 1920, Klein met another of Freud's close associates, Karl Abraham, and they were greatly impressed with each other. He encouraged her work and that prompted her to move to Berlin. In 1922, she read her first paper, 'The development of a child', to the Berlin Psychoanalytic Society. Freud was at the meeting though it is not clear he actually listened to her. If he had he would have been displeased. Klein had the chutzpah to challenge his timing of the Oedipus Complex; he had placed its start too late. Freud also claimed adults transferred their feelings and fantasies about parents onto the analyst. The patient loved the analyst as she had loved her parents but, for Klein, the baby's feelings were more conflicted as the baby both loved and hated its parents.

When her mentor Abraham died in 1925, Klein wrote it 'was a great pain to me and a very painful situation to come through'. A year later, Ernest Jones invited her to give lectures in England. He had no idea the trouble that would cause. Klein gave six which formed the basis of her first book, *The Psychoanalysis of Children*. Much of the material in this comes from her analysis of two of her children.

Klein wanted to understand how human beings evolve from the primitive pleasure-seeking impulses of early infancy and what could go wrong and produce neuroses. Babies are born weak, helpless and confused. Kristeva said Klein described the newborn's days and nights 'with the horror of a Hieronymus Bosch painting'. The infant cannot grasp people around it are in fact *people* and at first the mother is not even 'a mother' to her child. She is just a pair of breasts which come and go unpredictably. The infant experiences moments of intense pain (hunger) and then, for reasons it can't understand, moments of equally intense pleasure. When the breast is there and the milk flows, the infant feels calm and happy, but when the breast is not there and the baby wants it, she or he panics. The panic of the missing breasts makes the infant vengeful. This chaotic defenceless infant adopts a primitive defence mechanism against such intolerable anxiety. It 'splits' the mother into a 'good breast' and a 'bad breast'. The bad breast is hated with a passion; the infant wants to bite and destroy it. Klein's use of the word 'bite' may well be what suggested to Kristeva that Klein's ideas owed something to her memories of her mother selling snakes. By contrast, the good breast is sucked, licked, loved.

We do not, alas, know if Klein had enough milk to breastfeed her children. Or did she use a wet nurse?

Around the age of six months the baby reaches what Klein called 'the depressive position' as it begins to integrate its fragmented perceptions of its parent and develops a more integrated sense of self. Integration did not mean happiness, however. The 'depressive position' was a moment of soberness and melancholy when the growing child takes on board (unconsciously) the idea that reality is more complicated and that the mother cannot be neatly blamed for every setback; almost nothing is totally pure or totally evil; things are a perplexing mixture of the good and bad. Klein's theory highlights how we tend to reduce people into what they can do for us (give us milk, make us money, keep us happy), rather than what they are in and of themselves.

Klein was a mother who criticized Freud. Freud's loyal daughter had no children. Battle 'among the ladies', as Kristeva called them, was probably inevitable, especially as both tended to be jealous. Children could not free associate, and could not be analysed, Anna Freud decreed. They could only be taught. She told the Berlin Society in 1927 that it could be dangerous to analyse normal children. Klein, on the other hand, believed that analysis should be part of every child's education. Even by 1927, there was some evidence that favoured Klein; the play technique had produced good results with its insights into the inner worlds of children before the mites could speak.

Kristeva wrote:

> Some babies never achieve the depressive position and get stuck in a mode of primitive splitting Klein termed the 'paranoid-schizoid position'. These unhappy individuals cannot tolerate the slightest ambivalence: they must either hate or love. They seek scapegoats or idealise. They fall violently in love and then – at the inevitable moment when a lover in some way disappoints them, they come to hate him or her. The relationship between Klein and her daughter is an almost perfect illustration.

One of the striking features of Klein's autobiographical fragments is how little she says about her children. Melitta graduated from Berlin University writing a thesis on the history of homeopathy in Hungary. Though she depended financially on her mother, she dedicated her thesis to her father. It was a sign of trouble to come between the 'ladies'. Far worse was to come.

When he was 20 years old, in 1927, Klein's son Hans died in a climbing accident. His sister Melitta suspected the death was really suicide and blamed her mother. For Klein, who felt she had been blamed for her sister's death decades before, that was devastating.

The roots of the conflict between Klein and her daughter were also explored in Nicholas Wright's play *Mrs Klein*. When Hans dies, Melitta is convinced it's a case of suicide and holds her interfering mother responsible. 'Hans died because he couldn't bring himself to hate you', rages the daughter, adding vindictively, 'I can. I do'. Her mother remains impassive; detachment is important to her. How else can she see her children for the flawed creatures they really are? Klein also has to face an intolerable thought – that she had nothing to do with her son's death. Wright paints her as a Jewish diva with an ego the size of Everest. Hans was not playing out childhood traumas or expressing latent hostilities when he slipped; he just slipped. As Freud is said to have said, 'sometimes a cigar is just a cigar'.

In 1927 Klein also divorced Arthur and moved to England with her 13-year-old son, Eric, as well as Melitta and Melitta's husband, Dr Walter Schmideberg. Both were beginning to practise as psychoanalysts. Though he was Jewish, Walter had been accepted as a cavalry officer in the 1914 war, some achievement as many Austrian cavalry officers boasted there wasn't a Jew among them. During the war, Walter managed to get Freud his much-needed cigars – Freud felt he thought best when he smoked – so Walter earned his profound gratitude.

Melitta then went to Vienna in 1929 for a few months to study with Anna Freud. The trip was not a success as Melitta wrote a very intemperate paper about Anna's ideas, but this was the last time Melitta published anything that supported her mother. When Melitta came back to London, she continued in analysis – this time with Edward Glover. He seems to have encouraged her to assert her independence from her mother. Melitta wrote to her:

> 'You do not take it enough into consideration that I am very different from you'. I do not think that the relationship to her mother, however good should be the centre of her life for an adult woman.'

Melitta added that her own relationship to her mother 'until a few years ago was one of neurotic dependence'. War between mother and daughter burst into the open when Melitta was elected to the British Institute of Psychoanalysis. In her paper, 'The play analysis of a three year old girl', Melitta said the digestive difficulties of her patient, Viviane, were not due to constitutional factors as her mother's theory would claim, but to the fact that her mother had subjected her to over-zealous toilet training. Glover encouraged the feud. In the first volume of *The Psychoanalytic Study of the Child*, he described Klein's theory as 'a bio-religious system which depends on faith rather than science … a variant of the doctrine of Original Sin'. Schmideberg's paper won the Clinical Essay awarded by the British Psychoanalytic Society, which inevitably fuelled the feud.

Melitta did not need much encouragement to fight her mother. At one point she interrupted a lecture Klein gave, shouting, 'Where is the father in your work?'

Melitta then accused her mother of plagiarism. The British Psychoanalytic Society felt it had to set up a committee to judge but, in the end, found there was no plagiarism. The accusation was all that her mother needed. Klein sniped that her daughter's aggression was not just a question of theoretical differences. 'And there is one very obvious fact which I feel should not be mentioned nor even hinted at by any of us.' And that was 'Melitta's illness'. She did not give any further details.

The Kleins, however, did not begin to understand the rules of British society. It is just not done to accuse your mum of stealing other people's work and even less done to accuse one's flesh and blood of being mad. Freud's English translator James Strachey put it with nice irony, writing psychoanalysis 'is a game preserve of the Freud family'. Klein's views were fatally subversive. His letter ended with a very English 'bloody foreigners', which many of the analysts were. Strachey characterized the fighting positions of the ladies as follows: 'Your views are so defective that you are incompetent to carry out a training analysis or for the matter of that any analysis at all', says one protagonist.

Kleinians and Freudians were then, and still are now, very partisan. The Kleinians insist Melanie was a far more original thinker who had had to establish a reputation without having the benefit of being the founder's child. Anna Freud's book on the psychoanalysis of children, on the other hand, was at first rejected for publication. When it came out eventually, the only good reviews came from those close to Freud. She was daddy's child.

In 1932, Klein published *The Psychoanalysis of Children*. Her supporters boasted it was the most original work the Hogarth Press, run by Virginia Woolf and her husband Leonard, had published.

When, in 1938, Freud and Anna fled from Vienna to London, the conflict got worse. Klein sent Freud a letter of welcome but she was not invited to visit. Her daughter, however, was – and Freud even gave Melitta a present. Despite that, Anna found Melitta 'too asocial to co-operate with'.

In 1979, I interviewed Melitta when I was making a film on depression. She lived in a house stuffed with antiques and had fond memories of Freud, who was especially grateful to her husband Walter for the cigars he had supplied to him in the 1914 war. Melitta told me that after 40 years, she had come to the conclusion that the best form of therapy was to listen to patients' descriptions of their problems – and, whenever possible, to serve them wholesome soups. Too much theory, be it Freudian, Jungian, Kleinian, Reichian or of any other provenance, was of little help to either patients or therapists. I did not then know much of the rift between her and her mother so asked nothing about that. I did not know that there is not one word in Klein's autobiographical fragments about her fights with Melitta. To me Melitta exuded the wisdom of an old woman who had seen much, but smiled like a happy young girl when she showed me the silver spoon that Freud had given her.

Given the background described, it seems reasonable to read Schmideberg's classic paper, 'After the analysis', as a comment in part at least on her troubled relationship with her mother. She gave it to the British Psychoanalytic Society on 17 March 1937 and it then appeared in *The Psychoanalytic Quarterly* in 1938. Schmideberg began with a very accomplished overview, saying: 'Most patients come for analysis as for any other form of treatment with the concrete aim of getting rid of some definite symptom.' She divided patients into those who had 'on the whole a reasonable idea of what they can expect from analysis', and those 'for whom psychoanalysis has become the new religion', and who would 'never be satisfied with a mere alleviation of symptoms or any other simple tangible result'. This unrealistic patient

> expects that after being 'fully analysed' he will never have any more difficulties or disappointments in life, and never under any circumstances experience guilt or anxiety; that he will develop remarkable intellectual or aesthetic powers, perhaps even prove to be a genius, be blissfully happy, perfectly balanced, superhumanly unbiased and absolutely free from the slightest neurotic symptom, caprice of mood or bad habit.

Analysis was no panacea, Schmideberg countered. It was silly to imagine that a community, whose every member had been analysed, would be a paradise where there was no crime, no hatred and no neuroses. She added that 'Of course if you press so ardent an apostle of psychoanalysis, he will soon have to admit that he has never yet come across that marvel of perfection, "that fully analysed person"'. Such fantasies of perfection were, in fact, 'replicas of the child's ideas of what it is like to be grown up'. These fantasies saw adults as unutterably perfect; they could 'do no wrong, have no bad habits, make no mistakes ... are free from anxiety, from difficulties of any sort, and of course they are extremely clever'. These sections make one wonder whether this was what her mother had made her feel – that adults were indeed utterly perfect.

Children had one consolation; they imagined they would grow up and become such trouble-free adults themselves. Schmideberg added that:

> Analysis is for some patients an escape from life, a return to childhood. This type of patient lives almost literally only through and for the analysis; he wants to remain a baby and puts off any effort or unpleasant decision until the situation has been 'fully analysed'.

She added that 'The often "querulous" patient is really demanding compensation for all his past and present sufferings'.

Such demands, Schmideberg suggested, 'are largely a defence against guilt. The patient feels guilty for not getting better'. Again it is tempting to see her arguments as very personal because she had been through analysis with her mother. The patient

> feels that the analyst demands a standard of health which he can as little live up to as to the moral standards set by his parents. This is one reason for not giving the patient exaggerated ideas about the results of analysis.

Like Freud, Schmideberg identified as a Jew. On Yom Kippur, Jews atone. 'Analysis is regarded as an atonement', she wrote, and should be seen 'as a cleansing process, as a religious exercise; getting on in the analysis means doing one's duty, obeying one's parents, learning one's lessons, saying one's prayers. To get better, improve, is to be good'.

Analysts encouraged such illusions of total cure, when they clung to every detail of what Schmideberg termed the 'analytic ceremonial' and saw it as the 'only true therapy'. One of her women patients was especially anxious to be free from all neurotic symptoms or organic illnesses, and tried hard not to give way to any weakness. To be weak meant that she was babyish or feminine – and despised by her brothers. Schmideberg gave no more details about this patient. In another passage, Schmideberg may well be referring to herself or her personality after she broke off relations with her mother.

> With a really unsympathetic mother the only consolation she had had during her long childhood illnesses was the attention her father had given her. This combined with her mother's neglect came too near to the guilty Oedipus situation to make it possible for her to enjoy a repetition of the situation in later life. Being ill and neurotic also represented an identification with her very unhappy father.

One should remember that Melitta dedicated her thesis on homeopathy to her father.

Schmideberg made another critical point. 'The fantastic ideas entertained by patients as to the possibilities of analytic therapy are encouraged by the fact that analysts themselves are not always very clear in their minds on the subject.' All too often they did not want 'to describe the actual imperfect results achieved under the very imperfect conditions of real life'. She did not pull her punches.

> It seems almost as if there was sometimes a feeling that it is beneath the analyst's dignity to be too interested in questions of success, that it is bad form to claim good results, or again that to be sceptical is a confession of failure. Statistics such as those published by the analytic clinics are of little value because they do not explain what is meant by 'cured', nor do they give details of the cases.

Schmideberg hoped to see studies of patients some years after they had left analysis 'to find out if those described as "cured" showed any neurotic reactions' and to see how many could be regarded as permanently 'cured' or 'improved', defining the terms in detail, and which were the decisive factors for a favourable prognosis. She added:

> I believe that with certain patients an optimum result is achieved after a certain time which cannot be bettered to any considerable extent however long one persists with the treatment, at least with the same analyst. It seems to me that it is essential in therapy to know the right time to stop.

But some analysts found it hard to draw the line.

Melitta warned:

> I have heard of analysts who actually frighten the patient into continuing the analysis by warning him of the grave consequences of breaking off the treatment: that he may get worse, go mad, commit suicide, sometimes using direct or indirect outside pressure in addition. I think that the ill effects of such a procedure can hardly be exaggerated.

It is telling that Schmideberg often compares the patient to a child. She had, after all, been her mother's patient.

> The danger of our recent attitude of trying to make the patient go on as long as possible is that we behave very much like the possessive parents who make the child afraid of life because they do not want him to grow up and break away. There are those who claim that the fact that the analyst repeats an unfavourable parental attitude is of little importance so long as the fantasies stimulated by it are 'thoroughly analysed'. I do not share this opinion. The main danger of long analyses (six, eight, even ten years of analysis do not seem unusual any more) is that it estranges the patient from reality.

Freud wrote a famous paper on analysis terminable and interminable in which he discussed some of these issues.

Some patients even seemed to think a short analysis was a sign of failure. Edward Glover had told Schmideberg about one patient who fretted as his own analysis was 'a great deal shorter than that of his friends, had a dream in which he equated the "short analysis" with a short penis'.

Analysts had a perfect excuse as 'no one was without unconscious paranoid anxieties or an anal fixation. We must try to retain a sense of perspective with regard to the practical results we can expect'. Again, she compared the analyst to a parent. 'It is very natural that analysts should feel gratified if their patients excel in one way or another, just as parents are pleased if their children accomplish all they would like to have done themselves.'

Schmideberg then again turned to the question of parents. 'Some analysts seem to assume as a matter of course that analysed parents are also the best parents. This is definitely not the case', she said.

> All we can legitimately expect is that a person who has been successfully analysed will have a better relation to his child than before he was analysed. But this improved attitude is not necessarily better and is in fact often less good than that of a genuinely good parent.

Analysis, Schmideberg argued, could not 'remove every manifestation which might be regarded as a "symptom", but only those which really interfere with the patient's life'. A good analysis might have the result that 'the patient may remain homosexual or polygamous, continue to bite his nails, or to masturbate, though usually not to excess, without feeling guilty over it'. She continued: 'I believe that for most people it is more normal to have slight peculiarities, anxieties, minor neurotic symptoms or bad habits than to be absolutely free from them, provided they are in a position to tolerate them without difficulty.'

Analysts encouraged patients to become addicted to analysis. Schmideberg gave a telling example:

> A patient came to see me about a year after she had completed her analysis. She told me that she felt well and that her symptoms had disappeared but added that she would like to have a few months further analysis. I asked her why she wanted to recommence analysis if she felt well, to which she replied that feeling well was such a strain.

Analysts should not expect too much.

> A possessive attitude in the analyst is even worse than a possessive attitude in the parent. I consider it satisfactory that a number of patients whom I analysed successfully differed as fundamentally from me after the analysis as before it in their political, religious, social, and artistic convictions.

But analysts – and again it is tempting to see Schmideberg meant her mother – tended to be grandiose. She went on: 'we must admire the sense of proportion that enabled Freud to realize the limitations of analysis almost as much as we admire his creative genius in discovering it.'

Schmideberg ended with a nice story:

> A patient of mine told somebody at a party that she had been analysed. This individual looked at her with great amazement and said she could hardly believe it, because my patient was so free and easy and natural, quite like an ordinary person in fact, and unlike any 'analysed person' she had met before. I consider that for a patient to become 'just like anyone else' is the best result one can expect from analysis.

One note she added shows her scepticism. 'There is even some danger that the analyst may lose contact with real life if he has the same patients (usually comparatively few) over a number of years.'

Klein continued to be much admired by her admirers and hated by the Freudians. Melitta went to America in 1945 where she worked with delinquent children and then returned to Britain. In the mid-1950s she and Walter went to Switzerland where they were joined by Paula Heinmann who had been close to her mother and may well have been one of her lovers. Klein told Hanna Segal she was too destructive and booted her out of the Melanie Klein Trust in 1955. Melitta, Walter and Paula, like Jung, Emma and Toni Wolff, seem to have lived in a *ménage à trois*.

Klein wrote about envy and was envious herself. Kristeva argues she was envious of her mother, Anna Freud, Marie Bonaparte and Helene Deutsch, another pioneering woman analyst. 'I think my work will last', Klein said to Tom Main, a friend, as he walked her home one evening. 'I've done better than Helene Deutsch haven't I?' The artist Felix Topolski drew a picture of her which Kristeva claims gives her 'the look of a satiated vulture'. For her daughter, Klein seems to have been something of a vulture.

But the mother did leave her daughter some precious objects in her will.

> My gold flexible bracelet which was given me by her paternal grandmother, the single stone diamond ring given to me by my late husband, my gold necklace with garnets and the brooch which goes with the said necklace, both of which I received as a present on my 75th birthday and I have no other bequest to my said daughter because she is otherwise well provided for and by her technical qualifications able to provide for herself.

These were the most tender words Klein had said about her 'ill' daughter for 25 years.

Notes and references

As I have made clear, interviewing Melitta Schmideberg was fascinating and moving. Her relevant works are:
Schmideberg, M., The play analysis of a three year old girl, *Int J of Psychoanalysis*, vol. xx, 245ff. (1934).
Schmideberg, M., After the analysis, *Psychoanalytic Quarterly*, vol. 7, 122–42 (1938).
Schmideberg, M., *Children in Need*, Allen & Unwin (1948).

Melanie Klein's key works:
Klein, Melanie, *The Psychoanalysis of Children*, Vintage (1997).
Klein, Melanie, *Selected Papers*, edited by Juliet Mitchell, Penguin (1986).

The most useful books on Melanie Klein are:
Grosskurth, P., *Melanie Klein: Her Work and Her World*, Random House (1986).
Kristeva, Julia, *Melanie Klein*, Columbia University Press (2004).
Sayers, J. and Forrester, J., The autobiography of Melanie Klein. *Psychoanalysis and History*, vol. 15, 127–63 (2013).
Segal, Hanna, *Klein*, Other Press (1989).
Wright, Nicholas, *Mrs Klein*, Nick Hern Books (2009).

Other reference:
Glover, E., *On the Early Development of Mind*, Transaction (2009).
Edward Glover was one of the editor of the journal *The Psychoanalytic Study of the Child*. His 1953 book *Psychoanalysis and Child Psychiatry* (Imago) is useful. And Paul Roazen's *Oedipus in Britain*; Other Press; 2000 gives an account of the tensions Melanie Klein provoked.

7

JEAN PIAGET

His mother and psychoanalysis

'Hasn't analysis ever tempted you?' the journalist Jean Claude Bringuier asked Jean Piaget in 1975.

'But I was analysed', Piaget, a year short of 80, replied. 'Please one has to know what one's talking about when one speaks of something.'

In his often maddeningly impersonal *Autobiography*, Piaget writes that he could easily have been a naturalist and spent his life studying molluscs, if it had not been for his teenage crises. These were 'due both to family conditions and to the intellectual curiosity characteristic of that productive age'. The teenager who faced traumatic conflicts was intrigued by psychoanalysis.

Piaget became the most important child psychologist of the twentieth century. His biography remains unwritten 45 years after he died, however. His followers were very loyal and no one has attempted a biography, probably because he did not wish one written. Compared to many of those discussed Piaget had few secrets, it seems but one was that he spent some time in analysis with Sabina Spielrein, Jung's lover.

Eva Schepeler (1993) has tried to reconstruct some circumstances of Piaget's analysis. He told Bringuier it was 'a didactic analysis. Every morning at eight o'clock for eight months.... It was marvellous to discover all one's complexes'. Piaget added that he did not stop the analysis but that Spielrein did because they clashed over matters of theory. 'I didn't see the need for the interpretations she tried to impose', he said. Two years later, however, Piaget wrote a brief letter to his local paper, the *Journal de Genève*, saying he had finished his analysis to the complete satisfaction of his analyst. 'In the jargon of those days, I became a "grandson" of Freud.' Analysis often takes years but Piaget took just eight months to get what he wanted out of it. Was this psychic efficiency or arrogance?

Freud might not have welcomed a Genevan grandson and wrote to Spielrein: 'The people of Geneva are each and every one dilettantes to whom you must gradually transmit something of your analytic training. On top of that they never listened to advice.'

In the book which allows the reader to reconstruct best what he was like as a father, *Play, Dreams and Imitation in Childhood,* Piaget mentioned his analysis once but in an oblique way, writing that 'it is remarkable how many visual images come back with childhood memories'. The expert on childhood had a difficult childhood himself.

Piaget's father Arthur was a medieval historian and professor at the Neuchatel Academy. Rebecca, Piaget's mother, came from a family of wealthy industrialists in Paris but she became a socialist as well as a strict Calvinist. Piaget did more than hint at problems between them. 'My mother was very intelligent, very energetic and at heart really good but her somewhat neurotic temperament made our family life rather difficult.' The parallel with Emilie Jung and Melanie Klein's mother, Libussa, is striking. As a result of his mother's temperament, Piaget admitted he played much less than children usually did and concentrated on work 'to imitate my father but also to take refuge in a world that was both personal and not make believe'. Jean Piaget wrote that his father was 'a man who had a scrupulous and critical mind. He did not like glib generalisations. Among much else he taught me the value of systematic work even when it came to details'.

As a boy of eight, Piaget collected catalogues of motorcars which were not make believe, and dreamt 'of nothing but factories and machines ... I have always hated any flight from reality, an attitude that stems from the fact that my mother was not stable'.

When Piaget was 15, his mother insisted he follow a course of religious instruction. His father did not share his wife's faith and so, while he obeyed his mother's wishes, Piaget did the course in a critical spirit. But the question of why his mother was so difficult and the impact it had on the family meant that 'when I started studying psychology, I focussed my interest on psychoanalysis and pathological psychology'.

Eva Schepeler also found the text of a talk Piaget gave to the Alfred Binet Society. (Binet devised some of the first intelligence tests for children.) In his talk, Piaget describes the dream of an anonymous 22-year-old patient – he himself was 22 at the time – who is walking anxiously through a city to find a room after he had 'secret conflicts with his mother'. His mother was trying to bully him into religion, just like Rebecca was, while he needed to 'develop himself in a personal direction' and establish his independence, just like Piaget himself. Schepeler argues there were also sexual undertones to the dream, presumably Oedipal ones, though she did not specify any details.

About three years after his lecture to the Alfred Binet Society, Piaget tried to do something which no analyst seems to have ever done. According to Piaget's sister, Marthe Piaget-Burger, who eventually became an analyst herself, her brother tried to analyse his mother sometime between 1925 and 1929. The differences between this particularly bizarre episode and Freud and Klein's analyses of their children is one of authority. Piaget might act the analyst but his mother still had power over him. She stopped the analysis because she disagreed with her son's interpretations of her dreams. (Did Piaget suggest mama had incestuous fantasies or that she wanted to kill her perhaps dull husband? We shall never know.) What we do know is that 'Il aurait vivement ressenti cet echec', as Piaget's sister said, meaning Piaget would have felt this failure badly. Marthe is the only one of Piaget's sisters he mentions in his autobiography.

Piaget was a child prodigy. When he was ten, he saw an albino sparrow in a park and sent a short article about it to the *Rameau de Sapin*, Neuchatel's natural history journal. His article was accepted and 'I was launched', Piaget wrote with some irony. After the article appeared, he approached Paul Godet, the director of the local natural history museum, explaining that he was at school and asked if he could study the museum's collections outside normal working hours. Godet agreed and also invited him to accompany him on expeditions to collect molluscs. 'These studies, premature as they were, were very useful in my education as a scientist', Piaget said. He thought watching shellfish insulated him from the lure of philosophy.

When Piaget was 16, his godfather, the writer Samuel Cornut, introduced him to Henri Bergson's work. Piaget found Bergson, who many thought one of the greatest philosophers, disappointing. 'I was left with the impression of an ingenious construction' – he could have said confection – that was more frothy than factual. Bergson is mainly remembered today for his theory of comedy (when human beings behave like machines they become laughable) and his theory of vitalism. Vitalism claimed that living organisms are fundamentally different from non-living ones because they have some non-physical element, the mysterious élan vital. Piaget was not convinced. 'I think it was at that moment that I discovered a need in me which only psychology could satisfy', Piaget said.

When he was 16, Piaget was offered a job in Geneva as a specialist in mollusc research; he replied very politely he would adore to accept, but he still had three years of school to finish. He agreed nevertheless to edit a catalogue of all the molluscs in Switzerland, a catalogue which eventually ran to over 300 pages.

After leaving school, Piaget studied for two years in Paris where he learned how to interview psychiatric patients. In 1919, he moved to Zurich to attend Jung's lectures on experimental psychology. Then he went back to Paris and studied at the Sorbonne with Theodore Simon in Alfred Binet's child psychology laboratory. Piaget noticed that mistakes children made on intelligence tests had some pattern to them. Observing how the child's mind develops would offer great insights, he decided. No one had done this systematically before, he noted correctly. Darwin, after all, had only studied one of his children.

Years before he had children of his own, Piaget had learned how to talk to toddlers. From Paris Piaget returned first to the University of Neuchatel and then, in 1925, to the Institute Jean Jacques Rousseau; he began watching children play and talked to them in the ways he had seen psychiatrists talk to patients when they wanted to understand their thoughts and delusions. But there was a key difference. In one of his experiments, Piaget asked children, 'What makes the wind?' The children's answers were certainly not deluded, but they were also not those an adult would give. What was normal for a child was not what was normal for an adult. The following exchange is revealing.

PIAGET: What makes the wind?
JULIA (age five): The trees.
PIAGET: How do you know?
JULIA: I saw them waving their arms.
PIAGET: How does that make the wind?
JULIA: Like this (waving her hand in front of Piaget's face). Only they are bigger. And there are lots of trees.
PIAGET: What makes the wind on the ocean?
JULIA: It blows there from the land. No, it's the waves.

To say these answers are 'true or false' misses the point. Julia's replies were clever and coherent. 'Children have real understanding only of that which they invent themselves, and each time that we try to teach them something too quickly, we keep them from reinventing it themselves', Piaget wrote.

In 1923, Piaget married his brightest student, Valerie Chatenay. Their daughter, Jacqueline, was born in 1925. She and her siblings Lucienne (born 1927) and Laurent (born 1931) were studied from the moment they were born, and at a time when Piaget was psychoanalysing his mother. With a job at the Institute and a mother on the couch, it is not surprising Piaget's wife carried out many of the observations of their own children.

Piaget's first book, *The Language and Thought of the Child*, made his reputation, though he was only 27 years old. There was a key difference between Darwin and Piaget. Darwin's observations were studded with asides about how wonderful his children were. Piaget hardly ever said anything emotional about his. It is tempting to speculate this was a reaction to his emotional mother who exerted control yet again by putting an end to being analysed by her son.

I met Piaget's three children when they were invited to a conference in 1996 to celebrate the centenary of their father's birth. To my recollection, they did not address the conference.

Time for a perhaps strange comparison. A year after Jacqueline was born, Elizabeth Bowes Lyons, who had married Prince George, the future George VI, engaged a governess for her two daughters, Princess Elizabeth and Princess Margaret. Marion Crawford, or Crawfie as the royals called her, had had some training in child psychology in Edinburgh. After the 1945 war, she wrote her memoirs of the princesses' childhoods. Crawford had an acute eye. Reading the memoirs, it seems the princesses behaved much like Piaget saw other children behave.

Lilibet, as Crawford called Princess Elizabeth, was obsessed with horses. She and her sister had a collection of 30 toy horses, all on wheels. 'That's where we stable them', Lilibet told her governess. Each horse had its own immaculate saddle and bridle; the girls polished them and followed the routine of a top-class stable. Every night, each saddle was removed and the toy horses fed and watered.

Piaget often observed children reversing roles, even trying to act the parent. Lilibet did something like that. One of her favourite games involved putting a harness of red reins with bells attached on her teacher. Lilibet would then 'ride' 'Crawfie' as they went off delivering groceries. She recalls that 'I would be gentled, patted, given my nosebag and jerked to a standstill. Meanwhile Lilibet delivered imaginary groceries at imaginary houses and held long intimate conversations with her imaginary customers'.

Lilibet told Crawford that, as a horse, she had to 'pretend to be impatient. Paw the ground a bit'. The dutiful teacher dutifully pawed. Sometimes the roles would be reversed and Lilibet would prance around, being the horse, whinnying and sidling up to Crawford in the best equine manner. Piaget would have seen all this as nicely typical.

Studies of Piaget tend to treat his children as universal – not as his and Valerie Chatenay's individual children. But these observations offer the best, indeed the only, information we have on the Piagets as parents. Before examining those in detail, one needs to consider Piaget's theory briefly.

Piaget developed a theory of four stages through which children's minds develop. The four stages are in every textbook of child psychology – the sensori-motor stage, the pre-operational stage, the stage of concrete operations and finally the stage of formal operations where children have mastered the intricacies of logic. There was not a 'normal' age for a child to go into any of the stages and Piaget loathed the American mania, as he put it, for pushing children. Inevitably though, psychologists have tended to put average ages against the stages.

William James, one of the first men to set up a psychology lab back in 1879, wrote that babies were a blooming buzzing confusion. Piaget likened babies to primitive savages! No one in 1920 had heard of political correctness. Freud called the baby 'a little primitive'.

The newborn does not realize the most primitive fact of life. When I touch someone I know where I end and they begin – what is my skin and what is their skin. The newborn does not realize he is a separate being and that his body – and his self – stops at the ends of his fingers and his toes. The infant 'looks at his own body the way we look at a strange animal', because 'the baby is submerged in a chaos of interesting impressions without there being any distinction between his internal state and things outside' (Piaget, 1952).

Piaget was keen to work out when babies could first perform an intentional action as that baby would no longer be a mewling chaos of reflexes but on the way to becoming a human being. He saw the very first signs of 'intentional' action when Jacqueline was two weeks old. If he put his finger against her cheek, she turned her head and opened her little mouth as if to take the nipple.

At 23 days, Laurent searched for the nipple with his mouth. He would turn to the right to look for it if it brushed against him. None of that was fully intentional, Piaget argued, but it was the first step in that direction.

By three months of age, Piaget's babies were more coordinated. If they heard a noise, they turned their heads to see what made it. They stared at objects and reached out for them. Human intelligence starts with these motor movements, especially with eye–hand co-ordination, Piaget and his wife believed; they gave their infants objects to touch, then teased them gently by showing them balls and toys, then taking them back.

Babies did not have the concept of objects that adults do, Piaget claimed. When I walk out of my front door, I don't worry whether the petrol station opposite my house still exists when I'm not looking at it. Adults assume objects are permanent, but babies don't have the experience to make these assumptions. They are at the mercy of 'the here and now'. If they don't see something, it just does not exist.

Piaget then spotted something bizarre in the way his six-month-old babies behaved. In one of his most famous experiments, he hid objects. Sometimes, he and his wife let the baby see where he was concealing them; but sometimes, they did not. Remarkably this did not change matters much. Once the toy or ball disappeared, the baby under six months behaved as if that object had never existed. Piaget only had to throw a cloth over a toy, even while the baby was looking, for that to happen. The infant made no attempt to remove the cloth. Instead Piaget noted (1950, p. 132), 'the child acts as if the object were reabsorbed into the cloth'.

By ten months, the infants behaved even more peculiarly. When their parents rolled a ball behind some cushions, the Piaget children usually looked for the ball. But in the wrong place! A logical baby would look for the ball behind the cushions, but the infants started looking where the ball had been … before it disappeared. It was as if they believed the ball might reappear at that very spot by magic. It remains a very curious result.

The utterly innocent baby does not stay innocent that long and becomes capable of imitating. Imitation is not simple. To imitate what I have just done: first, you have to notice I am there; then, you have to register what I have done; third, you have to have the ability to reproduce my actions. At five months, Jacqueline was imitating her father quite clearly because when he stuck out his tongue at her, she stuck her tongue back out at him.

Play, Dreams and Imitation in Childhood, the book that allows us more insight into the Piagets as parents than any other, has some observations which suggest the home was friendly and that the children had fun, though the word fun seems to occur only once in the text – and there is no mention of Piaget loving his children. Yet the way he and his wife played and experimented on the children suggests there was much affection.

When Jacqueline was nine months old, 'I hung a celluloid duck above her', Piaget said. His daughter pulled a string which shook the duck, then grabbed a doll, then grabbed the duck again and finally started to suck the fringe of her pillow. All this energetic activity was not properly intelligent action but just activity, yet it was vital as it prepared the child's mind. A month after the duck, Jacqueline pressed her nose close to her mother's cheek which forced her to breathe more loudly. Piaget almost rebuked his daughter, for not being much of an infant scientist, as 'instead of merely repeating it or varying it so as to investigate it, she quickly complicated it for the fun of it'.

Rituals were important. Five days after her first birthday Jacqueline was slapping the bath water, a ritual she repeated. Such rituals were key to Piaget's thinking as they were a move towards symbolic action. At 15 months and 11 days Jacqueline was able to ask for her pot and laughed a lot when it was given to her. Tactfully Piaget said she indulged in some ritual movements playfully without specifying what these ritual movements were. One suspects she pretended to pee or shit.

The first true instance of play came when Jacqueline was 15 months old. She saw a cloth whose fringed edges were much like those of her pillow. She grabbed the fringe, lay down on her side like she would lie down on her pillow – and laughed hard. Then, laughing, she said 'Nene nono'. The next day she treated the collar of her mother's coat the same way. Two weeks later the tail of her rubber donkey represented the pillow. Make believe indeed. Three months later, Jacqueline rubbed her hands together, said 'oap' for imaginary soap and pretended to wash them.

When Lucienne was 15 months old she pretended to put a napkin ring in her mouth, laughed, shook her head as if saying no and then took it out. Four months later, she pretended to drink out of a box and then held it to the mouths of everyone who was there.

When Jacqueline was 19 months old, she was in bed sitting up and talking to herself. Piaget was listening as his daughter listed 'Look, look, Uncle G, aunty A, uncle G'. Then she lay down and said to herself 'Nono' and began again to list her relatives, adding 'mummy, daddy, grandma'. A few days later she repeated the list, adding 'Little Istine', referring to a cousin who had just been born. One gets a sense of Jacqueline being surrounded by a lively, loving family.

Piaget was also interested in the rules of games. When she was two years and two months old, Jacqueline threw pebbles into a pond and laughed. Six months later she filled a bucket with sand, overturned it and demolished her sand pie with a spade.

Her father clearly had a gift for talking to small children as the following exchange makes obvious:

JACQUELINE: What's that?
PARENT: A cowshed.
JACQUELINE: Why?
PARENT: It's a house for cows.
JACQUELINE: Why?
PARENT: Because there are cows in it, there, don't you see?
JACQUELINE: Why are they cows?
PARENT: Don't you see, they've got horns.

The first question was 'serious' but then his daughter 'just asked for the sake of asking'. As children will, Jacqueline often made up stories merely to contradict or to be naughty.

Piaget and his wife gave many examples of their children playing imaginatively with objects. A shell could become many things. When Jacqueline was a year and ten months old, she put one on the edge of a big box and made it slide down, saying 'Cat on the wall'. The day before she had seen a cat climbing a tree. Then she put the shell on her head and said 'tree' and added 'right at the top'. Three months later, she put a shell on the end of her finger and declared it to be a thimble. In the next five months Jacqueline was often playful. Piaget recorded what she said when she looked at a stone:

JACQUELINE: It's a dog.
PIAGET: Where is its head?
JACQUELINE: There.

His daughter pointed to a lump on the stone.

PIAGET: And its eyes?
JACQUELINE: They've gone.
PIAGET: But isn't it a stone?
JACQUELINE: Yes. Good for dog.

She went on to say the stone was a dog and then a lion. A few months later she was talking to a safety pin and said it was a grandmother. Lucienne for her part turned a small piece of material into her grandmother.

Piaget wanted to see how his children got a sense of self. When she was a year and a half old, Jacqueline ran after her shadow. A month later, she was sitting on Piaget's knee in their garden and said 'Jacqueline' when she saw her shadow. He asked her where Jacqueline was. She got off his knee, took a few steps towards her shadow, which moved with her, and then bent down and pointed to it. Three months later when Piaget made a shadow with his hand, she said 'Daddy'. These nice moments are interesting in the light of Darwin's work on when infants recognize their own reflections in a mirror, something chimps can do, it seems. No one seems yet to have investigated how animals react to their own shadows.

Some of the most interesting observations are examples of when the child pretends to be the parent, a habit I described in my own *The Development of Play* which was researched 50 years after Piaget started work.

When Jacqueline was 14 months old, a cousin called T said 'daddy' to her and she held out her arms to him like it would seem her father did to her. That same month, Jacqueline was in her mother's arms and said 'daddy' to a man and then 'mummy' to a strange woman, but there were few such confusions.

At 18 months Jacqueline was becoming more and more adept at persuading adults to give her what she wanted. When they refused or pretended not to hear, she grizzled. One of her grandfathers was most accommodating so that she started to use 'panana' to call him and also to indicate she wanted something even when he was not there.

Lucienne, when she was 26 months old, pretended to be her mother. She said to Piaget 'come kiss mummy' – and kissed him. These scenes were not always sweet, though. Sometimes Jacqueline was angry with her father and said so.

One day Piaget knocked against Jacqueline's hands with a rake and made her cry. 'I said how sorry I was and blamed my clumsiness. At first she didn't believe me and went on being angry as though I had done it deliberately. Then she said, half appeased: "You're Jacqueline and I'm daddy".' His daughter then hit his fingers and told him to say she had hurt him. Piaget did so, whereupon she said, as if she were him, 'I'm sorry my darling. I didn't do it on purpose. You know how clumsy I am'. She repeated his exact words.

Another of these reversals took place when Jacqueline was four years and seven months old. They were walking by some nettles and 'I told her to be careful', Piaget said. She then pretended to be a little girl who had been stung. That evening the following exchange took place after she had been playing with a pointed stick:

'Jacqueline: "Daddy say you won't cut yourself Jacqueline, will you?".' Piaget does not promise not to cut himself despite his daughter's anxieties.

Jacqueline was worried when she saw her father ride away on a friend's motorcycle. She put her fingers to her mouth in a way she had never done before and said to her mother: 'I'm putting my fingers like that so that daddy'll come back.'

Dolls played a big part in the life of the Piaget children and by the time she was six, Jacqueline had created an imaginary village, Ventichon, where her fantasies flourished. Coloured stones represented cows. She even put a cemetery in the village. Jacqueline created a number of characters, like Mrs Odar and Mrs Anonzo, as well as cousins, grandparents and visitors, though the husbands tended to stay in the background. There is little in Piaget's book to suggest that his children had to make up a village because they were compensating for traumas in the home. Ventichon was an imaginary place but not a refuge. Piaget's book suggests life in the family when his children were growing up was not as difficult as his own life had been when he was a child.

Piaget also discussed dreams. When she was two years and nine months old Jacqueline screamed in the middle of the night. Her parents seem to have gone to her. 'It was all dark and I saw a lady there', Jacqueline said, pointing to her bed. Piaget went on to say that, three months later, Jacqueline admitted dreams were not real but in her head.

Four months before her fourth birthday, Lucienne told him: 'I didn't have any dreams last night because it was quite light. Dreams are in the dark.' Three months later, she said: 'The dark's lovely. You can take everything you want in the dark and put it back afterwards.'

'Did you dream last night?' her father asked. His daughter replied she had dreamt a boat was flying. 'I saw it in the dark. It came with the light. I took it for a minute and then put it back.' Piaget unfortunately did not explain what he thought his daughter meant by putting it back.

These examples all suggest that while there may be ethical issues in studying children, observing them certainly makes one pay attention to them.

Piaget recorded fewer observations of his children as they got older.

The second stage of development he called the 'pre-operational' stage. It was defined by the fact that children, until they are about seven, are totally egocentric. He did not use the term 'egocentric' to mean being totally selfish or self-obsessed. Pre-operational children were egocentric as they couldn't imagine how anything might look from anyone else's perspective; they were slaves to 'the here and now' because they could not hold alternatives in their mind.

Children then moved through the stage of formal operations to intellectual maturity where they mastered logic. Piaget had what seems to us the weird idea that most teenagers are logically competent and can see the flaws in complex arguments. We do not know if Piaget's children ever managed that. If they did, they would have been exceptional. Fewer than 10 per cent of teenagers achieve mastery of logical operations.

Unlike Freud, Piaget did not found a dynasty. Two of his children, when I met them, had gone back to live in the family home in Switzerland where they had grown up and where their parents had studied them. Their claim to fame (not what one should judge any individual by) was that they were the children Piaget studied. Laurent Piaget worked for the foundation that archived his father's papers, one of a number of children of psychologists who spent much of their lives protecting their father's legacy. The subversive question is, does that show the father was a good parent? The good enough parent, it could be argued, makes their children free to lead independent lives.

Piaget became one of the most respected psychologists of his day but he did not become a famous public figure. The children of my next subject had to cope with the fact that their father was so famous he was once on the cover of *Time* magazine.

Notes and references

There is no definitive biography of Piaget as yet. Relevant works by Piaget, including interviews with him:
Bringuier, Jean Claude, *Conversations with Jean Piaget*, University of Chicago Press (1989).
Piaget, J., Un moineau albino, *Le Rameau du Sapin*, vol. 41, 36 (1909).
Piaget, J., *The Language and Thought of the Child*, Kegan Paul, Trench and Trubner (1952 [1929]).
Piaget, J., *The Psychology of Intelligence*, Routledge and Kegan Paul (1950).
Piaget, J., *Play, Dreams and Imitation in Childhood*, Routledge and Kegan Paul (1951).

Piaget did not want his biography written, but he did make some notes towards an autobiography. These have been examined by F. Vidal, *Piaget before Piaget*, Harvard University Press (1994) and J. Voneche, C. Barbisio and C. Quaranta, Jean Piaget and his autobiographies, *Transformazioni e narrazioni*, 25–30 (1995).

On his experiences in analysis:
Schepeler, E., Jean Piaget's experiences on the couch – some clues to a mystery, *Int.J of Psychoanalysis*, vol. 74, 255–73 (1993).

Other reference:
Crawford, Marion, *The Little Princesses*, Orion (2003).

8

BENJAMIN SPOCK

The conservative radical

When Benjamin Spock won an Olympic gold medal in 1924, he probably never imagined he would be tried for treason one day – and that his eldest son would admire him for that.

When the Vietnam War broke out, Spock protested against it publicly, to the fury of conservative minister and bestselling author, Norman Vincent Peale. Peale thundered that 'Dr. Spock's advice – hug your children, feed them when they are hungry, put them to sleep when they are tired' was the root of the problem. 'The U.S. was paying the price of two generations that followed the Dr. Spock baby plan of instant gratification of needs.'

Spock's two children, however, did not experience their father as a man who gratified their needs instantly at all. In 1970, his eldest son Michael told *Ladies Home Journal* that his father was demanding, rather inflexible and had never kissed him once. Watson also never kissed his sons, so it would seem that in order to write an American best-seller on parenting, a man must never kiss his sons! Watson was consistent at least. In his book and his life, he was against kissing children. Spock never kissed his boys but *The Common Sense Book of Baby and Child Care* recommended much hugging and some kissing at least.

Spock's book influenced parenting from the moment it was published in 1946. 'To most mothers, it felt like a complete revolution', Spock said. 'Don't be afraid to love (your baby). Every baby needs to be smiled at, talked to, played with, fondled – gently and lovingly', he counselled. 'You may hear people say you have to get your baby strictly regulated in his feeding, sleeping, bowel movements and other habits – but don't believe this.' Babies would fit in with the family before too long, Spock told a public that was ready for liberal advice. 'Be natural and enjoy your baby', he wrote. The advice is as sage as that given by Spock in *Star Trek*. Live long and prosper.

Prosper Spock did. His book has sold 50 million copies in 49 languages. He also wrote a book of guidance for teenagers. It would be naive, however, to assume that his expertise meant Spock was an easy or relaxed father. In 1968, Spock's grandson Dan even suggested his grandfather had something of a split personality. To his public, 'Ben' was warm and reassuring, the great doctor who knew everything about feeding, loving and playing with babies, but to his family he was rather remote.

The book's success made Spock famous and that fame became a problem. 'When someone is larger than life, when they are public property – an icon – they become untouchable in a way and difficult to deal with as a human being', Dan Spock said. Both his father Michael and his uncle John, Spock's second son, found that when they tried to deal with their father as a human being, 'he was always referring back to the icon and saying this is who I am'. Such a carapace suggests conflict inside.

Baby and Child Care was so successful, Spock himself suggested, because it was published at the end of the Second World War. By then Watson and Rayner's *The Psychological Care of the Infant and Child* seemed out of date. Many couples delayed having children during the uncertainties of the war. Now they wanted to know how best to care for their precious new child.

Spock was born in 1903 in New Haven; his father was a Yale graduate and the lawyer for the local railway company. Spock recalled his maternal grandmother, Ada, was extremely strict. She once locked one of her daughters in a closet, left the house and returned to find her child not just upset but almost crazed by the ordeal. Yet Spock wrote: 'A child psychologist would be certain since the children turned out well, that they not only felt their father's affection but must have recognised their mother's devotion and even love under her harsh exterior.' The strong grandmother also disapproved of sex, but even she could not control everything. One of her daughters had an illegitimate child. Ada objected to her daughter marrying the son of a carriage maker.

Given her severe mother, it is perhaps not surprising that Spock's mother herself was rather strict. He recalled: 'I was brought up by stern, puritanical parents.' When he was a toddler, his parents were able to afford a nanny but his mother chose a rather icy woman. Nanny, Spock said, was

> a terribly severe, awesome sort of person. She always wore a black dress with a high lace collar held up by whalebone. We had to tiptoe into her parlour where she served tea in cups of such thin china that we could see right through them. In a formidable voice she would say 'would you like a cookie?' I would say 'Yes Nannie'. Then she would hold out the dish of cookies and I would take one never two. Except for saying 'Thank You', I was never supposed to say anything else or ask anything else. Then I would turn and get out of the room.

As the oldest child, Spock had to help look after his brothers and sisters, which was perhaps unusual for a boy at the start of the twentieth century. At school he did well and he went to Yale, exactly as his father had done. He was not studying medicine at that stage, but history and literature. He was also an excellent oarsman and made the Yale crew. Their eight was picked to represent the United States for the Paris Olympics. One other member of the crew was a Rockefeller. They won the gold medal.

Spock was also inducted into Yale's senior society, Scroll and Key, whose previous members included William Bullitt, America's first ambassador to the Soviet Union, who wrote a book with Freud which proved (to their own satisfaction at least) that the Treaty of Versailles was so punitive because Woodrow Wilson had never been psychoanalysed. The men got much inside information on Wilson's neurotic behaviour because Edward Bernays, Freud's nephew, worked for the president.

After Yale Spock went to study medicine and graduated top of his class at Columbia in 1929. Despite his academic and sporting achievements Spock still felt his parents were not quite satisfied with him – and that was especially true of his demanding mother, who had had such a demanding mother herself. She wanted Ben to learn that sex was dangerous, an 'emotional bomb'. So she told him he was unattractive, that when he looked at girls he was 'disgusting'.

To cope with these feelings, Spock decided to be psychoanalysed. His first analyst was a failure. Spock then asked Sandor Rado to take over. Again the connections are striking. Rado had been a pupil of Freud's friend, Sándor Ferenczi, who had analysed Melanie Klein. This second analysis worked better and seems to have allowed Spock to express some of his negative feelings about his strict childhood upbringing.

Spock was good with the oars and good with the feet. He was an excellent dancer. In June 1927, before he finished medical school, Spock married Jane Cheney. The couple led an energetic social life even when she was carrying their first child. As they had little money, they and their friends organized 'The Dancing Academy'. For $40 a night they rented a hall and for $400 a 12-piece orchestra. Everyone paid $1.50 to get in. Spock liked to dress in a very old-fashioned way, wearing tails. He was a very popular dancing partner.

When he became a father, Spock reverted to his parents' traditions, despite his expertise and his years in analysis. 'Jane and I were obviously old-fashioned parents', he wrote. 'We believed that young children should be in bed at 7, not just so they can get a good rest, but also so that the parents can have a whole evening of rest and dignity and peace.'

Strictly scheduled feeding was the rule at the time so if their first son yipped for milk at the wrong time, he was allowed to cry for an hour before being fed. Michael said:

> When I was born my father was just starting out his practice in New York. The demands of New York living – parties, activities, everything – once made me complain to my parents that they went out more than the King and Queen of England. They replied that the King and Queen did not go out much.

Just as Freud had, Spock worked incredibly long hours. 'My father drives himself very hard – even to the point of answering his every bit of mail. He is the product of his own upbringing', Michael said.

> [Spock] would come home at 7 o'clock to a supper which had been waiting half an hour. Then phone calls started and he was forever on the telephone to mothers. My mother wanted him to be firmer with them but he never was.

But at times Spock did have time for his son.

> When my father was available I had as much contact with him as anyone. Times of intimacy and companionship were mainly in the morning and in the bathroom. We'd get up about seven. I'd sit in the bathtub while he'd shave and help me with my multiplication tables.

One nice detail was that Spock would pull out his son's teeth. 'If I discovered a loose one I'd make it really wiggly before going to my father to help me pull it out', Michael explained. Spock never hurt his son because 'he gently punched it and poked it out with his thumb'.

For all his conventional upbringing, Spock could be unconventional occasionally. Michael recalled that when he was five, he became fascinated with cigarettes. His father had him try one. He hasn't smoked since.

When America joined the Second World War, Spock spent two years in the Navy. Psychiatrists were told their duty was to treat battle-exhausted Marines so they could go back into action quickly, but those who were unlikely to manage that were to be discharged quickly, 'without making them full pension claimants all the rest of their lives because they were no damn good to start with'. Spock ended up working on a naval prison ward where he gave an unflattering description of the typical patient as 'an impulsive irresponsible person who had been deprived of love and care in early childhood'. Spock's patients had dismal histories; they played truant and rarely managed to stay in jobs long. 'You could write one of these discharge surveys in your sleep', Spock said.

On 20 April 1944, Spock was still working for the Navy at Bethesda Hospital when he got an urgent phone call. He took the milk train to New York and reached the hospital just about 20 minutes before John, his second son, was born. Attitudes to fathers were very different 70 years ago. 'You can't come in here', the head nurse barked, 'you're not Dr Spock now, you're just a father. Get out'. Spock never forgot this moment and used the incident to teach medical students to be kind to fathers – and not exclude them.

There was one advantage to working for the Navy. Spock could be sure of leaving at five in the evening to get home in time to see his new baby son. The rules by which John grew up were more relaxed than they had been for Michael. He did not have to cry for so long for the bottle. It is hard to know whether the Spocks had changed or fashions in child care had – partly, of course, as a result of his work. Equally Spock and his wife, like many parents, were less anxious with their second child as they had managed their first one.

Spock said that 'One trouble with being an inexperienced parent is that part of the time you take the job so seriously that you forget to enjoy it'. Bonding with your child provides an easy-going companionship 'that's good for him and good for you'. Spock never behaved towards his children as his grandmother had behaved towards hers; she, it will be recalled, locked one daughter in a closet. 'Discipline was not applied by spanking when I was growing up', Michael said.

Thomas Maier, who had Spock's co-operation when writing his biography, suggests that Spock often worked so hard so as not to have to spend too much time with his family.

Oddly, Spock insisted his children called him by his Christian name. 'Ben always dealt in absolutes. Something was either right or wrong.' The children were expected to behave. Michael explained that the limits were 'Don't be disruptive, don't butt in, don't be slow in dressing, don't forget to write thank you notes to Grandma'. The formidable grandmother still made her presence felt and 'was even more resolute in her convictions', Michael said, than his father.

Parents have to be firm — a word Spock liked — in their convictions. 'Parents who say, "I can't make him stay in his room" just don't have the courage to make them to do it', he said in one interview. Both boys had to take an afternoon rest, and if they didn't feel like sleeping they had to stay in their rooms for the designated time. 'I don't think they were particularly strict', Michael said, adding, however, that he was constrained as an individual because of his father's overwhelming personality.

For both his sons the idea that they had permissive parents appears absurd. In private Spock was reserved and rather demanding. 'I could always feel Ben's strong sense of disapproval if I did something wrong and I wouldn't think of attempting to talk him out of a decision', Michael said.

By the time the book had been out for about five years, however, Spock was 'alarmed at the misunderstandings on the part of some mothers'. Parents were feeding babies erratically — every time they screamed — and 'didn't put the baby to bed unless he practically asked to be put to bed'. Spock felt misunderstood. When he revised the book in 1957, he stressed children needed firm leadership. Parents who set boundaries would see their children grow up happier and better behaved. Happier was optimistic because Spock's oldest son had very mixed memories.

'The difficult thing for both of us — John and I', said Michael, 'was that he was such a strong personality. We were allowed a fair amount of freedom within strong limits that were set. The point was, he communicated without any question about where he stood on everything'.

'People who knew me as a child tell me I got away with murder', Michael admitted though. One reason was the fact, as described, that his father was so busy. Michael pointed out: 'My contemporaries had a lot of their time managed for them. But I was pretty much on my own from the time.' When he was nine, he started to go 'rummaging around in junk shops or to museums'.

Parents and children see things differently. Spock has said he did not try to impress on his sons that they had to be like him. He did not talk endlessly about his time at Yale or even his heroic rowing – he had after all won a gold medal – to his sons. Instead he talked about the amusing aspects of his time at the Olympics.

Being allowed some freedom did not make life easy, however, and Michael described his teenage years as 'the black phase of my life'. It was a phase that lasted some 15 years. As part of what he defined as his adolescent rebellion, Michael chose to go to Antioch College, a decision that surprised his father. 'It would never have occurred to me not to go to the college my father went to', Spock said, but he did not stop his son going to a different, and less prestigious, university.

Michael had a hard time settling into his studies. Doing examinations was excruciatingly hard. 'Nowadays they talk about an identity crisis. Then all I knew is that I was having a hard time keeping up.' His problem, he said, was that he had no idea who he was.

When Michael told his parents of his troubles, they suggested he see a counsellor. 'My mother was convinced it was important', but though his father had undergone analysis, Spock reverted to type and, rather like one imagines his grandmother would have done, thought it was really a matter of will power. In the end, though, his parents found him a psychiatrist in Cincinnati. Michael had to travel three times a week for his sessions. By the end of his analysis he had driven, he reckoned, some 100,000 miles.

'It was hard for my family', especially as he had done well at school. Michael had never seemed to be a troubled child. 'It was only when I left home that everything seemed to disintegrate. It takes a long time to wean yourself.' Eighteen is a remarkably young age to start analysis and his father, the convinced Freudian, made no problems about paying the bill. But the analysis was very much stop–start.

Michael dropped out of Antioch three times while he was seeing his analyst. He worked as a hospital porter, a petrol pump attendant and wrote copy for a store's advertising department. 'My parents were distressed.' In the midst of all this Michael met his future wife who felt he would never settle down. It took him nine years to get a degree in biology.

There was a telling flash-point during this period. One day, Michael came home from college with a beard. His father, the famous liberal, was not going to stand for excessive hair. 'It was', Michael's wife, Judy, later recalled, 'a kind of High Noon confrontation'. The beard came off. In a way this is such an odd anecdote as Spock was espousing a very radical cause – the anti-Vietnam movement. Spock himself, however, had an interesting insight on why he became so passionate about issues of conformity and rebellion. 'Looking back I can see I was an insecure and excessively ambitious person, quite ready to conform in any way to make the grade.' He was not proud of that and suggested his anti-Vietnam position represented 'a final rejection of my adolescent values'. No one, however, ever mentioned the beard again.

When he talked to *Ladies Home Journal*, Michael mused on why he had done nothing by way of protest during the McCarthy era when Senator McCarthy chaired a committee on un-American activities. Many famous people were summoned to be accused of being Communists. 'I never did make my wild stand.' He and Judy thought of joining a march at an airbase but they decided against it. 'This was before Ben's activist phase and we were afraid of embarrassing him.'

In 1968 Spock was put on trial for conspiracy as part of his opposition to the Vietnam War. This worried Michael, who told *Ladies Home Journal,* 'Our children know what Ben is doing. We will probably take them to part of the trial'. There was a risk, Michael felt, that some of those who supported Spock might themselves be accused of treason and put on trial. 'But even if he is branded a traitor my father would continue his stand', Michael said.

Michael asked himself if he was letting his identity as Spock's son stand in the way of his own beliefs. Spock's biographer, Thomas Maier, however, has suggested that not going to the demonstration was a kind of betrayal, but this seems rather harsh.

If one sees 1970s feminists as somewhat left-wing, Spock was attacked from the left as well as from the right. He made some changes to his book and said: 'I always listen to criticism, not because I am noble, but because I was criticized all through my childhood and I had to adapt one way or another to my mother's constant criticalness toward her children in general.'

Michael ended his interview with *Ladies Home Journal* with praise:

> I am grateful to my father for having established a clear cut set of principles by which to deal with people and to live. This is what I love him for in his Vietnam stand. I sincerely feel he is doing the right thing. And if I didn't agree with him, I would still be proud that, despite great personal risk, he speaks out for his beliefs. I would like to have his courage.

In 1970 Spock published a book that was a guide for teenagers. Many of his ideas were very reactionary, he admitted, and his grandmother would probably have approved. Teenagers should not date until they were 16 and should 'not go beyond kissing and embracing the person he loves until there is some kind of commitment to marriage'. Spock also encouraged teenagers to take showers every day (presumably cold ones), to be polite and to do chores without being nagged by their parents. He was also for the use of deodorants, a product that Watson had more or less created in his advertising days when he made Americans worry that if their armpits smelled, no one would talk to them. The great behaviourist launched Odorono on the world, a product whose name is both sledgehammer subtle and nearly a haiku poem:

Odor

Oh no

John felt he had an advantage being the second child as his parents found it more possible 'to let me exist as an independent person with their own outlooks than they were with Mike'. He was controlled less and insisted he was never a guinea pig for his father's theories. 'I wasn't spanked much, just isolated.' His parents, however, were 'very demanding, although it wasn't stated as such'.

One comment John made is harsh, however. 'We were a stiff family and were never particularly warm with one another though I really do love my mother.' She has kept a Valentine card her son sent when he was a schoolboy.

Even as a grandfather, Spock was severe. Michael's wife remembered one time when her son Peter was 18 months old and they were all dining together at a restaurant. Peter enjoyed singing at the table, and it had never occurred to his parents to discourage him. Singing in public places, however, offended Spock's ideas of how anybody ought to behave. He suggested rather strongly that Peter stop.

Peter ignored him. Spock then swept the small child up in his arms and marched out of the restaurant.

John decided not to go to Yale but to Harvard. He explained that 'excellence was the idea … excellence in school or in manners or in building a model boat'. He continued that this imposed 'very large demands on Mike and myself, some of which we were able to fulfil and some not, and then we felt very badly'. John added: 'My reaction has been to discard excellence as a motivation, I guess because I found it pretty uncomfortable.'

Michael, who had visited museums from the age of nine, became a very successful museum director and ran the Boston's Children's Museum. John became an architect.

Dan, Michael's son, said that his grandfather

> did not forget. I think there may be some part of Ben that feels everybody was ungrateful and petulant. Why couldn't they just enjoy being the sons of the great man? I think both my uncle John and my father struggled with that.

But the person who paid the ultimate price was Peter, Spock's grandson, the toddler Spock had stopped singing in the restaurant. On Christmas Day 1983 he jumped from the roof of Boston's Children's Museum. His father, Michael, was director of the museum. The family has remained tight-lipped about what might have made Peter kill himself. (Spock's biographer, Thomas Maier, stresses that Peter had schizophrenia.)

Spock's own childhood experiences affected his response to the tragedy. When Spock's favourite sister, Marjorie, learned Peter had committed suicide, she was horrified. Spock had spent recent visits with her reading aloud from Beatrix Potter but not ever discussing what was happening in the family. 'You don't come here again, ever, and just read Beatrix Potter to me. I've known Peter as a little boy and loved him very dearly. And I never knew, until he was dead, that he was in trouble!'

The family tensions – and faith in Freud – made the family decide to try family therapy, which forced Spock to face, yet again, the contradictions in his personality.

Notes and references

A thorough biography of Spock is Thomas Maier, *Spock: An American Life*, Basic Books (2003).

Other references:
Freud, S., *Introductory Lectures*, vol. XXX, Standard edition, Hogarth Press (1963).
Spock, B., *A Teenager's Guide to Life and Love*, Pocket Books (1970).
Spock, B., *Baby and Child Care*, Simon & Schuster (1978). Various editions exist as Spock tried to bring his original edition up to date.
Interview with Michael Spock, *Ladies Home Journal* (1972).

9

JOHN BOWLBY

The man with the bowler hat

At the start of the book, I quoted Bowlby's remark that 'children are so helpless, so vulnerable'. He is remembered for his theory of attachment. Children needed a secure base which was best provided by a caring mother. If infants did not get that security, they were liable to be disturbed and to become delinquent. Bowlby felt that children were vulnerable all his life, it seems.

'The first time the full significance of his work struck me was during a family walk in the Chiltern Hills in about 1958', Sir Richard Bowlby said of his father. It was

> just after his paper on the child's tie to his mother was published. He said to me: 'You know how distressed small children get if they're lost and can't find their mother and how they keep on searching. I suspect it's the same feeling that adults have when a loved one dies – and they keep on searching too. I think it's the same instinct that starts in infancy and evolves throughout life.'

'Well if you're right you're on to something big', Richard Bowlby remembers saying. He was still a teenager when he delivered this judgment. In fact, most of his father's work examined the consequences of separation and loss.

I have tried not to make simplistic assumptions about what drove psychologists to study a particular topic but it is plausible to argue that Bowlby's early harrowing experiences helped determine his career; his fascination with loss was the result of the losses he suffered himself, starting when he was a little boy. Bowlby's mother, like many upper middle class Victorian mothers, was not very present, and so Nanny was often left in charge of the nursery. But she left when John was only four years old. Freud too lost his nurse, Rosie Wittek, at the same age but it does not seem to have made him concentrate on loss. It may be that was because his mother was more present and Vienna's Jews had no tradition of sending their boys off to boarding school when they were seven or eight.

Bowlby's father was a famous surgeon who also did not see much of his children, though he did devote a few hours to them most Sundays. He joined the army during the 1914 war and then hardly saw his family for some five years. Richard Bowlby believes these absences affected his father profoundly.

There was then a tragedy at the school the ten-year-old John and his older brother were sent to; Bowlby's godfather dropped dead during a football match in front of his godson. Absent parents, nannies who left, and then sudden death. So much separation – and tragedy – left its mark. In 1944, Bowlby told his wife, Ursula, that he considered children to be 'so helpless, so vulnerable'. But Bowlby would also face unexpected loss as an adult.

In 1948, Bowlby's closest friend, Evan Durbin, drowned while on holiday after rescuing two children. Today Durbin is a forgotten figure but he was an important Labour politician after the war, a friend of Hugh Gaitskell and Harold Wilson. He and Bowlby had shared a house in London and they were each other's best man at their weddings. Bowlby helped organize a trust fund which supported Durbin's children's education (Holmes, 1993). According to Bowlby's wife, Ursula, the loss of Durbin was the worst loss Bowlby experienced in his life (U. Bowlby, letter, 29 April 1996).

Bowlby's response to these losses illustrates one of the perils of biography. In analysing Piaget's analysis Eva Schepeler suggested he concentrated on cognitive development to avoid examining the emotions surrounding his difficult relationship with his mother – perhaps especially after Maman refused to let him continue to analyse her. John Bowlby, on the other hand, seems to have studied loss because he had experienced so much loss as a child himself. Both arguments make some sense but logically they cannot both be right unless one resorts to an insipid 'well Piaget and Bowlby had very different personalities'. Psychology often struggles to provide precise answers to complex questions.

Bowlby was supposed to follow his father into medicine. He went to Cambridge where he first read Freud's *Introductory Lectures*. He found them fascinating and was already confident enough to pick holes in some of the theory. 'As a somewhat arrogant young man I was in no mood to accept dogmatic teaching', he wrote.

After three years, Bowlby stopped his medical training, left Cambridge and went to teach for six months at a school called Priory Gates where he worked with maladjusted children. Priory Gates 'suited me very well because I found it interesting. And when I was there, I learned everything that I have known; it was the most valuable six months of my life, really. It was analytically oriented', he wrote. He then went to University College Hospital to finish his medical training and decided to become a psychoanalyst too.

The British Psychoanalytic Society accepted Bowlby for training analysis but he then became embroiled in its battles as Anna Freud and Melanie Klein tried to stick their hatpins into each other's theories. (If Kristeva can call them the ladies, I can arm them with hatpins without being sexist.) Joan Riviere became Bowlby's analyst. She had been a patient of Ernest Jones and, in 1920, met Freud and eventually became one of the best translators of his work. She was 'the incomparable Joan

Riviere, that tall Edwardian beauty with picture hat and scarlet parasol', whose renderings retained more of Freud's stylistic energy than any others, according to John Strachey. Riviere was part of the inner circle of psychoanalysis. Bowlby should have been delighted but his relationship with her was not easy.

We know little, of course, about Bowlby's analysis but it must have examined how he dealt with the feelings provoked by the losses and separation he had lived through. Despite her eminence, Bowlby wanted to leave Riviere, but the Training Committee of the British Psychoanalytic Society warned that a candidate usually suffered when he did that. Melitta Schmideberg remembered that Riviere used every possible emotional trick to get Bowlby to stay with her. Another well-known analyst, Susan Isaacs, started crying when it seemed likely the young man would take to another couch.

The issue was not, Bowlby said, that Riviere probed too sharply into his feelings, but a matter of theory. Like most classical analysts and his supervisor, Melanie Klein, Riviere tended to ignore the real experiences of children. Play, dreams, the inner life, mattered far more than what children said or did. That was for him excessive theory and not enough observation of children. In the end, however, Bowlby stayed seven years with Riviere.

After he qualified as a doctor, Bowlby went to work at the London Child Guidance Clinic. There he began to see troubled children who stole and played truant. Like the children at Priory Gates these child patients would not be forgotten.

In 1939, Bowlby joined the Army as a Lieutenant Colonel. The military was using psychiatrists in recruitment, something which provoked Churchill, who managed his bouts of serious depression largely with the help of his long-suffering wife, brandy and cigars. In December 1942, he put his boot into the shrinks, claiming 'it would be sensible to restrict as much as possible the work of these gentlemen'. Psychiatrists could do an immense amount of harm and Churchill suspected some psychiatry was 'charlatanry'. He did not want the couch wallahs to 'quarter themselves in large numbers upon the Fighting Services at the public expense'. Most soldiers, sailors and airmen were normal and did not need to be plagued by 'the odd questions in which the psychiatrists specialise'. (Churchill himself suffered from depression, or the 'black dog' as he called it).

In 1941 Bowlby and Ursula became parents. Having children did not disrupt his schedule much, however. He worked from 10 a.m. to 6 p.m., but very often went to evening committees or went out after having dinner at home. His wife told him three evenings a week was enough and he agreed (U. Bowlby, letter, 7 September 1997). One of Bowlby's children asked Ursula if Daddy was a burglar because 'he comes home after dark and never talks about his work' (J. Hopkins, personal communication, 15 November 1994). As his own father had done sometimes, Bowlby did take long holidays with his family.

In 1946, Bowlby published the paper on 44 juvenile thieves that made his name. From the moment a baby is born, Bowlby argued, the love-needing baby should get the love he needs from his mother who is biologically driven to give that baby love. If a mother does not bond with her child, the baby starts life 'feeling' insecure.

A child needs a secure, 'attached' base from which to grow, learn and explore the world. Juvenile thieves were far more likely to have been separated from their mothers between nine months and five years of age than boys who did not get into trouble.

Bowlby reminded me when I interviewed him that Harry Harlow had shown a similar pattern of behaviour in monkeys. A young monkey might have the support of a group, but if he was separated from his or her mother, that monkey showed signs of extreme trauma and would even cling to a metal cage for comfort. Bowlby rejected the criticism that 44 was perhaps too small a sample to base such large conclusions on. 'This was work which was done before the war and I was the first to collect a sample of as many as forty four.'

Bowlby told me with some intensity:

> If you put an infant of between nine months and three to four years in a strange place with strange people, he is very frightened and upset. He cries for long periods and makes it obvious he wants to find his mother. This is the stage of protest. Then he begins to despair. He can become very apathetic, very distant. He may cease crying or even talking. When the child has been separated for 14 or 21 days and resumes contact, he tends to evade her. Sometimes, he tends not to recognize her. All the normal emotional reactions are missing.

Bowlby's research had a major impact on the British justice system. It made it very hard for a fair person to blame delinquents for their delinquency. The young hoodlum had no free will; he had been conditioned to become delinquent at his mother's knee or, to be more accurate, by the absence of his mother's knee.

There is a fly in the ointment, a counter example, that Bowlby must have been aware of. In 1936, Mark Benney's autobiography of his youth, *Low Company*, made a huge impression. Its author had been often left by his wayward mother, who was sometimes broke, sometimes flush, depending on how rich her latest lover was. At the opening of the book Benney had yet again been fostered out when, he wrote, 'A familiar voice came down the street like a grey fog, "Youy Ma-a-a-rk"'. Mrs Greensmith, one of Mark's many foster mothers – 'mother was rather remiss in paying the stipulated board money' – was standing by his real mother who looked 'like some rare visitant from kinder spheres in her expensive fur coat'. She had come to take her boy home. Mark had almost forgotten what it was like to be in a family as, for years, his mother 'had been more of a legend to me than a real person. Once in a month or so she had been used to come "to see 'ow I was getting on"'. She was like 'a comet in transit'.

Mark did, as Bowlby's theory required, become a juvenile thief and was sent to Borstal. But then came the transformation. Benney started to write, became acquainted with George Orwell and H.G. Wells, and then one of the important sociologists of the mid-twentieth century, David Riesmann, whose *Lonely Crowd* claimed that after the Second World War Americans became 'other-directed', seeking their neighbours' approval and were terrified they might be considered different. Some juvenile thief!

I had not come across Benney's book when I met Bowlby so I did not ask him about what it took to get over maternal separation as Benney had done. Bowlby had retired but was allowed to keep a room at the Tavistock Clinic. His office was stark, with only a painting of pheasants on show. There was, however, that emblem of the upper middle class, a bowler hat, on his book case. Bowlby insisted on having the right to see what I wrote for the *New Scientist* and struck out the mention of the bowler hat. I was not surprised as he seemed a little prickly, a trait that he seems to have passed on to one of his sons at least.

Bowlby rejected the accusation that he was propping up the status quo, male supremacy or the conventional family but emphasized that 'The stable family situation with one man and one woman is best for a child'. He cited research he reviewed for the second volume of his trilogy, *Attachment and Loss*. 'There were about twelve studies which correlated stable family life and cheerful, self-reliant effective children.' He didn't apologise for one second. 'It is looking at the nature of human nature', he smiled, and added that he had gathered evidence from Britain, France, Holland, Switzerland, the United States and Germany, which made his work 'transcultural'.

'There is always a hierarchy of preferences', Bowlby told me. The child makes a first choice. 'I've never known a child who doesn't just pick out one figure. That could be the father but that would be strikingly uncommon.' There was no case on record when 'a man was the principal attachment figure'.

After he had published his 1946 paper, Bowlby eloquently pleaded for governments to be aware of the dangers if their policies separated mothers and children, even if the mothers were incompetent. The World Health Organization then asked him to investigate the mental health of homeless children. What was crucial, he decided, was not being homeless, but that 'almost all the evidence concerns the child's relation to the mother which is without doubt his most important relationship during these early years'. The father was second fiddle at best. Bowlby added, 'and his value only increases as the child's vulnerability to deprivation decreases'.

Bowlby developed the theory with the Canadian psychologist, Mary Ainsworth. They wrote *Child Care and the Growth of Love* (1965) which detailed a test called the 'Strange Situation'. They observed a child playing for 20 minutes while its mother and strangers came in and left the room. They studied how much the child explored and played with new toys and how the child responded when his or her mother came back after having left the room. They saw three different types of reaction. A child who was 'securely attached' explored freely while his mother was there and interacted with strangers; he or she was upset when the mother left and happy to see her return. While she was absent, the child avoided the strangers. A child with what they called an 'anxious-resistant attachment style' was nervous of strangers and did not explore or play much even when its mother was present. If she left the room, the child became very distressed. When she came back, the child would try to get close to her but would show much resentment. A child with an 'anxious-avoidant attachment style' was very subdued and showed little emotion either when the mother left or when she came back. Such a child did not explore very much, whoever was in the room.

The test was yet more proof that the bond between mother and infant was universal. 'It crops up in many other species', Bowlby told me. 'Why? My answer is that it gives protection. It especially gives protection from predators and I emphasise the predators' part. Even a two-year-old elephant is at risk when he's alone. He can be eaten by lions quite easily.' In the kind of analogy that Freud, patron saint of the surrealists, sometimes made, Bowlby went on to compare lions with cars. 'The motor car is the modern analogue of the predator. The car may not eat children but it certainly kills them unless parents protect them.' The effects of the separation, Bowlby argued, could be mitigated. A grandmother or even a spare part father, could make it less traumatic but that was the best one could hope for.

Bowlby never wanted his name attached to attachment theory, however. His son Richard remembered a family supper when his father asked what he should call the theory. They groaned when he said he wanted to call it attachment theory. 'We all said he should call it love theory but he told us that love was far more complex than this very specific biological protection mechanism he was working on.' At one point the idea that the theory should be named after Bowlby himself was mooted, but Bowlby pointed out that theories named after those who devised them 'tend to become stagnant once they die'. A theory will 'sink or swim on its ability to explain the observed data'.

It seemed important to track down Bowlby's children and the obvious first step was to contact the Bowlby Centre which was then in Spitalfields. I rang and rang but never got an answer so I finally sent a letter. Finally I got a response. What followed was tense and dramatic.

Bowlby's son Richard phones while I am on a train. He says he does not understand what I'm doing. I start to explain what this book is about. He tells me it seems prurient but we agree, or I think we agree, that I will phone him again.

'Who is it?', he asks, when I stick to that arrangement. I am in Belsize Park on the way to meeting Skinner's daughter, Deborah.

He seems to have forgotten the arrangement. I suggest that we could meet and I could explain to him in more detail what I'm doing.

'Are you doing a research project or a book?'

I make clear it is a book. I add that I have written a book of interviews with great psychologists and two books on fathering.

But is this book on psychologists in general or famous psychologists, he wants to know.

I give him a list of those I intend to cover and tell him those whose children I have talked to. If I hoped this would butter him up, I'm wrong.

'Oh yes', he says, 'but I don't see what the value of what you are proposing to do is though, of course, I can see there may be some royalties'.

Humour may be the best policy. I suggest that this book is unlikely to be a bestseller. Royalties probably won't buy me too many holidays in the Caribbean.

'I can see that', he concedes.

I add again that I have written many serious books on psychology.

'I am being defensive', he concedes.

Bowlby's son sounds as if he wants me to say no, he's not being defensive. I say nothing because I hardly want to provoke him. Then he switches tack.

'When were you born?'

'1946.'

'I was born in 1941.' He adds that his father, like most military men, tended to be absent when his children were little. Talking of the military – I am still in major buttering mode – makes we wonder if we might have an acquaintance in common. Bowlby as a Lt Colonel in the Army probably knew Stephen Mackeith with whom I co-authored *The Development of the Imagination*. MacKeith became the Army's chief psychiatrist. I offer to send Bowlby the book. As butter this does not wash. 'I'm dyslexic', he says, dismissing my offer.

Bowlby explains that everything there is to say about his father is out there in the public domain, including at the Wellcome Trust. There is a massive amount of material, he insists, and he clearly has no intention of offering me additional homely touches.

Then he tells me that 'you are harassing me'. I point out that we had arranged for me to ring him but, by then, I know I won't get anything else out of this exchange.

Richard Bowlby did give an interview to Lisa A. Newland and Diana D. Coyl for the journal *Early Child Development and Care*. Despite having been impressed by his father's 'big idea' when he was a teenager, Richard Bowlby admitted: 'It was not until my kids were 8 or 9 that I started reading my father's work. Dad said don't start with volume 1 you'll find it very boring.' When Richard did get round to it, he disagreed, because he found chapter 11 fascinating. Yet what really made him engage with his father's ideas was when he had his first grandchild. Attachment theory 'doesn't account for fathers'. When Richard's son-in-law Matt became a father, 'he was playful and engaging with my grandson'. That prompted Richard Bowlby to ask his father 'about the role of fathers but he didn't have a well thought out opinion and finished by saying "well a child doesn't need two mothers"'. By 1980, John Bowlby 'rated fathers more', his son said, but he added that 'I suspect his intense focus on mothers has biased researchers and distorted cultural values'. Richard Bowlby, after he himself retired, became a passionate advocate of his father's work but also argued that the original theory needed to take into account the importance of the father.

Notes and references

Bowlby's work:
Bowlby, J., Forty-four juvenile thieves: their characters and home life. *International Journal of Psychoanalysis*, vol. 25 (19–52), 107–27 (1944).
Bowlby, J., *Attachment and Loss*, Pimlico (1997).
Bowlby, J. and Ainsworth, M., *Child Care and the Growth of Love*, Penguin (1965).

Relevant works on his family:

Cohen, D., Interview with John Bowlby, *New Scientist*, 9 September 1971.

Holmes, Jeremy, *Something Is There That Doesn't Love a Wall: John Bowlby, Attachment Theory and Psychoanalysis*, Analytic Press (1995).

Newland, L.A. and Coyl, D., Interview with Richard Bowlby, *Early Child Development and Care*, vol. 180, 25–32 (2010).

Other references:

Benney, Mark, *Low Company*, Caliban (1936).

Cohen, D. and MacKeith, S., *The Development of the Imagination*, Routledge (1992).

Freud, S., *Introductory Lectures on Psychoanalysis* (1917), available in Penguin edition of 2001.

Holmes, Jeremy, *John Bowlby and Attachment Theory*, Routledge (1993).

10

BURRHUS SKINNER

The man who caged his daughters?

'One night just as I was falling asleep the phone rang and a young man asked: "Professor Skinner is it true you keep one of your children in a cage"', B.F. Skinner wrote in his autobiography, *Particulars of My Life*. It was not that unexpected. 'For one thing the children of psychologists are always under inspection. Are the shoemaker's children poorly shod?' Skinner's ideas were controversial and he was often attacked. His two daughters were sometimes not well disciplined, he admitted, but they never had serious problems. 'I used to say I was not trying to produce a well behaved ten year old; I wanted a happy twenty year old.'

Skinner was the most influential American psychologist between 1940 and 1970. He built on the work of Ivan Pavlov, the Russian who conditioned dogs to respond in various ways to bells, and on Watson's rather more complex experiments. Skinner did many ingenious studies of rats and pigeons, and argued that children too are conditioned or 'shaped', the term he used, by the way they are punished and rewarded. One reason he became so controversial a figure was that he devised what his critics called a Skinner box, which they sniped was much like a cage one kept rats in. It was that which the late night phone call referred to.

I interviewed Skinner twice in the 1970s, first for *The Observer* and then for my book *Psychologists on Psychology*. I vividly remember he wore Bermuda shorts as we talked in his house in Cambridge, Massachusetts. He was infinitely less formal than any other of my interviewees. His daughter, Deborah, felt her father had never managed his image well, a failure that cost him dear.

When Skinner met his wife, Eve, he was 38 years old and had already built a reputation for himself as a leading behaviourist. She had been a brilliant student and went to the University of Chicago when she was only 16. Skinner himself was under pressure from his family to marry and have children. 'Come on Fred', Deborah told me her father's parents had nagged. So he and Eve married. 'Eve and I have continued to talk about our children perhaps excessively', Skinner said. But they did that partly because of 'the cage'. Nothing made Skinner as furious as the accusation that he and his wife had brought up their daughters in that.

Deborah, their youngest, is a fierce defender of her father's reputation. When I met her in Belsize Park some 30 years after I had last interviewed him, she gave me a copy of an article she wrote for *The Guardian* in March 2004. It was a riposte to the publication of *Opening Skinner's Box* by Karen Slater, a very critical book about Skinner, his ideas and, inevitably, about how he had brought up his children.

'By the time I had finished reading *The Observer* I was shaking', Deborah said.

> According to *Opening Skinner's Box* my father 'used his infant daughter Deborah to prove his theories by putting her for a few hours a day in a laboratory box in which all her needs were controlled and shaped.' But it's not true. My father did nothing of the sort.

Deborah was outraged that Karen Slater never contacted her to find out if these allegations had any substance.

The details were wrong, for a start. Skinner did not put his daughter in a cage but in a custom-made air crib. Deborah continued: 'I have heard the lies before but seeing them in black and white in a respected Sunday newspaper I felt as if someone had punched me in the stomach.' Her reaction was hardly surprising as the book also suggested Deborah was actually dead. 'I had gone crazy, sued my father, and committed suicide.' The story of her suicide 'did the rounds of psychology classes across America'.

Skinner wrote about these rumours himself. A psychiatrist had spread the cage lie. All this malice was whipped up, Skinner believed, 'by clinical psychologists who found it useful in criticising behaviour therapy'. Behaviour therapy tries to eliminate neurotic behaviour and especially phobias by first relaxing the patient and then gradually exposing her or him to the stimuli that provokes anxiety. Step by step, the patient learns not to panic. Skinner did not invent behaviour therapy, it should be said. It owed something to Watson and was later developed by Hans Eysenck, a German-born psychologist who came to London and whose son Michael I quoted in the introduction.

'The plain reality is that Karen Slater never bothered to check the truth', Deborah said. 'Instead she chose to do me and my family a disservice and at the same time to debase the intellectual history of psychology.'

Her early childhood, Deborah concedes, was unusual. 'But I was far from unloved. I was a much cuddled baby.' Her father devised the air crib as an alternative to the usual cot with its cage-like bars. With the crib there was no need 'for clothes, sheets and blankets which restricted a baby's movements and were "a highly imperfect method" of keeping an infant comfortable'. Deborah said; 'I was very happy too, though I must report at this stage that I remember nothing of those first two and half years.' She was told she did not once object to being put back in the crib. Through its glass front, she could see what was going on around her and 'luxuriated semi-naked in warm, humidified air'.

In an interview with the *Norwegian Journal of Psychology*, Deborah older's sister, Julie, remembered:

> the air crib was a wonderful place to hide in when my sister wasn't in her bed. I would climb inside and pull down the shade and no one would find me. The air crib was built to improve on the comfort of an infant, not to add to science. My father did no experiments with it. Air cribs are wonderful infant beds.

They were hardly Pavlovian devices for conditioning children.

Deborah believes, in fact, that her crib helped make her remarkably healthy, as she did not have a cold until she was six years old. She was surprised the contraption never became popular. A few air cribs were built in the 1950s and 1960s, and someone even produced plans for a DIY version but it was never marketed commercially. Julie used one for her two daughters. 'It kept out mosquitos and wasps and in the winter gave a warm place to give baths. When we visited my parents, we borrowed a standard crib and worried about limbs getting stuck between the slats.' The other problem was that 'Unfortunately they don't prevent colds, as my father assumed from comparing Deborah's lack of colds as an infant to mine'. In general, however, Julie felt sleeping in the air crib made babies happy.

The Observer review of Slater's book was critical, Deborah was glad to note. The reviewer suspected Slater had not been thorough. 'He realised she could have contacted me to confirm or verify what she suspected but plainly hadn't.' The reviewer concluded that she had gone into hiding. 'Well here I am, telling it like it is. I'm not crazy or dead but I'm very angry', Deborah said.

Memories of our childhoods are often memories of moments – and the feelings that we associate with them. Deborah smiled as she remembered her father's routine. He always woke at 4.40 in the morning, 'When the alarm went off'. He would work until about 7 in the morning when his wife put out 'A bowl of Cheerios. It was always Cheerios for him'. After breakfast he would work at home for an hour or so before walking to his office in Harvard.

Her father was 'self-contained' – except when it came to his children. She experienced her father as playful and affectionate, Deborah told me, in that he was different from his intellectual hero, Watson, who never hugged or kissed his children. When Deborah went to boarding school, Skinner always hugged her when they met again.

Her sister Julie also speaks of her father's affectionate nature.

> Growing up with him as a father was wonderful. I was very close to my father. When we were little, my father put both my sister and me to bed. I remember asking questions to keep him sitting longer on the side of my bed. For example, I once asked 'What is beyond space?' My father turned on the light, made a paper Mobius strip and let me trace a line around it to illustrate how space folds back upon itself. I got good at asking questions that required long answers.

Deborah also remembers a night during the McCarthy hearings; her father was tucking her into bed and she asked him whether Communism was good or bad. 'He was giving me a good answer saying well yes and no.'

Less politically, does the good enough father take his children to the dentist? Probably, and he also puts up with not being wanted too much. Skinner remembered taking Deborah to the dentist once and asked if he could go in with her, but she had the confidence to tell him to stay in the waiting room.

Her parents' marriage, however, did have problems, Deborah told me. Her mother had been a brilliant student but her career never took off the way Skinner's did. The fact that her mother was 'unfulfilled' bothered her. 'She always said she didn't want to have kids and he was the one who was pushing for it.... Father said to me once that he had never wanted to have boys.' She thinks they discussed that subject as she told him she was worried he minded the fact that his oldest child was also a girl. 'I wouldn't have known what to do with a son', Skinner replied.

Skinner encouraged his daughters in many ways. 'My interest in playing an instrument', Julie said

> began in Monhegan where, looking through a Sears Roebuck catalogue, I saw a guitar and told my father I would like one. A $9.95 Silvertone guitar arrived in the mail a week later. It came with a pamphlet called, 'How to Play the Guitar in Five Minutes.' Five minutes later I still could not play the guitar and gave up. My father picked up the guitar and started going through the little book, but he had even more trouble placing his fingers than I had. I said, 'Here, Daddy. Let me show you'.

Julie did just that and soon had mastered two chords 'with which I could accompany myself singing songs like "Streets of Loredo"'. Julie sang in the Harvard Radcliffe chorus and even once performed with the Boston Symphony Orchestra. 'My father sat in the audience with, he later told me, tears in his eyes.'

Deborah's memories are also often touching. Her father watched her as she learned to ride a tricycle. 'The nicest memory I have of my father is of him teaching me to make an origami pigeon', she added. It would be a pigeon as Skinner's experiments often involved pigeons. He conditioned them to learn ping pong and even, during the 1939–45 war, to guide a missile, in theory at least. (The full story of the weird plan to put pigeons in a missile and train them to peck to keep it on course is told in Skinner's autobiography.) The origami pigeon was splendid, Deborah told me, because it could actually fly if you pulled on the tail. Her father gave it to her because he had received a box of oriental treasures.

As Deborah grew up, her school reports often complained of a lack of motivation. Her father blamed himself; he had failed to reinforce her properly. But 'when she found something that she could do well the problem was solved'. What she could do well was draw. Skinner encouraged her talent for drawing. He gave her a set of magic markers which allowed her to draw splendidly straight lines. Deborah's other fond memories include summer holidays spent on Manchego Island off the coast of Maine. 'It was a wonderful island. No cars. No electricity. We spent our summer holidays there. It's where I first learned to draw. My father and sister built me a row boat.' During those summers, Julie said for her part, 'my father taught me to sail, made me a workbench complete with vise and taught me how to use hand tools. In the pine woods called "Cathedral Forest", he built moss houses with my sister and me'.

Once Deborah's talent for drawing was clear, Skinner was very supportive. She recalled that once he hung an unfinished etching of hers in his study. He was in no way 'embarrassed' and told her how good it was. 'He was so biased and so chuffed', she smiled.

Her father was also good in a crisis. When she was a teenager, Deborah broke her leg when she was skiing. After she had showered 'and made myself decent', she would sit with her leg in a cast, get it up on the edge of the bath and 'Dad would wash my toes'. After the accident, she went to summer school at Harvard and once, after a difficult evening, her father wrote her a letter, some of which is worth quoting.

'I think our discussion last night was profitable in spite of the Kleenexes which strewed the floor afterwards.' The letter shows a father trying to right his relationship with his daughter. He told Deborah that if she did want to get a college degree, he did not mind. He was not embarrassed by any of her 'supposed shortcomings or afraid that you will prove to the world that I am a bad psychologist. Live your own life, not mine. Be yourself'. He added that he liked her Self as her Self was. When he offered to help or gave advice, he was not criticizing her. 'You are still developing, learning about life. I am an old timer.' They should not start to reverse evolution by shying away from discussing their experiences and differences. Man became the dominant species because he learned to store and pass on his experiences, Skinner continued. It was a touching letter from an old timer who could treat his teenage daughter as an equal.

Skinner also had intellectual discussions with his other daughter while they went on long walks. Julie recalled that 'My father would tell me about whatever he was writing. When I later read his articles, I would think, "I remember that homunculus. We talked about it walking around Fresh Pond"'.

Skinner enjoyed his fame – and Deborah enjoyed it too. She flew down once to spend a weekend with him in New York. They met Kate Mostel, the wife of the famous comedian Zero Mostel – the families were friends – and, 50 years on, she remembered having a wonderful weekend. They went to have dinner at Asti's, a swish showbiz restaurant, which had photographs of many stars.

Skinner believed in reward not punishment, something he stressed in his utopian novel, *Walden Two*. Writing the book went some way towards fulfilling an early ambition. Skinner told me that before becoming a psychologist, he wanted to be a poet. Deborah is a successful artist. Julie became an educationalist and developed some of her father's ideas. She wrote:

> To me, the foremost issue is shifting educational practice from aversive control to positive contingencies. Shifting to positive practices requires designing

learning activities so that individuals at all levels of proficiency succeed and *see* their improvement. Teachers too, need to see their students enthusiastic and successful. Few teachers have been taught to be sensitive to the timing of postcedents and to properties of antecedents that are critical for progress. Recently a student told me of a procedure of 'prompting' a student to ask for a break when he showed signs of an imminent 'meltdown.' The time the student spent in 'breaks' did prevent tantrums, but a better analysis of contingencies was needed. Instead of prompting breaks when pre-tantrum behavior occurred, break prompts could be timed to reinforce academic skills.

But Julie argues that behaviour analysts 'underestimate the power of seeing oneself conquer a new level of performance. When consequences depend on the student's own activity rather than solely on teacher-controlled consequences, students respond with what people call "self-esteem", "intrinsic motivation", and "self-discipline"'.

Skinner was very proud of both his daughters. In *Particulars of My Life* he quoted a critic who praised Deborah's landscapes in an 'extremely worthwhile exhibition' as being 'a complex and profound statement for the eye'.

Julie and Deborah were both distressed when their father was diagnosed with leukaemia. Julie took leave of absence from her university 'so I could spend his last nine months with him. Even now, going through all the photographs, notes, datebooks, manuscript drafts, awards, and other memorabilia I am amazed at how much time he spent with us'. He was certainly a good enough dad.

Notes and references

I interviewed Skinner twice and he looked over the draft of the interviews before allowing them to be published. He was charming, helpful but careful. He pointed out to me that no one had written a biography of John B. Watson, which spurred me to write one. Skinner's interview is in D. Cohen, *Psychologists on Psychology*, Routledge (1977). I also talked at length to his daughter Deborah.

Skinner's relevant works are:
Skinner, B.F., *Particulars of My Life*, Jonathan Cape (1976).
Skinner, B.F., *Walden Two*, Hackett Press (2005; originally published 1948).

Material relating to the controversy about the Skinner box:
Skinner, D.B., in *The Guardian*, 12 March 2004.
Slater, K., *Opening Skinner's Box*, Bloomsbury (2003).
Vargas, Julie, Interview in *Norsk Tiddskrfit fro Atferanalyse*, 119–26 (1970).

11

R.D. LAING

Violence in the family

Ronnie Laing offered a radical vision of psychiatry in the 1960s. He argued that schizophrenia was not really an illness like cancer or the measles, but a desperate attempt to deal with conflicts, usually in the family. His first book, *The Divided Self*, was a brilliant attempt to understand the minds of schizophrenic patients. He then co-authored *Sanity, Madness and the Family: Families of Schizophrenics*, a detailed study of 12 families which showed that complicated and poisoned family relationships often led to one member of a family not so much becoming mad as acting mad.

In an interview with the *Sunday Times*, R.D. Laing's daughter, Karen, revealed that her father once beat her so viciously that her brothers had to intervene to save her from serious injury. Laing, the author of three important books on psychiatry, subjected his children to a reign of terror, she claimed.

'I was injured after it but it was also the impact that it had on me emotionally and psychologically that was very damaging. It wasn't just myself – there were other incidents', she said.

Her father was a Jekyll and Hyde figure, Karen Laing said, compassionate and caring towards his patients but cruel and abusive to his own family. 'I have sat in on sessions with my father while he was working with clients and experienced his genius as a man who could relate to another human's pain and suffering', she said.

Her brother Adrian also experienced the wild side of their father. As far as I can tell Laing is the only father of the psychologists herein who had to be rescued from a police station by one of his children.

Adrian became a barrister and Karen became a psychotherapist. Both are struck by the differences between Laing the theorist and Laing the father. Karen Laing said:

> There seems to me to be a huge void and contradiction between R.D. Laing the psychiatrist and Ronnie Laing the father. There was something he was

searching for within himself and it tortured him. It makes me feel very sad that he could relate to other people but he couldn't relate to people in his own family and see what was happening within the family network.

After the death of a half-brother in 2008, following a suspected drugs and drink binge, Adrian called his childhood 'a crock of shit'.

Laing himself wrote that when one was tempted to blame the parents for the fact that a child suffered psychiatric problems, one should never forget that her or his mother and father had parents of their own with their own screw ups and screw looses. I could say disturbances, difficulties, schizophrenias, fits-o-frenias or any other of the myriad terms for mental problems, but Laing had ambitions to be a poet, so why not frolic a bit with the stiff medical language? Laing's complex ambitions were the product of a complicated childhood. In one of the playlets in his collection *Do You Love Me?* the mother tries to kill the father until the son intervenes. As drama it's a little basic but it does fit in emotionally with some aspects both of Laing's childhood and his behaviour as a father.

Laing's mother managed to be as neurotic in Glasgow as any Viennese hausfrau Freud ever saw. She did not tell anyone she was pregnant with 'Ronnie' until the day he was born. Laing's mother, it seems, did suffer from depression among other things.

Laing himself saw the child as a victim of everything, starting with her father and mother and moving on to bourgeois society and capitalism. In *The Politics of Experience* (1970), he wrote:

> From the moment of birth, when the Stone Age baby confronts the twentieth-century mother, the baby is subjected to these forces of violence, called love, as its mother and father, and their parents and their parents before them, have been. These forces are mainly concerned with destroying most of its potentialities.

From 1951 to 1971, Laing's potentialities were not destroyed as he wrote and co-wrote three books, one with David Cooper, perhaps an even fiercer critic of psychiatry than Laing was. It is a sign of the impact Laing made on the culture in general that there have been 11 books about him and his ideas.

Many conventional psychiatrists, however, were acutely critical of Laing and *The British Journal of Psychiatry* did not review *The Divided Self* until 1984, a delay that was outrageous as well as silly. After 1971, however, Laing got increasingly lost in a haze of drink, drugs and mysticism.

For his children, he was utterly contradictory. Though her father took drugs copiously, Karen Laing said he flew into a rage when he came back from holiday and was told she was high on drugs. She should have been baby-sitting for his second wife, Jutta. Furious, Laing rampaged back to Glasgow to confront his daughter, a confrontation that ended in his attacking her.

This was the same person who, according to Diane Cilento, the ex-wife of Sean Connery, asked for 'a great deal of money, complete privacy, a limo and a bottle of the best single-malt Scotch' before he and the man who played Bond took a six-hour LSD trip together. Connery was anxious about his career. One could argue Laing was worth every penny the actor paid. Like Carl Jung, Laing had two personalities – or at least two

Late in his career, Laing wrote an autobiography of his early life; he also gave a very extended interview to Bob Mullan as preparation for a biography, and his own son Adrian Laing published a frank, often engaging, biography. Adrian Laing, it seems to me, often throws up his hands in despair and laments almost Biblically, 'Why oh Lord did you land me with this lunatic but charismatic father?' His father identified and worked with the family as the cause of many mental traumas, yet he 'had nothing to do with his own family'.

Yet Laing clearly liked being a father as he had ten children by four different women and lived in a family all of his life, apart from occasional expeditions to ashrams and hermitages where he could meditate in search of his soul. In the *New York Review of Books*, one of Laing's biographers, Daniel Burston, admitted he had said little about Laing as a father

> though not for lack of interest or desire to say more. The fact is that after interviewing Anne (Hearne) Laing, and two of her children, and Jutta (Werner) Laing, and sending them copies of a preliminary draft, they wrote to inform me that they did not welcome any further inquiries or correspondence from me, and refused me permission to quote anything I had previously gleaned from discussion with them. Prudence and tact compelled me to say little on this point.

The silence can be interpreted in many ways. I wrote to them and so far have not had any answer.

I did talk to Adrian Laing when his biography was first published, but when I approached him this time, he was polite but said he did not want to add anything to what he had told me then.

Adrian Laing catalogued a very flawed father who felt unable to seek help when he knew he was depressed, drinking too much and aggressive. Karen Laing agrees, saying that 'There was a lot of violence when we were young – vicious, nasty stuff – and at times it certainly felt an unsafe place to be'. Again the ambivalence surfaces as she said 'There were so many different parts to my father. He was a tortured soul, he was tormented and he took that out on other people who were around him'.

Laing gave a detailed account of his own childhood in his last book, *Wisdom, Madness and Folly*, which had none of the success of his earlier works. He was the only child of a seemingly quiet Presbyterian couple whose behaviour, however, was anything but quiet and would have raised eyebrows in the kirk if anyone had known about it. His father was a senior figure in the Scottish electricity industry and also a fine amateur singer; his family thought he had not married well.

He was raised in what seemed to be a disciplined house. Laing said: 'I was punished for disobedience and for what I did wrong.' Disobedience was wrong in itself and, in addition, 'I had done which I should not have done because it was wrong in itself to do that whether I had been told to or not'. He gave a long list of what was forbidden – picking his nose, slouching in a chair – and added that he learned 'not to put a finger in my ear, to blow my nose properly, how to brush my teeth, comb my hair, tie my shoe laces, do my tie always to have my socks pulled'. That was not all he also learned 'how to shit properly and wipe my arse properly'. From when he was seven years old he was expected to 'get up in the morning, do my teeth, wash my hands, arms, face, neck, gargle, pee and do no 1' – the long list ended up with Laing setting off for school spruced up, with a clean handkerchief as well as a pen, pencil and geometry set.

Amelia, Laing's mother, was demanding. He suffered from eczema and she insisted that some foods would make his rashes worse and should never be touched. Fatal temptation. On his first day at school he had swopped one of his rusks for a devilish white roll filled with jam. When he got home, his mother suspected he had sinned. She made her son look her in the eye: 'Did I eat anything I had promised not to today at school?' Amelia demanded. 'No', said Ronnie. 'Is that the truth?' Amelia wanted to know. 'You've lied to me Ronald and I'm going to tell your father when he comes home – and he'll give you a thrashing for breaking your promise to me.'

Thrashings came on a scale; Laing got a 'sound' one, which was one degree more severe than a 'good' thrashing. Some of Amelia's habits were truly odd. She often burned the family's rubbish inside their house so that the neighbours would not get to rifle through the garbage. The kirk would also have been surprised because there were what Daniel Burston, one of Laing's biographers, describes as 'brutal physical scenes in the parlour', as Laing's father and grandfather sometimes fought. Amelia was a confusing mother; sometimes she was perfectly normal but, at other times, simply nasty. She destroyed her son's toys when he was a boy.

Ambivalence seems to have been ever present. Long after Laing was a little boy, Amelia insisted on barging into the bathroom when her son was in the tub and rubbing his shoulders. Laing was not allowed to lock the bathroom door. By the time he was 15, to hide his sprouting pubic hair, he would make the bath water as dirty as possible so that his mother could not see his genitals.

Laing used one story about his mother in *Self and Others*, though he did so anonymously. He said it was 'one of her wiles – the last one I hoped I would be caught in'. A boy of seven was accused by his father of stealing his pen. The boy protested his innocence. His mother told his father their son had confessed he had stolen the pen; it was a mercy that while he was a thief at least he was not also a liar. This confused the boy, who began to wonder whether perhaps he had stolen the pen after all and lied about it. His mother eventually realized her son had, in fact, not stolen the pen at all. She said that to her son, but not to his father, who went on thinking his son thieved.

'Come and kiss your mummy and make it up', the mother said to her son. But the boy felt he was being forced to comply.

Even horrific childhoods – and Laing's was not that – can be a mixture of good and bad. The boy, with this ambivalent relationship with his parents and especially his mother, would sit down after tea and listen to the radio with them. *The Brains Trust* was a favourite; the trust often included an anonymous Scottish doctor who Laing later discovered was Edward Glover, Melitta Schmideberg's analyst. Yet another unlikely connection.

'Provided I looked all right, smelt all right, and sounded all right, as long as my thoughts were good and my heart was pure, I was free as a bird', Laing wrote, but this was not the whole truth. He was under pressure to please. When he went to Hutcheson's grammar school, one of Scotland's best, he excelled at classics and also dabbled in evangelical Christianity. By the time he was 15, Laing was reading Voltaire, Marx, Nietzsche and Freud. He also played rugby and was such a good pianist there was some talk of him trying to make a career as a musician. His parents, however, were always prickly. Once his class had to write an essay on their home life. 'Mine began "Time lies heavy on my hands".' His parents were upset and could not understand how he could write that when he had his schoolwork, his music and played rugby as well. 'And it shows how ungrateful you are for all we have done for you', they told him, though he does not seem to have got a thrashing. The ungrateful son turned dutiful and changed the first line of his essay to 'life is full of interest'. He listed all the fabulous things he was learning – Homer, Greek irregular verbs and Chopin. The revised essay got 8.5 out of 10, which made his parents very happy, but, Laing added, 'That sort of deception, dissimulation, compliance, some people find intolerable'. He found it intolerable, it seems.

In 1945, Laing went to the University of Glasgow to study medicine and graduated in 1951. He turned his experiences of eczema to his advantage as he came first of his class in the exam on skin diseases. National Service was compulsory and he worked as a psychiatrist in the Army. Freud often skived off when he had to do National Service in Austria, but Laing was a model officer by comparison. He obeyed the orders of his medical superiors, interviewed hundreds of soldiers, treated many with the drugs that were then available and did not challenge orthodoxy much. Laing sometimes labelled men as 'mad' so they could be discharged on medical grounds. But he was beginning to develop considerable empathy for those he saw.

Laing wrote of one soldier:

> On admission he said nothing. He was completely mute. He blew out his cheeks till he was blue in the face. 'The patient tried hard to speak but could not even whisper.' He then cried, beat his head and tore his hair.

For the next five sessions, he was in much the same state and Laing gave him a heavy dose of sedatives. Then the man regressed so much that he had to be fed and taken to the toilet. The most astonishing thing was that the soldier wanted to play with toys. 'He asked for a yoyo.' One of the lessons Laing learned was that regression had its uses.

Young as he was, Laing was sharp. Four of his patients reported what was taken to be a mad delusion that they were being beaten up. It was no delusion, however, Laing found out. The four had indeed been beaten up by a corporal and a private on night duty; the two were duly court martialled. Laing does not draw out the conclusion that he could be effective and do good within a system.

After the Army, Laing worked at the Glasgow Royal Mental Hospital where he began to be sceptical of orthodox psychiatric ideas, especially the usefulness of schizophrenia as a diagnosis. He started to write the book that made him famous – *The Divided Self* (1961). Two other influential books followed – *Sanity, Madness and the Family: Families of Schizophrenics* written with Aaron Esterson and *Reason and Violence* written with David Cooper. Laing and Aaron Esterson interviewed 12 schizophrenic patients and their families at length. They concluded that a person was diagnosed as schizophrenic because of what was happening in his or her family 'nexus'. They could have written 'the nexus wrecks us'. The 'madness' was a means of coping with an impossible situation. It wasn't crazy. Rather it was an understandable strategy, the only way out of intolerable contradictions.

By 1965 Laing had left Glasgow and come down to London. He established an alternative psychotherapeutic centre where no one used the words 'psychiatrist' and 'patient'. There were no locks on the doors, and anti-psychotic drugs were banned – though LSD was administered to release buried childhood traumas. It was not illegal at the time. Psychotic behaviour was seen as an expression of distress rather than an illness.

Laing was clearly proud of the centre. 'Just before my parents split up, my dad took me to Kingsley Hall', Adrian recalls. He was under ten at the time.

> He said there was a special person he wanted me to meet and he took me downstairs into what I can only describe as a dungeon. There, in the corner under a blanket, was a woman. I was terrified, but my dad had this way of sitting in silence as if nothing was going on. He called it being an active presence.

The woman was Mary Barnes, Kingsley Hall's most famous resident, who was regressed to infancy there for a time, smearing the walls with faeces and being fed with a bottle. She later became a well-known artist and poet. 'I came to know her well', wrote Adrian. 'She would send me her paintings.'

Laing left Adrian's mother in 1965, and had little to do with him for the next decade. His sister Karen said:

> It was an awful culture shock when my parents separated, leaving our schools and friends in London and arriving in Glasgow in the early 1960s, which then had a frightening reputation for gang violence. We had occasional visits from my father, which always ended in rows. I felt hurt, angry and confused he couldn't be there for us.

The books he published in the 1960s made Laing famous. I went to a lecture he gave at Friends House late in that decade; the large hall was completely full. Then in 1968 *The Times Educational Supplement* asked me to see if I could get an interview with him. They doubted it was possible but the literary editor knew a man called Zeal who was a disciple of the great man. Zeal might even have his phone number – and might even be willing to part with it. When I rang, Zeal hesitated: he was not sure Laing would approve as he didn't want sensational press. *The Times Educational Supplement* is hardly a sensationalist rag, which may explain why, a few days later, Zeal telephoned to give me the number. When I rang, an efficient-sounding secretary told me to come to an address in Wimpole Street. I might have been booking a dental appointment. Freud would then have smiled as the psychopathology of everyday life intervened and I lost the address. I did not dare ring Zeal up again. With no idea what to do – and sure *The Times Educational Supplement* would never ask me to write anything ever again if I failed – I looked in the phone directory.

It couldn't be.

It was.

We had all assumed the guru's number was ex-directory, but the number stared me in the face: R.D. Laing. Laing, the great critic of mystification, had become so mystified himself I had thought it impossible to reach him except by the most tortuous means.

Laing's consulting room was conventional – he sat facing me and chain-smoked Gauloises. He ran quickly, efficiently, through his views as he had obviously done often in many interviews. The hour came to an end. I was dispatched to make way for a patient.

Five years later, when I interviewed him again, Laing had moved to a house in Belsize Park that his son Adrian describes as palatial. He was working from a dark-green room that was lined with books. A.J. Ayer jostled with Indian mystics on his table. Laing said he spent a great deal of his time here as he liked to work in the midst of his family, which showed how wrong it was to see him as somehow hostile to the family. His colleague, David Cooper, who wrote *The Death of the Family* (1972), was the anti-family man, though ironically Cooper ended up living in the house of his ex-wife, Juliet Mitchell, who took him in when he was in distress. Cooper acknowledged the irony to me.

For Laing, the link with Cooper could be irritating. He said:

> some people seem to confuse me with David Cooper and his attitude towards the family particularly as expressed in *The Death of the Family*, condemn the family. His spirit, that spirit, isn't my spirit about the family. You're interviewing me right now in the midst of my family. I enjoy living in a family. I think the family is the best thing that still exists biologically as a natural thing.

He would not like to see 'the family disrupted by state control or interfered with, as could very easily happen if you adopted the slogans of the sixties' psycho-politico anti-psychiatry anti-family left and used that has an excuse to take over'. He spiralled into fantasy, imagining a future where parents would

> have to have a licence to be allowed to have a child. I have someone who comes to see me who goes along to a psychiatric facility because she's distressed, emotionally disturbed. The first thing they do is to test her. They test her and they find that she's very emotionally disturbed and one of the things that she's disturbed about is the possibility of having a child, whether she's a suitable case for maternity. So, they say, OH NO, NEVER, on no account, never have a child! Unless she passes her psychological aptitude test, she won't be one of those who are allowed to have a child.

I should have pushed him more on what seems, even now, a slightly paranoid account. In the 1970s, we had seen far fewer tragedies where social workers had failed to take children at risk into care.

> The family is, I think, potentially a great thing, potentially a place where adults can play and be with children and the child can be with some people who are still a bit more human than a lot of those they will run into later. If the kids and the adults who make up a family get it off together well, then it's absolutely great.

In 1964 Laing met Jutta Werner. By 1977 Laing's radical insights had turned to mystical mush and what my late son Reuben mocked as dreadful poetry. Sixteen years after the success of *The Divided Self* Laing published a book with no pretensions, recording conversations with two of the children he and Jutta Werner had; it was a riposte to those who imagined he felt the family was crippling. 'The other side of the story has not been looked at nearly so much. The language of the happy dialogue of intelligent beings has evolved to an amazing degree of intricacy and complexity', Laing wrote. The family did not have to be suffocating. 'It is the free and open space between us where we can play with reality together, where we question and answer, inquire into what is the case and what is not for the sheer heaven of it.' Laing did not record the conversations with a tape recorder, as that would have been inhibiting; instead he wrote them down immediately after they happened. He knew that would expose him to the charge that he embellished the conversations, but they sound largely convincing and often give a cute picture of family life – perhaps too cute.

One of the early conversations with his three-year-old, Adam, took place when the family had gone to India and Sri Lanka:

ADAM: I want to go to Kandy and kill people and cut them up and eat them for breakfast with a big steel gun and a stiff trigger.
DADDY: Why?
ADAM: Because I want to shoot a lot of people and kill them so they'll be dead. Like I did last time.
DADDY: How do you mean last time?
ADAM: Last time I was here.
DADDY: Here.

ADAM: Last time I was alive.
DADDY: How do you know?
ADAM: Come on, come on Swear, Swear. Let me hear you swearing.
DADDY: Come on come on yourself. I don't feel like swearing. Why do you want to hear me swearing?
ADAM: I want you to swear.
DADDY: I don't want to swear.

Adam pressed on, wanting to hear his father swear. And Laing resisted his son's demands. During the trip to Sri Lanka and India Laing sometimes left his family to study with the guru Gangotri Baba who claimed to possess occult powers.

In July 1973, back from the East, six-year-old Adam was again pressing his father. Now the subject was how one would cope with various indignities.

ADAM: Come on daddy it's your turn.
DADDY: If someone shoved spaghetti up your nose.
ADAM: And how would you like it if someone mixed up sand and water into some kind of cement and poured it down your throat? [Adam seems to have been unusually precocious on some technicalities.]
DADDY: And how would you like it if someone put you in a large tub – as large as this room – of treacle?
ADAM: And how would you like it if someone cut off your nose?

Laing is right that such games are fun and often the violence is mere play. In the end Laing noted of Adam, 'He's got me on the run'.

In one sweet conversation Laing's daughter Natasha comes into his bedroom and insists on him taking her back to her own bed. She insists on him saying her prayers, which Laing did, even though in other conversations God is dismissed as a fantasy. Jutta certainly did not run an anarchic house. At one point, she told the children to 'tidy your beds, straighten your pillows and fold your sheets'. In another Adam moans – he is now eight – about being told to go and get some milk and butter from what seems to be another part of the house. But in the end Adam did as he was asked.

There were also jokes in the family.

NATASHA: When does the snow dance?
RONNIE: I don't know.
NATASHA: At the snow ball.

And later:

NATASHA: What did one candle say to the other candle?
RONNIE: I don't know.
NATASHA: I'm going out tonight.

The conversations record darker moments, too, but none of the violence Karen Laing described. Laing wrote of one outburst of sibling rivalry when Natasha wished Adam were dead. Biblically, Natasha added 'I wish his seed had been crushed'. 'But Adam's your brother, you'd miss him', Natasha's mother said.

'I want to miss him', Natasha replied. A brilliant and dramatic last word.

Natasha was more poetic than Jung's four-year-old girl who just said she wanted her brother killed.

Talking to me long before he published these conversations, Laing said:

> My attack on the family is aimed at the way I felt many children are subjected to gross forms of violence and violation of their rights, to humiliation at the hands of adults who don't know what they're doing, and are so arrogant in their ignorance, they're not likely to get the point.

He never mentioned his own violence. Rather, he added that it was in the family that human beings could be most themselves. When I suggested this was at odds with what he wrote, he blamed what he saw as an unfair interpretation of *Sanity, Madness and the Family*.

About ten years after his parents had split up, Adrian spent a year living with his father and his second family and found it confusing. 'I could never work out when an event in the house was therapy and when it wasn't. Someone was always turning up and doing breathing exercises or yoga. Everything could be called therapy.'

Laing seemed to want to draw Adrian back into the fold. Adrian was just out of university when his father again took him to a hall. He recalls:

> We were in an old church hall opposite this palatial London house my dad had in Belsize Park. It was meant to be a practice session for his helpers, who were all dressed in pastel-coloured tracksuits and emitting a kind of unified moaning noise.
>
> They surrounded me at my back, at my hips, at my shoulders and at my head, where they pushed their hands down on me to simulate a womb opening. I had to push to get out from between them while they tried to stop me. The idea was to relive the struggle I had had to be born.

Adrian was not frightened. 'The whole experience made me feel better, more alert, that I could see things more sharply. It was a very primitive form of catharsis, as if you'd had a really good cry.' That, of course, was not the formal way of putting it. 'My father called it the physical realisation of your existential impasse', Adrian added.

In the mid-1970s and 1980s, Laing's work became more esoteric and he was annoyed that his books did not sell well. He once persuaded Carl Rogers to put up a few thousand pounds so that they could stage a debate between them at the Dorchester. Rogers liked the idea as he had staged a very successful debate with Skinner, but Laing simply filched the money. He was driven to such dishonesty because he was no longer earning large royalties. He wrote a book, for example, which looked at birth and described his own attempts to re-experience his birth but it sold poorly. Laing was in reality becoming more disturbed, partly because he had lost his status as a radical hero. He also had what Adrian called 'warrior fantasies' and was planning a book called the *Way of the Warrior* which was never finished.

After the year where his father tried to mend their relationship, the two drifted apart. Adrian was called to the Bar. He did not expect his father to become a client, however, but Laing was living 'life with the brakes off'. At 11.30 p.m. on 27 September 1984 Adrian was summoned to Hampstead Police Station. His father, more than a little the worse for alcohol, had thrown a full bottle of wine through the window of the Rajneesh Centre in England's Lane and sat down muttering obscenities about 'orange wankers' (followers of the Rajneesh wore yellow). When he was taken to the police station, Laing was told to empty his pockets. A brown substance presumed to be cannabis was found. He was charged with possession. Adrian rang the lawyer for the Rajneesh Centre who agreed to drop any charges as long as the broken window was paid for and he paid 'a social visit' to the orange-robed to sort out what they called his 'spiritual disturbances'. Adrian was more worried about disturbances in the nick as his father acted out to the full the stereotype of a drunken Scot. Being clearly an effective barrister, Adrian persuaded the constabulary to let him take his father home, guaranteeing he would bring him back once they had analysed the brown stuff.

Getting Laing to return to Hampstead Police Station involved Adrian putting up with his foul moods, making sure his dad put on a suit and 'the now routine argument as to whether the cab was to be paid cash or "on account"'. When he got to Hampstead Police Station, Laing ranted at the police and the duty inspector, a sensitive soul, said he was deeply insulted that Laing should turn up drunk. Adrian had to persuade the police to let his father go home again on the understanding that if he did not turn up sober the next day, he 'would be detained in the cells'. Adrian was furious, but his father then surprised him, for once in a good way, as he 'gave me one of the few hugs I ever had of my dad and said "Aw come on". The son's anger "subsided" and they laughed all the way to the pub "like two eighteenth century cavaliers"'.

The harmony did not last. Before his case came up on 27 November 1984, 'Ronnie was boasting he would beat the rap and intended to plead not guilty', Adrian said. He knew a full blown trial would attract bad publicity and he knew his father was being unrealistic about his chances of being acquitted. Adrian persuaded a senior barrister to meet his father. The three spent hours tearing Laing's defence to shreds and he finally agreed to plead guilty. He got a 12-month conditional discharge.

Then Antony Clare, the psychiatrist who wrote *Psychiatry in Dissent* and hosted a radio programme called *In the Psychiatrist's Chair*, persuaded Laing to be one of his subjects. Clare, with deadly gentleness, got him to admit taking drugs and drinking to excess. Clare knew this would destroy Laing's medical career, and he was indeed reported to the General Medical Council who withdrew Laing's licence to practise medicine.

Laing did not just suffer public humiliation. At this time his ever ambivalent mother made an effigy of her son, an effigy she called a 'Ronald doll', and started sticking pins in it. According to Adrian, she wanted to induce a heart attack in her boy because he had offended her by including swear words in one of his books. It was Laing's father who died instead. Laing's mother then wrote to her son to say she never wanted to see him again. He wrote back on a large piece of paper on which he drew a heart and said 'I promise'.

When Amelia herself died, for all the difficulties they had had, Laing wept out of control at her funeral. Adrian pointed out with compassion that his truly grieving father then had to endure the mockery of his friends. One man ribbed that Laing was weeping because he had just been hit with the hotel bill.

There was less drama when Adrian got married. His father 'behaved himself and delivered an appropriately amusing speech from the high table'. After that father and son stayed in telephone contact and they spoke in July 1989, when Laing tried to persuade Adrian to help Bob Mullan with the biography that he was planning. That was 'something I was reluctant to do despite our friendship. I had always made it clear to Ronnie that the day would come when I would write my own book'.

In the end Adrian wrote a novel as well as a biography. *Rehab Blues* often yo-yos between poking fun at his father and then softening the satire as it follows the celebrities who come through the doors of The Place, next to Hampstead Heath, a therapy mansion that owes much to his father's Kingsley Hall in the East End. 'Great' parents often leave a legacy of great ambivalence. Adrian Laing has remained married for 24 years, and has five children. 'That's been my therapy', he laughs.

On 6 May 1988 Laing's last child, Charles, was born. A little later, Laing went to Austria. A new child seemed to help him promise to turn over a new leaf. He stopped drinking and started to work with Bob Mullan on his biography, which he hoped would earn some much-needed cash. Then, at the end of August 1989, Laing went to St Tropez to stay with Robert Firestone. Before they met Laing had agreed to write a preface to Firestone's *Compassionate Parenting*, a preface it is worth detailing given Laing's troubled times with his own children.

In the mid-nineteenth century, Robertson Smith, in *The Religion of the Semites*, suggested that infanticide, the killing and eating of children was, wrote Laing, 'the dark totemic pole right at the dead centre of the Mesopotamian origins of Western social organisation'. Relations between children and their parents were still poisoned, Laing suggested, a very different line from that he had taken in his interviews with me.

Firestone had 30 years of clinical experience, backed Robertson Smith and characterized, Laing said, 'a great deal of parental so-called "love" as parental hate and hunger. He documents here ways in which parents kill and eat their children, not physically but psychologically'. It was a desperately sad book, labelling parents as psycho-cannibals, but, Laing hoped, the next generation of parents would do better. That would seem unlikely if they followed his advice. 'Babies and infants have to be defended against', Laing declared, making one of the most bizarre statements ever made in psychology.

> The smile and outstretched arms of the normal baby are a 'demand'. Their genetically programmed evocative qualities, programmed to elicit happy,

effortless, complimentary. Returning, reciprocal responses in the adult are experienced by the normal schizoid, narcissistic, autistic, paranoid parent as assaultive, demanding, draining.

Firestone was expressing in prose perhaps what Laing's mother had expressed in many of her ambivalent actions towards her son.

By 1989, Laing had lost much perspective. Firestone, however, thought there was still some magic to him.

Towards the end of the foreword Laing offered yet another poem:

> Last night I dreamed a dreary dream
> Beyond the Isle of Skye
> I saw a dead man win a fight
> And that dead man was I.
>
> Aye indeed.

In St Tropez, Laing and Firestone played tennis and Laing was winning four games to one when he felt extremely unwell. Firestone asked Laing if he was all right or whether he wanted a doctor.

'Doctor what fucking doctor', Laing said.

By the time Laing's then partner and Charles' mother appeared, Laing was dead. His death made the front page of some papers.

Just as his father was ambivalent about his parents, Adrian seems ambivalent about his father. 'My father still prompts such violently diametrically opposed views about whether he was a genius, a madman or a charlatan', Adrian reflects.

> I feel bitter and sweet about him at the same time. My dad did have an exceptional desire to find noble truths, but he couldn't handle the adulation he attracted. He loved sitting up on a stage, with disciples at his feet, being adored but never challenged. He loved being treated as a guru – too much for his own good.

Adrian said pointedly that his relationship with his father 'improved greatly after his death'.

In this chapter, I have quoted Laing's conversations with his son Adam. In 2008 *The Guardian* reported that his decomposed body was found by police on the island of Formentera. Adam was found in a tent. 'Next to him lay a discarded vodka bottle and an almost-empty bottle of wine.' It was first assumed Adam had killed himself after his relationship with a German diving instructor broke up, but the *post mortem* showed he had died of a heart attack.

Of all those covered in this book, Laing is the most tragic. He ended up squandering his great talents and, even on the most generous interpretation, he could not be called a good enough father.

Notes and references

When I interviewed Laing, I was not aware of all his family issues. That interview is in D. Cohen, *Psychologists on Psychology*, Routledge (1977). I also interviewed Laing's son Adrian when his biography of his father appeared, and talked briefly to his daughter Karen who was not willing to be interviewed. Adrian Laing, *R.D. Laing: A Life*, Peter Owen (1998), remains a good, if often sad, book.

Works by Laing:
Laing, R.D., *The Divided Self*, Penguin (1961).
Laing, R.D., *The Politics of Experience*, Penguin (1970).
Laing, R.D., *Do You Love Me?* Random House (1976).
Laing, R.D., *Conversations with Children*, Penguin (1978).
Laing, R.D., *Wisdom, Madness and Folly*, Macmillan (1985).
Laing, R.D. and Cooper, D., *Reason and Violence*, Pantheon Books (1971).
Laing, R.D. and Esterson, A., *Sanity, Madness and the Family: Families of Schizophrenics*, Penguin (1971).

Adrian Laing went on to write a novel based on some of his father's experiences: *Rehab Blues*, Gibson Square Books (2013).

Other references:
Burston, Daniel, *The Wing of Madness*, Harvard University Press (1990).
Clare, A., *Psychiatry in Dissent*, Tavistock (1976).
Cooper, David, *The Death of the Family*, Pelican (1972).
Dinnage, Rosemary, Review of Burston, *The Wing of Madness*, New York Review of Books, vol. 18, no. 43 (1996).
Firestone, R., *Compassionate Parenting with an Introduction by R.D. Laing*, Glendon (1990).

12

CARL ROGERS AND UNCONDITIONAL PERSONAL REGARD

Carl Rogers had a glittering career. His early work was on children but, in 1940, he left his post in Rochester, New York where he worked for the Society for the Protection of Children and went to the University of Ohio. He developed what has come to be known as humanist therapy and wrote a number of successful books on counselling.

Rogers was critical of the way he fathered his two children when they were small. 'I would rate myself only fair as a father then … in those days I was concerned with whether they were disturbing me rather than whether what I was doing was in the direction of promoting their own growth.'

Rogers coined the phrase 'unconditional personal regard', by which he meant that the therapist had to suspend judgment of the inevitably flawed human being he or she was trying to help. Rogers' motto also influenced his ideas about furniture. You could not have unconditional personal regard if you were staring down at the patient lying in a submissive position on the analytic couch. So sometime around 1942, he decided clients – he disliked the word patients – had to sit opposite him as equals.

In abandoning the couch, Rogers resembled a man whose politics he would have detested, Matthias Goring, the cousin of Hitler's second in charge, Herman Goring. Matthias was a psychoanalyst who also did not want patients to lie supinely on the couch while the all-knowing therapist looked down on them. Matthias Goring was both a fervent Christian and a fervent Nazi. As a Christian he believed that the healer and the sufferer had to face each other as equals. Rogers never claimed religion was the reason he changed the seating arrangements but Rogers, I argued in a critical biography, had many blind spots about himself. (My late son Reuben did much of the research, spent months in the Library of Congress reading Rogers' papers and would often get exasperated by them. Rogers left the library 117 boxes of papers including the bank books which he opened as a teenager. Reuben turned his experience into a fine novel, *Theo's Ruins*.)

The man who thought his every note was worth gifting to the nation was bitterly disappointed not to win a Nobel Prize in the 1980s. He thought he deserved it for some well-meaning attempts he made to offer encounter groups to the Catholics and Protestants in Ulster during the Troubles. If only they could give each other unconditional personal regard, they might stop murdering each other, he believed – not an unworthy ideal.

Rogers had considerable understanding of the loyalties that religion inspires. He was born in Chicago in 1902 into a devoutly Christian home. His daughter Natalie wrote that it was

> a strict, puritanical environment where the family gathered each morning for prayers and bible reading. The six children sat in the parlour taking turns reading paragraphs from the Bible. After the reading each person knelt on the floor, hands folded on the chair in front of him, to get a final blessing from his parents.

After that the family ate breakfast – starting with a prayer. They went to church every Sunday, of course.

Natalie said – and, of course, she was basing this on what her father said – that it was a household

> built on faith in God and with strict rules of moral conduct: no drinking, no smoking, no cards, no dancing and as far as I can tell no discussion of sexuality. The five boys rose early in the morning to feed the pigs and milk the cows.

Rogers noted proudly that when he was 12 his father made him responsible for a few acres of land on the family farm. The youngster's task was to farm these acres profitably. 'A strong work ethic pervaded the Rogers' household', Natalie wrote.

There was an unexpected finale to this religious upbringing. In 1922, when he was just 20, Rogers was chosen to travel to China to meet fellow Christians for a World Student Christian Federation Conference. He kept a diary of his travels, which has only recently been published with an introduction by Natalie. Her introduction reveals some important facts both about her father and his relationship with his children. China excited Rogers and that was reflected in enthusiastic prose. He wrote:

> For the life of me, I can't realize that I am really off for six months of high adventure, with great experiences, and tremendous opportunities ahead of me. I can't help but wonder how much the trip will change me, and whether the Carl Rogers that comes back will be more than a speaking acquaintance of the Carl Rogers that is going out.

In her introduction, Natalie added:

> Sitting on the train or up nights on the boat he recalled the sights, the people, his impressions and his shifting views of the world and his religious beliefs. It

seems apparent that as he wrote he was talking to family and colleagues as well as to himself.... This dedication to documenting and integrating his inner reactions with learning from life experiences continued until the end of his life and is one of the many reasons he was, and still is, widely read and appreciated.

Natalie marvelled at her father's self-confidence in China. Rogers never said

> anything about being nervous or having to prepare for these (meetings), even when the audience was 600 people. His self-confidence when it came to intellectual ideas and his zeal for the mission apparently made it easy for him in these situations.

Rogers did not even get dazzled on the final day of one conference when he debated with leading politicians. He wrote:

> I am afraid that I would have liked to differ again with the Ex-Chancellor of the German Empire. He and I had a hard time agreeing, all the way thru. At 11:30 I had to speak for the American delegation, giving our message.
>
> *(April 10)*

'It seems Carl was challenging the Ex-Chancellor throughout the conference! No wonder he was seen as a leader. He had the courage to confront his elders of high rank', Natalie said. But the tone of the diary was a great surprise. 'In the diary, Carl often speaks of his faith in God, his love for Jesus and the urgency for Christian morals to help shape a peaceful world.' She highlighted one section where her father said 'It isn't until one is facing a big job alone that one appreciates all that his faith in a Heavenly Father means to him (February 15)'. There can be little doubt of his very conventional faith in 1922. He also wrote:

> I am sure that there is a God, who is a loving father. I am sure that Jesus Christ is my leader and Lord, and that I want to follow his principles of brotherhood. I am sure that his kingdom, as he calls it, offers the only solution for the problems of the world.
>
> *(February 25)*

Natalie was amazed:

> My brother, David, and I grew up in a home where our parents Carl and Helen [his wife] did not *have* a bible, and I never heard either of them discuss God, Jesus, or faith in an Almighty. We didn't say prayers, nor did we ever go to church. I was left to figure out what I believed, on my own. If I had read this diary as a teenager I surely would have had a lot of questions to ask my father.

Natalie was disappointed her father had not really told her of his once-fervent faith. She added:

> When I read, 'it was more imperative than ever that we set aside an unhurried time, each day, *for communion with God* in order to renew our spiritual strength, to develop our power of vision to develop our power for helping others ...' (February 20th), I asked myself, 'Is this really my father?' At this stage of my life (I am 83) I feel a bit cheated that I did not get some element of this from him as I grew up.

I have written about this at length as it illustrates one of the contradictions about her father that Natalie has had to deal with. Rogers preached openness but it seems he was far from open with his children. Later on in his life, Rogers regretted the fact that he had been so obsessed with work that he left most of the child rearing to his wife, Helen.

Natalie commented:

> I wonder, even now, how it could be that a man of such deep religious faith would close the door to initiating discussions with his family and colleagues about God and Jesus. (As a youngster, I always thought Jesus was a fairy tale made up to placate those who didn't have inner strength.) When he was asked, later in life, 'Are you religious?' I remember him saying, 'I am too religious to be religious.' While I believe this to be true, to the questioner it could feel like a closed door.

Despite all that, Natalie was generous:

> Overall, it has been a delight for me to be with my father in his youth, experience his energy and passion for life, and read about his intellectual fervor as I try to understand his early devotion to Christianity. During this journey he was also courting my mother, Helen, by mail, which is another story. (And a successful one!)

She continued:

> In this personal writing we see many of the characteristics that stayed with him for life: his interest in observing and documenting his experience and his interest in challenging his own and other people's beliefs in order to come to some new self-understanding.... The big question in my mind, as I read and re-read this diary is, 'How did his journey to the Orient change young Carl's views and beliefs about Christianity?' I found myself wondering to what extent did this trip create the path between his faith in the Almighty to his faith in each human being.

That second faith was central to his belief that the therapist had to give the client unconditional personal regard.

In 1924, Rogers graduated from the University of Wisconsin. To decide just what work he wanted to do, he went to a seminar on *Why am I entering the Ministry?*

It was a decisive day as he decided not to become a minister. His father objected and, as a compromise, Rogers enrolled at Union Theological Seminary, but he was becoming set on studying psychology. He then went to the Teachers College, Columbia University, where he got his PhD. While working on his thesis, he began to study children and especially the way children completed the many tests psychologists gave them. In 1930, Rogers became director of the Society for the Protection of Children in Rochester, New York.

By then Rogers had married Helen. Their son David was born in March 1926. He and Natalie grew up mainly in Rochester. Natalie remembers her father as not being demonstrative. She had very little memory of him cuddling her. But, typically, she was generous, adding that Rogers was 'much too hard on himself' when he blamed himself for not being around that much. Her brother David was also mixed, recalling that Rogers was 'gentle but not around very often'. But he also added his father was 'almost every night accessible' and that he was interested in him and proud of what he was doing.

On Sundays the family often went on picnics with Rogers' brother, Walter, and his family. Natalie's mother encouraged her to paint and sculpt, which would influence the direction her work would take.

Between 1928 and 1932, Rogers published a series of tests for children. The tests codified what any good psychiatrist or psychologist 'skilled in children's behaviour might use in an interview'. Rogers became skilled himself and soon discovered that a number of young children had more sexual knowledge than one might expect. Rogers had read August Aichorn, a friend of Freud, who was a teacher and gifted at dealing with delinquent children. Aichorn argued that when children misbehaved seriously they usually had emotional conflicts. Rogers suspected some of the children he saw had been abused but, rather like Freud 30 years earlier, he did not stress what he had found. At first he let himself be more than a little blind to the facts.

Rogers' book *The Clinical Treatment of the Problem Child* (1939) gave an interesting account of 24 problem children he had seen; three were clearly sexually abused but Rogers knew he would court controversy by making too much of that. He also carried out a useful study of what made good foster parents but he was becoming disillusioned.

His children were also growing up. David had gone to medical school and, after some time in the Navy, became a specialist in infectious diseases. Natalie graduated from high school when she was only 15. In 1940, Rogers left Rochester and became professor of clinical psychology at Ohio State University, where he wrote *Counseling and Psychotherapy* (1942). He suggested that the client, by establishing a relationship with an understanding, accepting therapist, could achieve the insight needed to change his life. These radical ideas would make his name. In 1945, he was invited to set up a counselling centre at the University of Chicago. The therapist had to make an almost equal relationship with a client. Natalie remains an advocate:

> Carl was a verbal therapist and a revolutionary, a pioneer in his own way. And he has, even long after his death, been voted the most influential

psychologist in America. His work was so profound in bringing forth the idea that within each person there is the ability, the capacity for self-development, self-insight and growth. So he changed the whole psychological counselling world.

Her father rejected 'the so-called medical model which assumed that any form of psychological distress was like a physical illness'. The good doctor and the good therapist had to ask the right questions and then devise a plan to heal the sick. The professionals had all the power. Natalie Rogers said her father developed a radically different view which needed therapists to give up power. She added that they often 'have a very difficult time really letting go of their ego as a therapist, and their ego saying, "Oh, I must have the answers for this person"'.

Counseling and Psychotherapy became a best-seller and, in 1947, Rogers was elected President of the American Psychological Association. His election required some suppression of reality as Rogers did not always live up to his high ideals. He once literally ran away from a patient because he could not cope with her mental condition – a flight not quite fitting for a leader of his profession.

Rogers' next two books, *Client-Centered Therapy* (1951) and *Psychotherapy and Personality Change* (1954), established his reputation with a wider public – and one of his students used some of his ideas to set up the Parent Effectiveness Training (PET) movement. The effective parent learned how to communicate more effectively with his or her children and became wise enough to ensure family conflicts were defused. Less trauma, more happiness.

As a father Rogers was, as he admitted, all too often not there. And as an author he was less than frank. His official biography by Howard Kirschenbaum leaves out some crucial episodes in his relationship to his children. David married his childhood sweetheart, Corky, when he was just 20. The marriage would cause problems to David, to Rogers and to their own relationship. We know a good deal about David's difficulties, not just because there are letters in the Library of Congress but because Rogers kept detailed notes of his conversations with his children even when these were on the phone. These notes are also in the library.

The record of these conversations show Rogers trying to help his son and his daughter-in-law but often with little success. In 1951, for example, David criticized his parents for not coming to see them when Corky was ill, as she often was. In the next few months Corky took to drinking and to taking barbiturates – as a doctor's wife she presumably had easy access to them. David felt he was a failure and wrote to his father: 'I realise once again how uncomfortable it makes me to discuss my unhappiness with you.' Despite that, David was often on the phone to his father, complaining of migraines and depression. By then David was a doctor on the USS *Leyte*. Part of the trouble, as David saw it, was that his parents had the perfect marriage. When he and Corky had problems, David told his father that his parents were so happy, 'they had little sense of the struggles of other couples' and by comparison 'others are bound to feel dazzled and small'.

In fact, Rogers and his wife Helen did not tell the children of their own considerable marital problems. We would not know the details if Rogers had not given his notes to the Library of Congress and placed no restrictions on access to them. Helen complained, for example, that he always insisted on making love in the morning and in the missionary position.

Rogers did try to help David by talking to Corky but she told him that she had married into a family 'so godamned creative it kills me'.

By 1959 David had published 20 scientific papers and was becoming recognized as an authority on infectious diseases. He wrote his father a self-absorbed letter in which he said he had many resentments and problems that he had never dared admit before. 'I don't think I ever vocalised to you I was afraid I'd blow apart.' David blamed his father for being uncommunicative in the past, though he admitted things between them were better now.

By the 1960s Rogers wrote that he regretted leaving so much of the parenting to Helen but he and his daughter (who was also having problems in her marriage) became closer now.

In 1964 David had a coronary at the very young age of 38. His father had somehow got wind of advice that the then President Lyndon B. Johnson wrote to the Chief Justice of the Supreme Court, after Frankfurter had had a heart attack. Trying to reassure David, Rogers stressed how Johnson had changed his lifestyle after he had his first heart attack. Johnson, a long-time workaholic, only worked 16 hours a day which allowed him eight hours of good sleep. The future president also cut back on the booze. Rogers did not just have to reassure David and Corky; he also had to cope with the anxieties of a second woman in David's life as his son now had a mistress. Rogers talked to Corky but seems to have blamed her for David's coronary as she was demanding, unstable and had in effect made his son's life miserable.

On 12 April 1969, Rogers received a letter from David's mistress saying David's life was 'a mess' and that David was 'withering inside'. As usual Rogers made notes. He was also aware that he was drinking too much and that, after talking to David's mistress, his blood pressure rose. It would seem Rogers often measured his blood pressure.

The fact that, for all his unhappiness, David had a number of extra-marital relationships also may well have made his father feel that he had missed out on much. Rogers had been a faithful husband until he reached his sixties but he then began to regret missing out on the permissiveness of the 1960s. By then Rogers was 67 and his attempts to catch up on the sex he felt he had missed would make him sometimes ridiculous and also lead to problems with Natalie especially.

By 24 July 1969, David told his father that he could no longer stand his marriage. He was being made to feel responsible for Corky. In the next few months Rogers would help his son devise a less than honourable plan to escape from his wife to stop her being awarded the whole of their family home in any divorce settlement. By 1970 his son was 46 years old, and yet, Rogers went to see a lawyer on his son's behalf.

To suppose psychologists should be more ethical than others would be naive but Rogers was also the author of *Becoming Partners*, a marriage manual. Rogers told his son that, despite Corky's troubles, he should not have her committed. It was all part of a cunning plan. David should leave Corky and find work in California, a ploy which would put Corky off her guard and make sure she would not get all the property they owned jointly, especially their house. David followed his father's advice. In 1972 he went to California where he became President of the Robert Wood Johnson Foundation. Corky felt abandoned.

On 2 January 1973 Rogers had a long talk with Corky. His daughter-in-law, whom he had known for over 20 years, protested that she belonged to one man and one man only – David. And David had now left her. A month later one of Corky's relatives rang Rogers to warn that she was suicidal. Rogers rang her and was sure he had helped.

The next day Corky was found dead – she had indeed committed suicide.

Natalie's marriage did not end in such tragedy. In 1950, she had married Larry Fuchs, a Jewish political scientist who revered Rogers. Fuchs became director of the Peace Corps in the Philippines and Natalie accompanied him to the Far East. As Rogers was a famous therapist, the couple turned to him for advice when their marriage got into difficulties. He did not manage to stop them divorcing.

Rogers wrote Larry that he understood each of their feelings about their conflict.

> I think what I am trying to say is that I love and care for each of you, not as perfect creatures but as very fallible imperfect persons. And as a very fallible imperfect person I expect to go on valuing each of you.

Some years later Larry was shocked to read Rogers' how-to book on marriage, *Becoming Partners*. Though all the couples were anonymous, the book described many scenes which Rogers only knew about because Larry and Natalie had confided in him. Anyone who knew them, Larry complained, would recognize them. He did not imagine for one moment that his father-in-law would write up his daughter's marriage as a case history – and particularly not without telling her ex-husband.

Larry wrote an outraged letter to which Rogers replied by suggesting he had done nothing wrong as he did make the couples anonymous. A furious Larry replied that anyone who knew him and Natalie would have recognized it was the collapse of their marriage that was being described. Rogers did not reply to that letter. Kirschenbaum criticizes my biography of Rogers because I used this incident 'to damn the great communicator for refusing to communicate'. I did so but, more seriously, I condemned Rogers for abusing confidences. Unconditional personal regard, this was not.

Natalie was far less bitter about Rogers' reply to her former husband, and the publishing of much intimate detail about their marriage. But not everything was well between father and daughter, partly because Rogers was being critical, even cruel, to her mother. In the 1970s, Helen became very ill and Rogers became her rather resentful carer. Natalie wrote to her father to say he seemed to be covered 'with a thin foggy veil around you so I can't get very close to you'. He was drinking too much and, in his continuing attempt to catch up on the sex he had missed, had been pursuing a woman called Bernice Todres who is never mentioned in Kirschenbaum's biography. Todres never let Rogers sleep with her so the great therapist spent much of his early seventies in a state of perpetual frustration.

Natalie did recover from these years of distance between her and her father. She was then quite happy to work with him though. From 1974 on the two of them and three psychologists, Maria Bowen, Maureen O'Hara and John K. Wood, ran residential programmes in the United States, Europe, Brazil and Japan, which used Rogers' Person-Centered Approach. Natalie eventually recorded *A Daughter's Tribute* in which she introduced excerpts from 16 of her father's books and 120 photographs that spanned his lifetime. David Rogers died in 1994 and, following his father's example, left boxes of papers to an archive.

Rogers died in 1982, much honoured, though it could be argued he had many flaws. After he died, Natalie pointed out her differences with her father in an interview she gave to Dr Van Nuys. She told Van Nuys: 'I feel my work has embodied Carl's theory of creativity; embodied and enhanced it. But I particularly like the word "embodied" because it's using the body in the creative process. We don't become creative by talking about creativity.' One key difference between father and daughter is physical. Natalie invites people to get up out of their chairs, to move,

> to help people get acquainted with their body, to express themselves through their body. I start with movement often, because in this culture – particularly the American and some of the European countries – we are so used to sitting and talking and telling our story.

It is hard to imagine Freud, for example, doing a knees-up with his patients. Rogers never asked people to get up out of their chairs.

As with many others in this book Rogers was not quite the father he wished to be. Few of us are.

Notes and references

My late son Reuben spent months researching him in the Library of Congress. I relied on his excellent work heavily. Reuben also used some of this material in his own novel, *Theo's Ruins*, which will soon be published.

Rogers' relevant works are:
Cornelius-White, J., *Carl Rogers: The China Diary, with an Introduction by Natalie Rogers*, Createspace (2013).
Rogers, Carl, *The Clinical Treatment of the Problem Child*, Houghton Mifflin (1939).
Rogers, Carl, *Counseling and Psychotherapy*, Houghton Mifflin (1942).
Rogers, Carl, *Client-Centered Therapy*, Houghton Mifflin (1951).
Rogers, Carl, *Becoming Partners*, Houghton Mifflin (1960).

His daughter recorded:
Rogers, Natalie, *A Daughter's Tribute*, CD ROM available from Psychotherapy.net (2002).

Biographies:
Cohen, D., *Carl Rogers: A Critical Biography*, Constable (1999).
Kirschenbaum, H., *Carl Rogers*, PCCS Books (2010).

13
THE GOOD ENOUGH PSYCHOLOGIST?

This book cannot pretend to be a methodologically pukka study. I chose the subjects which any critic could suggest is bound to reflect my own prejudices. Furthermore, there is no control group. Anne Roe (1958) compared the careers of, and influences on, psychologists, biologists, physicists and chemists. It was not my aim to see whether psychologists were better parents than physicists or footballers, so this study lacks a control group.

To make matters more complicated, I have used a smorgasbord of sources – letters, diaries, autobiographies, biographies, as well as material from interviews, some mine, some by others. A methodologically sound study or, to adapt Winnicott's phrase, 'a good enough study', would include accounts by all the children of their parents. Piaget's and Jung's children, however, said little, while Anna Freud never said anything critical about her beloved papa. Nevertheless it is possible to see some patterns, good and bad, if those terms do not sound judgmental.

Crucially, none of those studied abandoned their children. Watson's father, Pickens, did abandon his family but his son did not imitate him. After his divorce from his first wife, Watson stayed in touch with both of their children. Melanie Klein did not cut her daughter off; Melitta did that. Jung, despite his compulsive womanizing and living with two women, stayed close to his children. R.D. Laing was the most inconsistent and violent parent and saw little of the children of his first marriage when he re-married. Still, his book of conversations with his children is at times touching and he took Adrian to see his work a number of times. It is also true that all those discussed were professional people and there is less tendency for that group to abandon their families.

There is one acid test for any parent – and I write here as a father who has lost one of his children. Making sure your children survive so they bury you and you don't have to bury them. Here the record of this sample is saddening. Darwin lost three of his ten children to illness, which was high even for Victorian times. Freud lost his daughter Sophie to typhoid. He was unlucky in many of his relatives too. Sophie's son, who Freud adored, died when he was six. Two of Freud's nieces committed suicide, as did one of their husbands. Freud had had one niece, Cacilie, committed to an asylum some months before her death. Freud's cousin and brother-in-law Moritz also killed himself.

Watson's son Billy committed suicide while his daughter Polly made a number of suicide attempts. Melitta Schmideberg, Melanie Klein's daughter, believed her brother killed himself. Rogers talked to his daughter-in-law Corky the night before she committed suicide. One of Laing's daughters died of natural causes when she was 20.

This sombre list means that only Jung, Bowlby, Piaget and Skinner did not have to bury a child, the spouse of a child *or a grandchild*. Even though there is no comparison group of say architects or bankers, the tally of tragedies is striking. Kreitman *et al.* (1991) found there were more suicides in lower social economic groups. The children of psychologists were largely middle class. It is surprising, therefore, to find such a high level of suicide among these successful professionals.

The ideal parent loves and then lets go so that the child can flourish as her or his own person. In her novels about the Church of England, Susan Howatch describes some characters who want their offspring to be 'replicas'. Does the solicitor's son become a solicitor? My friend, the late James MacKeith, for instance, was a third generation psychiatrist. He had a fine career and his work on false confessions helped free the Guildford Four and the Birmingham Six. Nevertheless he was always somewhat in awe of his perfectionist father and delighted when he could help him achieve one of his serious ambitions – to get his work on paracosms or imaginary worlds published. I experienced Stephen's need for accuracy and perfection when we wrote that book together.

Letting go, it seems, is not easy for the children of famous parents. A number of Darwin's children, Francis and Horace, worked with their father. James Watson became an industrial psychologist. Anna Freud became a psychoanalyst. Despite her anger with her mother, Melitta Schmideberg also became a psychoanalyst, if a very eclectic one. Richard Bowlby is devoting part of his retirement to popularizing his father's work. Piaget's son Laurent worked for the Piaget Foundation much of his life. Natalie Rogers also worked with her father. One of Laing's daughters became a psychotherapist; his son Adrian has written a biography of his father. Skinner's eldest daughter, Julie Vargas, runs the Skinner Foundation. Billy Watson became a psychoanalyst before he killed himself. Love and let go may be the most important lesson we can learn.

Freud, Watson, Skinner, Spock, Klein and Piaget developed theories of child development and four had fairly definite ideas on parenting. It is worth contrasting Watson and Skinner, both of whom used behaviourist ideas with their children. Watson's son Billy was depressed and rebelled against his father by becoming a psychoanalyst. Billy blamed many of his problems on his father's theories. Skinner, on the other hand, used much the same theories; he put one daughter in an air crib. Yet he has left two seemingly happy children.

Finally is there anything we can learn from the parenting of those discussed here? I believe there is one lesson which challenges loving parents. You need to provide love and attention when the children are small, but you need to give them the confidence to get away from you. Love and let go. I know from my own experience how hard that can be. A final word. My late son Reuben was a fine editor. He would have nagged me, corrected me and made this book much better. I am no Eliot and he was no Pound but he was as well as much loved 'il miglior fabbro' (the better maker), as Eliot's famous dedication goes.

References

Eliot, T.S., *The Waste Land*, Boni and Liveright (1922).
Howatch, Susan, *Glamorous Powers*, Harpers (2010).
Kreitman, N., Carstairs, V. and Duffy, J., Association of age and social class with suicide among men in Great Britain. *J of Epidemiology & Community Health*, vol. 45, 195–202 (1991).
Roe, A., *The Psychology of Occupations*, John Wiley (1958).

INDEX

Abraham, Karl 77
Adler, M. 40
Aichorn, August 137
Ainsworth, Mary 109
anal stage 48
Andreas Salome, Lou 68, 77, 79, 80
Anne, Queen of England 11
anima 71
Antigone 46, 53
anti-Semitism 64, 73, 79
anxiety 4, 14, 15, 27, 32, 48, 67, 81, 114
Aptekmann, Esther 77
archetypes 63
astrology 63, 72
autism 4
Ayer, A.J. 125

Bair, Deirdre 74
Baldwin, Mark 34
Barnes, Mary 124
Batesburg Institute 32
Beard, Mary 7
beating fantasies 53, 55, 67
Beeton, Isabella 16
Bergson, Henri 88
Benney, Mark 108, 109
Bergmann, Gustav 42
Berkeley, Bishop 10
Berlin Psychoanalytic Society 64, 77
Bernays, Berman 47
Bernays, Edward 61, 98
Bernays, Eli 46
Bernays, Emmeline 47

Bernays, Jacob 47
Bernays, Martha *see* Freud, Martha
Bernays, Minna 48, 49, 58
Berra, Tim 16
Biblical references to fathers 6, 49
Binet, Alfred 87, 88
Bismarck, Otto von 1
Bleuler, Eugene 66, 67
Bonaparte, Princess Marie 75, 79, 80, 106, 107
Bowen, M. 141
Bowes-Lyon, Elisabeth 89
Bowlby, John 3, 12, 15, 16, 105–12
Bowlby, Richard 105, 106, 111
Bowlby, Ursula 106, 107
Bringuier, Jean Claude 86
British Psychoanalytic Society 75, 79, 80, 16, 107
Buchanan, George 8
Bullitt, William 98
Burlingham, Dorothy 57, 58, 59, 60, 61
Burston, Daniel 121, 122

Chagas Disease 15
Charles I, when he was a mere prince 10
Chatenay, Valerie 89, 90
child abuse: studies of 137; suppression of 137
China, Carl Rogers' trip to 134–5
Chopin 123
Churchill, Winston 16, 61, 107; grandson 61
Cicero 7

Cilento, Diane 120
Clare, Anthony 129
cocaine 47, 48, 57
Cohen, Reuben 5, 126, 133, 145
Coles, Robert 57
concrete operations: stage of 90
Connery, Sean 120, 121
conversations with children 39, 91–4, 126, 127, 128, 131, 143
Cooper, David 120, 124, 125
Cornut, Samuel 88
Coward, Noel 64, 74
Coyl, Diana 111
Crawford, Marion 89, 90
Creon 46

Darwin, Anne 14, 24, 26
Darwin, Charles 2, 3, 12, 14–30, 45, 61, 88, 89, 93, 143, 144
Darwin, Emma 15, 16, 21, 22, 23, 25, 26, 27, 28, 61
Darwin, Francis 14, 26, 27, 144
Darwin, George 14, 27
Darwin, Henrietta 14, 22, 27, 28, 144
Darwin, Horace 15, 26, 27, 28, 144
Darwin, Leonard 15, 27
Darwin, Susan 22
Darwin, William 14, 15, 16, 17–23, 24, 28, 34
day dreams 56
delinquency 84, 105, 108, 137
depression 15, 42, 43, 65, 76, 80, 107, 120, 138
depressive position, the 78
Descartes, René 10
Deutsch, Helene 58, 85
Dewhurst, Jack 11
discipline 7, 33, 39, 100, 113, 118, 121
displacement activities 4
Disraeli, Benjamin 1
Donne, John 10
Du Bois Redmond 29
Durbin, Evan 106

Edinburgh, Duke of 3
Ehrlater, Christian 1
Eitington, Max 57, 58
Electra Complex 48, 49
Elisabeth II, as a young girl, nicknamed Lilibet 89
Erasmus 7, 8, 10
Ernst, Edzard 63
Esterson, Aaron 124
Eysenck, Hans 5, 114

Eysenck, Michael 5, 114

Fainting: among psychoanalysts 66
fear 8, 19, 33, 23, 29; of the dark 32, 35, 36; of snakes 72
Ferenczi, Sándor 52, 76, 98
Fichtl, Paula 45, 60
Firestone, Robert 130, 131
Fliess, Wilhelm 45, 49
formal operations, stage of 90, 95
Fox, W.D. 20
Frankfurter, Justice 139
Freud, Alexander 46
Freud, Amelie, mother 46
Freud, Anna, daughter 1, 3, 6, 43, 45, 46, 50–62, 67, 75, 76, 77, 78, 79, 80, 85, 106, 143, 144
Freud, case histories: Dora 54; Emma Eckstein 54; Fanny Mauser 54; Lucy R. 54
Freud, Clement 61
Freud, Cacilie 144
Freud, Ernst 58
Freud, Julius 38, 46
Freud, Lucian 61
Freud, Martha nee Bernays 1, 45, 46, 47, 52, 56, 58, 59
Freud, Martin 2, 45, 48, 49, 50, 51, 52, 58, 59, 60, 61
Freud, Mathilde 47
Freud, Oliver 50, 57
Freud, Sigmund 1, 3, 6, 9, 12, 17, 27, 29, 38, 40, 43, 45–62, 64, 66, 67, 68, 70, 71, 72, 73, 74, 75, 77, 78, 79, 80, 82, 83, 84, 86, 87, 90, 95, 98, 99, 103, 105, 106, 107, 110, 120, 123, 125, 137, 141, 143, 144
Freud, Sophie 1, 12, 49, 51, 57, 144
Fuchs, Larry 140

Gaitskell, Hugh 106
Gangotri, Baba 127
Gallup, Gordon 18, 19
genital stage 48
George, Prince of Denmark 11
Glover, Edward 79, 83, 123
Godet, Paul 88
Goering, Hermann 64
Goering, Matthias 64, 133
Goethe 6, 58
Graf, Max 48
guilt 48, 54; in psychoanalysis 81, 82, 84; of parents 8, 39, 58
Gully, Dr. 24, 25

Harlow, Harry 108
Hartley, Marietta 43

Index

Hartley, Polly 31, 43
Heinmann, Paula 84
Helmholtz 29
Henry, Prince 8–10
Henry VIII 7
Hitler, Adolf 50, 58, 64, 133
HMS Beagle, Darwin's voyage on 15, 16
Hobbes, Thomas 10
Hohlman, Leslie 41
Holmes, Jeremy 106
Homer 123
Hooker, Joseph 26, 27, 28
Hopkins, J. 107
Hume, David 10, 23
Huxley, T.H. 28

Ickes, Harold 33, 35
Ickes, Mary, later Watson 33, 40
imitation in children 8, 91
Intelligence 5, 11, 27, 90
I.Q. tests for children 87, 88

Jocasta 46
J. Walter Thompson 35, 41
Jackson, Edith 59
James I 8, 9–10
James II 11
James, William 2, 90
Jenkin, Lewis 11
Johnson, Lyndon B. 139
Jones, Ernest 45, 51, 71
Jones, J.D.F. 67
Jones, Mary Cover 35, 37
Jonson, Ben 10
Jung, Agathe 66, 69, 70, 72
Jung, Augusta 64
Jung, Carl Gustav 3, 6, 63–74, 80, 84, 86, 88, 121, 128, 143, 144
Jung, Emilia 69
Jung, Emma, nee Rauschenbach 66, 68, 69, 70, 71, 72, 84
Jung, Franz 69, 70, 72, 73, 74
Jung, Gret 68, 70, 72, 73
Jung, Johann 64
Jung, Paul 64
Jung, Ruth 73, 74

Kant, Immanuel 10
Keynes, Margaret 15
Keynes, Randal 2, 24
Kingsley Hall 124, 130
Kirschenbaum, Howard 140, 141
Klein, Arthur 79
Klein, Eric 76, 79
Klein, Hans 79

Klein, Melanie 2, 3, 6, 12, 75–80, 84, 85, 87, 98, 106, 107, 143
Kristeva, Julia 75, 76, 77, 78, 85

Laing, Adam 126, 127, 131
Laing, Adrian 2, 3, 6, 119, 120, 121, 124, 125, 128, 130, 131, 143, 144
Laing, Amelia 121, 122, 130
Laing, Charles 130, 131
Laing, Jutta 120, 121, 126, 127
Laing, Karen 119, 120, 121, 124, 127
Laing, Natasha 127, 128
Laing, R.D. 2, 3, 12, 119–32, 143, 144
Lamb, Charles 29
language: development of 16, 89, 126
Lashley, Karl 41
Le Bon, Gina 6, 57, 61
Leibniz 10
Lieb, Ruth 42, 43
Little Albert 35, 36, 37
Little Hans 29, 48, 49
Locke, John 10
LSD 121, 124

McCarthy Joseph, Senator 101, 116
MacKeith, James 144
MacKeith, Stephen 111
Main, Tom 85
Mann, Thomas 1, 64
Mary, Queen of Scots 8
masturbation 40, 53, 54, 55
Merritte, Douglas 36
Milton, John 10
Mitchell, Juliet 125
Mobius, Professor 20
Montaigne, Michel de 8
Morris, Desmond 3
Mostel, Kate 117
Mostel, Zeno 117
Mozart 40
Mullan, Bob 121, 130
mushroom expeditions 50

Napoleon 3
Newland, Lisa A. 111

Ochwiay, Biano 72, 73
Oedipus 37, 38, 46
Oedipus Complex 37, 38, 46, 48, 49, 77, 82
O'Hara, Maureen 141
oral stage 17, 48
Orbach, Susie 63
Orwell, George 108

Pack, Mrs, wet nurse 11, 48

Padel, Ruth 2, 16
Pavlov, Ivan 113, 115
Peale, Norman Vincent 96
peekaboo 19
Piaget, Arthur 87
Piaget, Jacqueline 89, 90, 91, 92, 93, 94
Piaget, Jean 3, 6, 36, 86–95, 105, 143, 144
Piaget, Laurent 89, 90, 95, 144
Piaget, Lucienne 89, 92, 93, 94
Piaget, Marthe Burger 87, 88
pigeons: as a means of missile guiding 2, 116
play: as a means of therapy 59, 77, 79
Plutarch 7
Preiswerk, Helena 66
pre-operational stage 90, 94
Prince Charles 63, 73
Prince William 63
psychoanalysis 1, 42, 46, 52, 53, 68, 69, 70, 76, 77, 80, 81, 86, 87, 107
psychoanalysis of children 3, 51–3, 77, 87

Racine, Jean 10
Radcliffe, John 11
Rado, Sandor 98
Rayner, Rosalie 31, 34, 35, 39, 97
Reiss, Diana 19
Reissland, Nadia 21
Reizes, Emmanuel 76
Reizes, Libussa 76, 87
Reizes, Moriz 75
Reizes, Sidonie 76
Resor, Stanley 35
Riviere, Joan 58, 106, 107
Roazen, Paul 53
Robertson, Smith 130
Roe, Anne 143
Rogers, Carl 2, 3, 128, 133–4
Rogers, Corky 138, 139, 140, 144
Rogers, David 135, 137, 138, 139, 140, 141
Rogers, Helen 136, 137, 139, 140
Rogers, Natalie 2, 3, 134, 135, 136, 137, 138, 139, 140, 141, 144
Rogers, Walter 137
Roosevelt, Eleanor 1
Russell, Bertrand 40

Sauerwald, Anton 60–1
Schepeler, Eva 86, 87, 95, 106
Schmideberg, Melitta 3, 6, 75, 76, 78, 79, 80–5, 143, 144
Schmideberg, Walter 79, 80, 84
Schopenhauer, Arthur 50
Searle, E.R. 5
Segal, Hanna 76, 84

sensori-motor stage 90
Shakespeare, William 10, 51
Sheridan, Richard 21
Skinner box 2, 113
Skinner, Burrhus 2, 3, 4, 5, 42, 110, 113–19, 144
Skinner, Deborah 2, 5, 6, 110, 113, 114, 115–17, 118
Skinner, Eve 113
Skinner, Julie 115, 116, 117–18
Slater, Karen 115
smiling in babies 16, 19, 24, 34
Socrates 7
Speilrein, Sabina 64, 67, 68, 69, 71, 86
Spinoza 10
Spock, Benjamin 3, 96–104, 144
Spock, Dan 6, 97, 98, 103
Spock, John 97, 99, 100, 102, 103
Spock, Michael 96, 97, 98, 99, 100, 101, 102, 103
Spock, Peter 103
Spock, William 97
Star Trek 96
Strachey, John 80, 107
suicide 12, 43, 79, 83, 103, 114, 140, 144
Sully, James 29

Taine, Hippolyte 16, 20, 21
Tinbergen, Niko 3, 4
Titchener, E.B. 36
Todres, Beatrice 141
toilet training 39, 79

unconscious, the 9, 38, 46, 48, 49, 52, 57, 63, 65, 67, 68, 70, 72, 77, 78, 83

Vago, Klara 77
Vanbrugh, John 21
Van der Post, Laurens 63, 73
Van Nuys, Dr 141
Vargas, Julie 2, 144
Vietnam War 96, 101, 102

walking expeditions 70, 72, 94, 117
Wallace, Alfred Russell 28
Wassing, Anton 1
Watson, Billy 36, 37, 38, 39, 41, 42, 43, 144
Watson, James 31, 34, 41, 42, 43, 144
Watson, John 33, 40, 42
Watson, John Broadus 3, 6, 12, 29, 31–44, 96, 97, 102, 113, 114, 115, 143, 144
Watson, Pickens 31, 40, 143
William, Prince of Wales 11
Wilson, Harold 106
Wilson, Woodrow 61, 98

Winnicott, D.W. 2, 64, 74, 143
Wittek, Rosie 105
Wolff, Toni 64, 71, 72, 84
Wood, J.K. 141
Woolf, Leonard 80
Woolf, Virginia 80
word association test 67, 68

World Health Organization 109
Wright, Nicholas 79, 85
Wundt, Wilhelm 2, 67

Young Bruehl, Elisabeth 52, 57

Zeal, Paul 125